10667108

RAGWINGS
and HEAVY IRON

Other Houghton Mifflin Books
by Martin Caidin

NOVELS

The Last Dogfight

Whip

NONFICTION

Kill Devil Hill: Discovering the
Secret of the Wright Brothers
(Harry B. Combs, with Martin Caidin)

RAGWINGS
and HEAVY IRON

The Agony and the Ecstasy of
Flying History's Greatest Warbirds

MARTIN CAIDIN

HOUGHTON MIFFLIN COMPANY · BOSTON
1984

Library of Congress Cataloging in Publication Data

Caidin, Martin, 1927–
Ragwings and heavy iron.

1. Caidin, Martin, 1927–   2. Airplanes,
Military—Collectors and collecting. 3. Aeronautics,
Military—Exhibitions. I. Title.
TL540.C29A37 1984   623.74′6′0750973   84-3758
ISBN 0-395-36141-9

Printed in the United States of America

V 10 9 8 7 6 5 4 3 2 1

*for showing me the way to
a new world of flight*

this book is for

Major Karl von Strasser

Contents

RAGWINGS
and HEAVY IRON

Out of the Sun!

If you're going to fly a warbird, be
humble, or else that sucker will screw
you straight into the ground.

TERRY RITTER

A swelling roar pushes down against the airfield, throaty and coughing, the first wave of a great explosion tugging at clothes and pushing like a soft pillow against bodies everywhere. The booming thunder swells in volume, louder and deeper as the source of the crashing sound rushes closer. All across the airbase heads turn to the north, seeking shapes in the bright sun and thin blue sky, trying to pick out form from the haze that swims and shimmers brightly over the trees. Eyes strain, but for long moments there is only that ever-louder swelling of sound. Then, a thin wail, piercing all else, begins much closer at hand, the frightened cry of the siren calling the air raid alert, a sound that slips behind the ears and heightens the sense of fear another notch. Other sounds now; men shouting and calling to one another, feet pounding on concrete, jeeps racing like square-boxed, noisy little muppets as they carry pilots to planes. A loudspeaker crackles tinnily and a voice calls out hoarsely, imploring the pilots to bring their fighter planes to life, to save the field and all those so vulnerable to attack.

From the north rolls the thunder, so loud now as to make further conversation almost impossible, and the noise spews forth from three bombers like waves breaking, huge and crashing, marching low through the sky, winged shapes of impending disaster. "There

1

they are!" voices cry out shrilly, excited and frightened, tremulous with the moment. "To the north — over there!" "Quick! Turn those flak guns around!" Men scurry to swing long-barreled antiaircraft guns in the direction of the three speeding bombers, now close enough to make out the twin-engined shapes, the broad wings jutting from shoulder positions of the bodies of the planes, two huge engines, twin tails. Machine gun barrels jut from the slab fuselage like lethal quills of a porcupine. Sunlight glints from the curving Plexiglas.

"Ach! Verdamnt B-25 machines!" The loudspeakers placed across the airfield crackle and boom with the thick accent. *"Gunners! Schnell! Open fire! Open fire!"* Waspish cracks of sound whip forth as flame tears away from the flak guns. *"All pilots! All flieger! Man your planes! Man your planes! Rauss!"*

Heads turn as fighter pilots hurl themselves into the cockpits of Messerschmitt fighters, engines already turning over by the mechanics who have remained ready for any emergency. They, the pilots, aren't even wearing parachutes! No time, no time! The fighters begin to taxi seconds after the pilots are in the cockpits, snapping home seat belts and shoulder harnesses, yanking the canopies closed. It's a race against time as the fighters trail dust, taking off on taxiways and dirt overruns, desperate to get into the air. The tires are barely off the ground and the fighters turning away when the three bombers race into position.

The B-25 Mitchell bombers have been painted in a crazy-quilt pattern. The first is a desert sandy-pink, an immaculate machine that looks as if it has just flown from the factory. On its right wing is a battered older airplane, paint peeling, a scruffy-looking plane that clearly has seen better days. And off the left wing flies the third bomber, with a huge painting of a lovely naked woman on each side of its nose. Where there should be the star-and-bars insignia of the U.S. Army Air Forces there is, totally out of character, a huge crumpled beer can for an insignia. But there is time for only a glance at these maverick paintings, for the bomb-bay doors of the B-25s are open, and tiny gouts of flame spit from the machine guns as the bombers strafe the field before them and to their sides. The Messerschmitt fighters curving away in steep banks try frantically to gain airspeed to escape the sudden fire. All but one make it, and smoke trails the last fighter, which has taken a long burst into its innards.

A tremendous sheet of flame rips along the flight line, where bombs cascade and tumble against the earth, spilling into hangars and vehicles. Another roar of flame, and yet another, and terrible explosions tear in all directions, hurling people backwards, bringing exclamations of surprise and fear. The sound crashes against hangar doors and walls, and the new sound of tortured metal adds to the increasing din. More bombs! Flames erupt in a steady stream down the target run. Thick smoke boils greasily into the sky.

The German fighters have swung around and they race under full throttle for the hated American bombers. Two fighters close to pointblank range, and the sound of cannon fire mixes with machine guns as the German fighters blaze away at their slower targets. Black smoke pours suddenly from an engine of one bomber, and it skids in a sick, slewing motion, disappearing beyond the tree line. The two remaining B-25s swing sharply to the east, breaking away from the combat, hoping the fighters will have to end their attacks because of the next bombers coming in.

It works! Again the voice shouts over the loudspeakers, alerting the antiaircraft crews on the ground, the same message transmitted by radio to the German fighters. "Return to the field! Return to the field! *Schnell!* Bombers coming in from the north! *Achtung!* Bombers from the north! *Attack! Attack!*"

A motley formation, more a loose cluster of heavy warplanes bunched together in the sky, pours in from the north. It is a combined-force strike this time. A huge Boeing B-17G Flying Fortress thunders along the left side of what loosely passes for a formation, the pilot flying as if he doesn't care who else might be in the air with him. As he dives in a shallow descent against the German airfield other planes swarm about him. Two dark-blue Grumman TBF Avenger torpedo bombers fly tightly wing-to-wing, as if one hand were on the controls. Off to the side and below are two great single-engined shapes, Douglas AD Skyraiders, one a pale gray and the other a shining blue. Each Skyraider is festooned with bombs and rockets, and they dive as though madmen were at the sticks, barely flying above the treetops. In the midst of the attacking force is a machine rarely seen in combat, a high-tailed, twin-engined Douglas B-23 Dragon, bright red-and-white stripes on its tail an unexpected flash of color in the sky. It races after the B-17 to gain a protective position from the/ four-engined bomber's bristling guns.

Faster than the others are two sleek, all-black shapes, flat-bodied,

3

each with two huge engines and high tails, loaded with machine guns and napalm tanks and bombs, their engines a higher-pitched thunder than all the others; these are maverick Douglas A-26 Invaders, and they make their approaching strike in complete disregard of the other aircraft.

And then, the cloud of bombers smash the airfield, machine-gun fire ripping along the ground, the heavy bombs erupting in huge gouts of flame and thunder. Debris rips skyward, followed by massive swirls of dark smoke. Sirens scream as fire engines and ambulances dash and weave about the airfield, medics rushing to casualties, the fire crews pouring foam and water on the more critical targets. The antiaircraft fire dies away as the gun positions are hammered with strafing runs and bomb after bomb in their midst. Bodies fly wildly through the air, tumbling like lifeless straw dummies, smacking sickly back into the ground.

But the defending fighters race into the gaggle of attacking American bombers, and this time the Messerschmitts are joined by six Japanese Zero fighters! The Mitsubishis, red balls shining in the sun, dive in a beautiful attack formation against the bombers, racing in and out of the fleeing American aircraft, blazing away at their targets. The B-17G seems to stagger as its far right engine explodes in a shower of smoke, and the airplane turns away, fighters relentless in their attempts to shoot it down. Another bomber trails smoke, and still another as the Messerschmitts and Zeros claw and batter the American planes.

But not for long! Now the American fighters are on the scene, howling in from the north in fierce dives, unstoppable, their pilots hungry for enemy blood. In the lead of the mob of American fighters are four North American P-51D Mustangs, their Merlin engines howling like banshees as the pilots throw themselves at the Messerschmitts and Zeros. Two Zeros hurl black smoke on the very first pass, breaking away frantically as the Mustangs hit them like an avalanche. The other Zeros have already turned sharply to escape the Mustang assault, but there is no safety from the other fighters still pouring in. A big twin-engined Lockheed P-38L Lightning is right behind the Mustangs, and its nose becomes a huge sphere of twinkling, flaming gases as four machine guns and a cannon roar, sending a Zero rolling violently as smoke trails behind the hapless fighter.

And still they pour in from the north! If the words *motley* and *beautiful, casual* and *vicious,* could all be applied to the continuing

4

attack, this is the moment, as a crazy-quilt formation rips through the defending fighters, now falling one after the other. Two Bell P-39Q Airacobras and a single Bell P-63 Kingcobra, holding perfect formation, pour heavy cannon shells into the fighters trying to escape their wrath. A loose gaggle punches into a Zero and Messerschmitt that have broken sharply to the east; there is no way they can escape the combined fury of two Vought F4U-4 Corsairs, a General Motors FM-2 Wildcat, a gleaming Hawker Sea Fury, two shark-nosed Curtiss P-40N Warhawks, and a dark-blue Grumman F6F-5 Hellcat, every plane flown by a pilot lusting for enemy blood.

Two Grumman F8F-2 Bearcats sing a cry of deep thunder as they speed low over the runway and bank steeply into curving turns that become near-vertical climbs. Behind the Bearcats is a big Grumman F7F-3 Tigercat, faster than the other fighters with its two huge radial engines. The fighters scissor and turn and claw with fatal results against the Messerschmitts and Zeros; a few of the more fortunate enemy pilots have managed emergency landings, the pilots abandoning the planes and running for their lives to the safety of slit trenches.

The great cloud of fighters and bombers end their passes across the burning, exploding, smoking airfield, and the moment yields to a new thunder from the north. Eyes turn in disbelief as a large formation rumbles slowly into view, holding position at about fifteen hundred feet above the ground. There is no way anyone can mistake the three Douglas C-47 Skytrain transports in the lead, main cabin doors yawning wide open, holding a perfect Vee in the sky. *Transports?* It must be a paratrooper assault against the field! The C-47 transports continue slogging along, and holding protective formation about the slow and helpless transports are modified North American T-6 and SNJ Texan trainers, sixteen of them, each armed with three machine guns, weaving slowly as they crisscross back and forth, above and behind the transport planes.

As the Skytrains move into final position, a cluster of five ground-attack planes sweep ahead of them in a final strafing run to knock out ground fire. Big, chesty North American Nomads, blunt nosed and high tailed, spreading out to hit anything that moves on the ground — and in their midst an arrow-emblazoned, red-starred Yakovlev Yak-11C howling like a mad dervish right on the ground, the propeller barely clearing obstacles, machine-gun bullets ripping up the earth in stuttering bursts ahead of the speeding plane.

5

Right engine "smashed by enemy gunfire," the Ju-52 bomber is "trapped" by a bevy of vengeful American warplanes. That's Martin Caidin flying the Ju-52, Jim Patton in NASA's T-28A, and Pete Sherman in the big Lockheed P-38L Lightning. *Photo by Steve Rock, U.S. Navy*

And now the Skytrains are overhead, each transport disgorging twenty heavily armed paratroopers in perfect rhythm, multicolored parachutes blossoming in the bright sky, the troopers with their assault weapons at the ready. They land in the middle of the field, shucking their harnesses, gathering in perfect discipline to concentrate their firepower. Almost immediately they are attacked by German ground troops, rushing to the scene in trucks and jeeps, on fire engines and water pumpers; on anything that can move and carry men fiercely defending their airfield. The sharp reports of automatic weapons and rifle fire bang across the field as the two groups tear at one another. Bodies fall on both sides. The casualties are terrible as several surviving antiaircraft guns are brought down to ground level and open pointblank fire into the American paratroopers. The carnage is horrible.

The battle seesaws back and forth across the field, men cursing, men screaming in pain as bullets thud into their bodies. By now the American planes are all gone, the skies for the moment empty. But not for long! The people on the airfield and along its edges listen with sudden hope as the loudspeakers that are still "hot" carry the radio messages from Field Defense Control. *"Verdamnte geshtunker flieger! Schnell! Schnell! Attack at once! I repeat, attack at once! If ve do not gedt der paratroopers schnell, all is lost! Rauss!"*

Low over the tree line to the north new shapes appear in the sky, coming in fast. This time all the planes have black crosses and swastikas, and it is impossible to miss the shape of the biggest machine, holding the lead position as it thunders over the trees and then pulls up sharply, leveling off at a thousand feet. A great three-engined Junkers Ju-52, the famed *Iron Annie* with the massive corrugated body; as fast as it levels at a thousand feet, it holds position as if it were on rails, right down the runway, and suddenly it disgorges a cloud of dark shapes, German paratroopers tumbling away, chutes opening at once as they float down to reinforce their own forces taking a beating on the ground. Overhead, nestled in a swarm of Messerschmitt Me-108, 109, and 208 escorts, the Ju-52 rattles the ground as it swings about in a sharp turn and then, to the astonishment of everyone, dives steeply at the ground! This is a transport! What's it doing in this kind of crazy dive? As it howls lower, flat pitch of the propellers keening loudly like a buzz saw gone mad, the leading edges of the wings sparkle with machine guns firing in long staccato bursts. Again the spouts of dirt and grass erupt across the field as the Ju-52 races low, wheels slicing through bushes at the edge of the field perimeter, men falling in all directions. *Whose* men are they? Germans? Americans? No one can be certain as the madmen in the trimotored bomber rock and bank crazily, forward guns blazing, the gunner in the top turret hammering out long bursts of fire at anything in sight. In the widely yawning rear cabin door, a crewman braces himself, hurling out hand grenades in rapid succession as the Junkers rumbles down the runway. The Messerschmitts speed by, the pilots walking rudders to spray their machine-gun and cannon fire in the widest possible area.

The Ju-52 pulls up to a hundred feet, and an enormous ball of fire thunders across the field and for a moment envelopes the iron-crossed airplane. *"Verdamnte schweinhunt!"* The voice screams with rage through the loudspeakers. *"Dumbkopfs! Schmeggeggies! They haff bombed our own fuel tanks!"*

That's not all. Dead center in the field is a small building, obviously an outhouse or a Porta-John, used for the convenience of the German troops when things were quiet. But when nature calls, there's no denying it for *too* long. A German soldier runs across the field in the midst of the bombing and strafing, the flames and explosions and the firefights, dodging and twisting to reach the outhouse. He is inside only a few moments when the Ju-52 roars overhead, shaking the world, the madman in the open doorway still hurling grenades with wild abandon. One explodes about twenty yards from the outhouse; after a moment the German soldier stands in the doorway — from which the door has fallen off — looking with bewilderment about him. A split-second later a grenade whirls into the outhouse, which erupts with a sheet of flame and a deafening blast, hurling the soldier through the air. He staggers to his feet, his clothes smoking, and holding up his pants, he runs for his life, to uproarious laughter from everyone watching.

Wait a moment . . .

What the hell kind of air battle is this, anyway? The Sea Fury isn't an American aircraft; it's a carrier-based fighter of the British Fleet Air Arm. And a *Yakovlev* Yak-11C? That's a Russian fighter-trainer developed from the Yak-9 fighter of the Second World War!

What are Messerschmitts and Zeros doing at the same airfield? Not to speak of the fact that these are Messerschmitt Me-108 and Me-208 fighter-trainers mixed in with the sole Me-109G fighter. And look at the mixed bag of warplanes, both army *and* navy, flying in their wild formations to attack an enemy that shouldn't have been there in the first place. After all, when do you get Wildcats and Lightnings flying together? Well, they *did* fly and fight together in World War II, starting with Guadalcanal . . . But Kingcobras and Hellcats? That *is* stretching it a bit. How about the Tigercats and Bearcats and Skyraiders and Trojans? That's stretching it just a bit more, because these were all American fighters and attack bombers and advanced trainers (that became fighter-bombers; we're speaking of the North American T-28 Trojan) that came into being at the end of the Big War but never had the chance to get into battle before it ended in August of 1945.

Hey, those Zero fighters! Aren't they just a bit short to be real Zeros? True, true. Actually, they're modified North American T-6

Texan trainers, made to look like Zero fighters for the war film, *Tora, Tora, Tora.* Just as Japanese dive bombers and torpedo bombers were modified from Vultee BT-13 and BT-15 Valiant trainers (better known as Vibrators), so T-6 trainers fit a variety of needs with the help of expert sheet-metal workers and mechanics.

But this is an air battle and there's something very wrong here . . .

Well, not wrong, but *right.* Because the year is 1983 and the airfield suffering its battering from bombs, machine guns, cannon shells, rockets, hand grenades, and all manner of automatic weapons is immediately to the west of the Kennedy Space Center, just across the railroad tracks and U.S. 1 that flow north–south along the Florida east coast. The occasion is the annual gathering of warbirds — all kinds of warbirds, more than one hundred of these rare planes — that make up the combat airshow of the Valiant Air Command. Not only the pilots, aircraft owners, mechanics, crewmen, and all the ground support people of the Valiant Air Command who live in the southeastern United States, but members from throughout the country, and with friends and their planes from other warbird organizations from all across the United States, joining together to put on a dazzling display before nearly 100,000 fascinated, excited, thrilled, and cheering spectators.

This is living history on the wing. It is also the best damned warbird airshow in the world that in the space of only a few years has become a legend in its own time. At the annual bash of the Valiant Air Command there are pilots and crewmen, and their aircraft, who join in from the Confederate Air Force, Rebel Flying Corps, Warbirds of America, American Heritage of Flight, Yankee Air Force, Canadian Warplane Heritage, the Combat Museum of the Air, the Experimental Aircraft Association, and the Antique Airplane Association, and a dozen other assorted clubs and organizations.

This is the gathering of the ragwings and the heavy iron, masterful flying, simulated combat bombing runs, thrilling attacks and swirling dogfights between fighters, booming explosions and guns hammering, flame sheeting into the air, acrid smoke boiling across the field, assaults by American troop transports disgorging paratroopers and by German troop transports disgorging *their* paratroopers and, of course, by a convenient switch in the "tide of battle," possession of the airfield changes, all described with the gravel voice and nonstop eloquence of the narrator, an old hand at flying warbirds himself, the hulking, bearded Ted Anderson.

It is, first and foremost, great fun. It is stunning in its fury, awesome in its skills, daring in its execution, and a thunderous, crashing action event that lasts for two days, and overwhelms the tens of thousands of people who have come eagerly each year to become part of the legend themselves.

Because this is a plunge *back into time*. For the veterans and the oldtimers it is nostalgia at its most bittersweet as they watch, often in disbelief, the same warplanes in which they once flew and fought, or witnessed in action. More than one gruff old veteran, with a fistful of medals buried somewhere in a bedroom dresser, has stood unashamedly with tears running down his face as history stumped full force back into his feelings.

And with all those propellers whipping their keening cry through the air, and the powerful engines roaring, from the barking heavy roar of old radials to the honey-smooth song of the twin Allisons of the Lightning, it is truly breathless time travel for the youngsters (and that includes *anyone* who never flew in these machines). During these two days while the Valiant Air Command and its sister organizations are mustering up the past, they are enabling the veterans to relive that past and all those who have seen the great and classic machines of history only in films or in magazine illustrations to experience it, short of combat.

In this furious, crashing air battle of two days' duration there's a new creed: *Warbirds like these are no longer birds of war.* No one flying at the controls or manning the guns, or performing the myriad tasks of support on the ground, is out to hurt anyone — least of all their best friends and members of their own families! Behind the smashing explosions and towering geysers of flame and thick, acrid smoke, this *is* a gathering of men who flew these machines in combat, but mostly it is a gathering of the men and women who did *not* fly them in combat, but have been mesmerized by the siren song of flying the greatest combat machines ever to take to the skies.

☆

If there is any one factor, above all others, that makes the Valiant Air Command unique, as compared to the other warbird organizations in the United States, it is the avowed goal to *share* as much as possible the thrill, the agony, and the wonder of these great machines with the public. This is no small issue. Most airshows, especially the other warbird presentations throughout the country, are affairs where jealousy is almost rampant. *Keep away! Don't touch! We're the heroes and you're the unwashed public!* Or so goes the bleat of the special few who insist upon a great moat of distance and diffidence between themselves and the people who lay out their hard-earned dollars at the admission gate and bring their kids with true hero-worship in their eyes.

There is much to be said for protecting both airplanes *and* visitors from one another at any gathering, and it would seem that both are equally vulnerable. Obviously, safety is paramount and *must* be the single most demanding factor at any warbird (or any other type of airplane) gathering and affair. A turning propeller is nothing less than a ghastly and terrible mangler and destroyer of flesh and bone, and there is no way to mitigate that reality. Tons of metal rolling on taxiways and grass with pilots who can't see directly before them are to be avoided like rampaging elephants. Exhaust pipes and tubes of newly landed airplanes can peel the skin off unsuspecting fingers and hands like a runaway apple peeler.

So when things are turning, moving, or hot, you keep *everyone* away. But when they're still, stopped, and cool, you can bring in the admiring thousands to meet the pilots and crews, to have pictures and autograph books signed, to touch and feel and *ooh* and *aah*. Watching the pilots and crewmen of the Valiant Air Command as they lift children of every age (and their grandparents) into cockpits or walk them through the larger aircraft is an event that will stay with you forever. Sure, it requires more effort, it demands attention and a lot of time, and there's always the chance you'll have scuff marks and perhaps even some annoying repairs to make after a crowd rumbles about your airplane.

There's the heart of the matter, really. That crowd is made up of all kinds of people, and not all of them are the kind you'd let sit on your front lawn or invite into the house for dinner. So the rule is: Extend the welcome hand to the vast majority of people who approach you with wonder and dreams in their eyes. With courtesy and a bit of awe of your own, greet the old man who slides his hand in a caressing manner across the curving metal of your wing, and when you see mist in his eyes it's time to travel back with him in time to when he flew and fought in this craft. We had one old fellow come up to a Mustang on the line with the other fighters. Hell, he didn't look as if he could drive a pickup truck, let alone had ever flown an airplane. And a *fighter?* No way! He had a week's growth of beard and a beer gut and a kid (his grandson, as it turned out) perched on his shoulder, and he chewed a battered cigar stub; you knew he was just some happy old bum *until you looked at his eyes.*

Deep, pale-steel blue, crow's feet at the corners of those eyes, and you knew, oh, you just *knew* he had looked through curving Plexiglas at 40,000 feet somewhere, and that gnarled right hand so casually holding the beer can had also gripped a stick in some fighter cockpit long ago and far away. "Nice machine," he said ever so casually, and you could feel the sudden chill, because you knew you were in the presence of someone who had been there and done it all. In this particular case, every instinct, every feeling was right. He had flown Warhawks in North Africa and Lightnings over Italy, and then he climbed into Mustangs; he was a hotrock in his day and had shot down twelve and maybe twenty confirmed, all fighters, and twice he'd bailed out of fighters and come home on that thin nylon in a canopy over his head.

Funny. His grandson looked at *us* in awe and almost every one of us looked at the kid's grandfather in awe . . .

The truth of the matter was that the old man with the beer can and the cigar and the beer gut and the stubble and the pale blue eyes had been an ace, a killer, like every great fighter pilot of every country, *long before most of the pilots flying this airshow had ever been born.* And here on this field, this day, this moment, he looked out through those wrinkle-creased steel-blue eyes and saw the same fighters he had flown and some against which he'd flown in life-and-death flying; he was here on a sunny day with lots of years behind him and his grandson riding his shoulder, and he was a happy and a satisfied man to whom the fates had given all these years.

So the Valiant Air Command and its pilots and crewmen and ground support people live by their motto: Be kind, be gentle, be warm. You never know when the man you invite to touch your machine and sit in your seat may be one of the heroes who brought you into this business!

☆

So after the opening peals of thunder and the screaming props and roaring engines, the explosions of gasoline and powder charges and corkboard and oil, ever so carefully packed into the ground for maximum boom and smash and absolutely no danger to anyone,

Smoke chokes the air and the excited crowd presses closer to be part of the action as the big German bomber waits for its signal to make a "combat emergency" takeoff. Half the fun is being in the midst of the thunder and the fury. *Asgard Flite Photo*

Ted Anderson at the microphone discards his *ersatz Cherman* and the deep, warm tones of a "good ol' boy" roll through the loud-speakers, nice and friendly-like, and Anderson's mellow tones bring everyone right into the middle of the great circus act going on before, above, about, and all around the shouting and laughing and applauding crowd.

Through radio it's possible to bring the many thousands of people right into the cockpits of the warplanes going through their deafening maneuvers and simulated combat runs. Anderson flips a few switches, and all transmissions between the pilots and the airshow traffic controller, Bill Noriega, are patched into the loud-speaker system. It affords a marvelous touch of immediacy, of sharing, even of intimacy, to the people who've paid their good money to stand behind the crowd lines.

Noriega, who's controlled air traffic out of Ft. Lauderdale and Miami in some of the most heavily congested areas of the world, gets the word from the pyrotechnics specialist: "We're all set," he tells Noriega. "All charges in place. You can bring them in anytime."

Noriega glances at his watch. They're still right on time. To everyone else this is an airshow. To Noriega it's a terribly complicated orchestration of many parts and pieces, all moving in different directions; and every part and piece must be coordinated in time down to the second. Noriega nods to Anderson, who can now start his spiel to the crowd to explain what's happening. Then Noriega turns his full attention to handling the many airplanes in the sky along with others waiting to take off to return to the fray. He thumbs his radio transmit button, and his voice is heard simultaneously in all aircraft.

"Okay, you guys. This is Control. You paying attention up there?"

There's always a fast and brief chorus of "Yeah, sure," "Gotcha," "Go, baby," "Let's have it," or just microphones clicking.

"You people wiped out the crapper and a hamburger stand and scared the bejesus out of all the old ladies. Everybody else fell asleep, so let's have some sharper action from here on, okay? Let's have the B-17 and the Ju and the rest of the bombers come in from the north in a bunch. Use the preplanned formation. The single-engine bombers follow in trail. All you Skyraiders and Avenger pilots, got that? You work in trail behind the heavies and mediums."

A chorus of confirmation crackles over the air waves. "I want the 28s to follow the second group. Then the transports with the Sixes flying escort. You people got that?"

Robby Robinson, in the lead C-47: "Transports got it, Bill." A moment's hesitation, then Jack Kehoe in the lead T-6 calls down: "Sixes confirm." Short, simple, clear; no nonsense.

"Fighters, you on the line?"

Scott Smith's gravelly voice rumbles over the radio. "This is Mustang Lead. Go ahead."

"I want a break between the transports and Sixes, Scotty. Orbit to the northwest at fifteen hundred until I call you in. The way we'll work this is that after the transports and Sixes come by we'll have the ragwings do their thing. Then you people in the fighters come in just as we briefed." Pause. Then, "Ragwing Leader, you copy?"

"Uh huh. Gotcha, Bill." The calm voice of Vern Renaud, who makes his living driving a huge Lockheed 1011 jumbo jet for Eastern Airlines, now doing what he likes best — flying an old fabric-covered Stearman PT-17 biplane and leading a small cloud of grumbling, popping, stuttering, growling, snarling engines and fabric bodies around the sky at 800 feet, over the river to the northeast of the field. "As soon as the bombers start in, the ragwings are

14

to make their turn and come on in. Be careful, you people; be cautious for wake turbulence from the big guys."

Noriega glances at his watch. It's time. "Heavies, start your run now. Remember, you break out to the left and above, and twelve hundred feet is your ceiling."

Scott Johnson in the B-17 begins hauling the heavy bomber around on his final run. "Ah, Control from the Seventeen, confirm our run at three hundred."

"You got it, Big Man. Let's see some flying, mister." Scott Johnson laughs. He drives a Douglas DC-9 jetliner for Ozark Airlines for his bread-and-butter; now he is in heaven behind the controls of the Flying Fortress.

"Everybody keep in mind that we're setting off some heavy charges on this run, except for the rags," Noriega warns. He looks through binoculars to the north, where a swarm of specks in the sky slowly expands into familiar shapes. In a few moments Ted Anderson will punch in the music tapes and "Stars and Stripes Forever" will boom out through the loudspeakers. Between the music and the engine thunder and the swarm of warbirds, the crowd will be on its feet, cheering madly.

This is the aerial parade, the pass-in-review of the day. Until this point most of the warbirds have been screaming by at full power, jinking and maneuvering wildly, and there's been so much action that now it's time to give the crowd a good look at the planes. So they'll come in low and slow, giving everyone a good look at the many different types, and the crews will be waving at the crowd and they'll all be waving back and shouting as if anyone could hear anything in all this bedlam.

The "heavies" come in first, and everyone agrees the broad-winged B-17G absolutely must have lead place. The Queen of the bombers, the grand old Flying Fortress herself, her engine fires mysteriously extinguished, makes her pass down the runway, the four Cyclone engines smoother now than anyone remembered, and as she slides past the cheering throngs, only 300 feet up, the pilot begins a sudden curving climb to the left, away from the crowd, and they get a marvelous view of the old bomber sliding upward into the blue.

The others follow, the B-25 bombers in tight formation, the B-23 flying alone, the A-26s as a team, then the two TBFs and the two ADs, the Ju-52 rumbling along, gunners hanging out all over the machine and waving; and behind the heavy iron the T-28 Nomads

15

come in, Indian-file, chunky and snarling and pulling up steeply as they clear the south end of the runway. Immediately behind the long file of Nomads the now-familiar cloud of radial engines that focus into the three Douglas C-47 transports and the swarm of no less than sixteen T-6 trainer-fighters, holding 500 feet above the runway, and then they're wheeling off to the side into orbiting position to keep the airfield clear.

During this time, lower to the ground, the ragwings are making their move. Vern Renaud leads the cloud of midges made up of Stearman PT-17s and a bunch of old Pipers, Aeroncas, Stinsons, Taylorcrafts, Vultees, Fairchilds — all former trainers, artillery spotters, and liaison planes — toward the field. Nineteen small planes, sounding like mosquitoes and flies and wasps and hornets screeching full blast, appear no more than a hundred feet over the trees and settle slowly, doing everything but flap their wings. The ragwings stretch out their loose formation and ease closer, and then in a loose gaggle of what could pass for drunken geese floating to the runway, they're all down and rolling instead of flying, the pilots moving toward the offramps to clear the runway.

Bill Noriega confirms that everyone in the fabric gaggle is down. "Fighters, it's all yours. C'mon in, you guys, let's wake up the people."

The Messerschmitts streak past to open the razzle-dazzle, followed by the Yak-11C, and behind the red-starred machine come the Wildcat, and then the Sea Fury, the Warhawks, with the Bearcat and the Hellcat following. John Silberman takes center stage alone in the silver P-38, the Allisons singing their unmistakable cry of honey. The Tigercat follows and then the Airacobras and the Kingcobra, then all the fighters have gone by except the Mustangs, and Scott Smith and John Baugh bring in the ponies with a howl that shivers the bone behind a person's ears, and they come up sharply, straight up, some breaking to the left and others to the right, the pilots rolling steadily as they climb away.

That is the grand finale — except for the surprise, as a Lockheed T-33, descendant of the grand old line of Shooting Star fighters, tears down the runway at 500 miles an hour, a jet thrust from the past into the present, and if that isn't enough, a red-white-and-blue, star-spangled, sweptwing Republic F-84F Thunderstreak follows, pulling up into a torchlike rasp of power, straight up, whirling around and around as it punches for the heavens.

Bill Noriega is busier than a one-legged man in an ass-kicking

16

contest as everyone makes the move to come home to roost. The ragwings are well off the taxiways and into their parking positions, and now Noriega is back in his element, running the tower from the announcing stand. He brings in the jet fighters first because you never fly an airshow without giving full thought to the cost of fuel, and jet fighters at low altitude don't just *burn* fuel, they gulp the expensive go-juice in prodigious quantities. Then the heaviest iron, the bombers with all those multiple engines going, followed by the rest of the gang.

The ground crews keep the crowd back, away from those whirling propellers and huge wheels and wingtips and tails turning suddenly, the minor storms of dust and rocks as the machines dip on their shocks to park. Engines are run up to move propellers into desired positions and to clear the plugs, and then, one after the other, mixture levers are brought into idle cutoff positions and the great blades whirl finally to a stop. The silence is so sudden it's shattering.

In the quiet that follows, a long moment of hush while everyone waits to move up to the planes to touch, to feel, and to talk to the pilots and crews, a new sound, much closer at hand, demands attention. It is a crackling, pinging, crinkling sound of superheated engines cooling down, of stubbed and long exhaust stacks giving away their heat, of Allisons and Lycomings, Cyclones and Continentals, of Pratt & Whitneys and Merlins and Jacobs, Daimlers, and Renaults and Potez, all cooling down and accepting a rest that will be theirs for the long night to come.

The pilots and crews slide the chocks beneath wheels and attach the tiedown ropes and the control locks and prepare for the human river to enfold them, for the questions and the autographs and the tales to be spun. The security crews take down the barrier ropes, and thousands of people move forward to envelop the warbirds; this is the one-on-one element of the airshow to wind it down.

A few hours later, most of the crowd has gone. The long lines of cars, campers, trucks, vans, and busses have thinned, the long shadows have yielded to the early blanket of night, the field is again owned by those who live and visit here. For the Valiant Air Command it is just the next phase. Cleanup crews move slowly across the field, picking up the inevitable debris of so large a throng. Trash cans are emptied into trucks, the barriers are replaced, the fuel trucks move along the line to fill the tanks for tomorrow's early dawn patrol that precedes the airshow, coffee

The crowd is gone for the day, and it's time for the care and feeding of the now quiet giants. The Ju-52 crew goes to work to "rejuice" the big bomber. *Photo by Becky Ritter*

trucks bring steaming java to the crews, mechanics and pilots perform maintenance or other work on their warbirds, the debriefing of the airshow goes on constantly. The word passes through the professionals that the inspector from the Federal Aviation Agency — the FAA — is pleased, that everything went off with full compliance of safety regulations, to say nothing of common sense.

There will yet be dinner parties tonight, and great uproarious beer parties (and something stronger than beer), and the people will gather round and tell great and wonderful lies to one another; but this is the quiet moment, the stillness of aftermath, with the eastern horizon sunk into dark and slivers of the fading day streaking orange along the western sky.

Suddenly there are shouts and pointed fingers, toward the east, and everyone turns as a brilliant yellow-orange-white glow soars majestically from the horizon and begins a light-pulsating ascent into the heavens. It is unreal and incredible, taking place in silence. From the edges of Cape Canaveral a secret U.S. Air Force satellite has begun its breathless rush up into and through and beyond the heavens, riding the long prow of a huge Titan 34-D booster. The blazing rocket flame is a coruscating bowl of man-made fire, an artificial sun that banishes darkness as it spears the ultimate mountain of night. Long after it has levitated above the planet the thunder rolls down and across the airfield with the silhouetted warplanes. The light in the sky fades to a glowing ember and then winks out, leaving the night to the stars.

"It's hard to believe it's real," someone sighs into the darkness.

A man's voice, disembodied, speaks in reply. "Jesus, it makes me feel *old*."

Down the line a Merlin coughs and barks, spits away mechanical phlegm, misses, catches again, and then settles down to a powerful roar as the ground crew tests the engine for tomorrow's show.

"I swear I don't know which is real," a woman says. "I just watched something rush away from this world. It's *gone*." Her voice catches for a moment as she looks down the long row of wings and propellers. "Look at me. I'm surrounded by ghosts."

The Merlin screams under full power and comes back to a comfortable, subdued thunder. It's very sure of itself and it sounds good.

It *is* good.

These ghosts are real.

What's a Warbird?

The only right way to rebuild a warbird
is to buy one that's already been rebuilt.
That way you won't go crazy.

JOHN SILBERMAN

Scratch a warbird and most likely you'll discover a decrepit bank account. Ask the warbird owner how it got that way, and you'll cringe from the shrill and often hysterical laughter you receive in response. Talk to the warbird owner's wife and she'll tell you that her new house, swimming pool, Porsche, braces for the kids' teeth, piano, ocean cruise, and everything she dreamed of for years were all smelted down and reborn in that unmentionable hunk of scarred aluminum standing like a frozen bulldog on the flight line. She'll snarl when she expounds her miseries and woes, and probably kick you in the shins as she walks away — carrying a bundle of rags and liquid wax to put a new shine on that old, scratched, and beloved aluminum.

There is no sanity or reason when it comes to owning a warbird. Even that demands its own definition. *Owning* is the least of it, you see. There's the matter of locating the winged thing, negotiating the price, and then buying it. Easier said than done. Banks close their doors when you try to get in to talk about a loan on a warbird. Bankers you've known all your life suddenly have never heard of you when you bring in this madness. So you've got to raise the scratch from anywhere. After selling your soul, there's the matter of checking out in the damned thing. You don't leap into a World War II fighter or bomber "just like that," and launch into the wild blue. No way, friend. You have to know what you're grabbing by the shorts. You've got to read the book, talk to the people who've already gone through this exercise, and try to get checked out, sanely and thoroughly. Then you fill the mother with fuel and the average of two bucks a gallon comes home with a vengeance when you find out that even a small twin-engined bomber has fuel tanks bigger than those in the *Queen Mary*.

Then there's the little matter of insurance. Don't shrug it off, friend. Insurance companies in this country don't want to touch warbirds. They're a bit benevolent when it comes to the littler warbirds like the ragwings and trainers, but the moment you step up in weight and class something sets off alarm bells and sirens, and *they're* doing *you* a favor by *taking your money*. The problem is that if you haven't purchased your scarred aluminum outright, if you don't own the winged beastie with clear title, that means you have to carry insurance to protect the people who did loan you the scratch to get into this business. You *must* insure the thing for hull damage and liability in flight and liability for passengers and liability for whatever damage and battery you might do to innocent buildings, cars, cows, and people who get in your way should you need to descend to earth suddenly and with little choice of where to alight.

If you have a warbird with some element of rarity to it you encounter one of the Catch 22s in this business. Not that many of the heavy irons have been certificated as civilian aircraft. If yours is one of those beasties with an experimental or restricted category, the insurance tab goes up like a runaway rocket. You're going to carry passengers in an airplane that hasn't been certificated? You're mad, and you're going to have to pay for that right and privilege.

All right, let's do it by the numbers. We'll use the airplane I fly — the Junkers Ju-52/3m, the three-motored German machine that began life as a commercial airliner and because of its extraordinary versatility was pressed into service as a combat and assault transport, seaplane, and heavy bomber. Consider that it's one of the safest, toughest, most reliable, and strongest airplanes ever built, that no one, *ever*, broke a Ju-52 in the air. Consider that it flew as a major commercial airliner in more than forty-five countries around the world, including Germany, Norway, Sweden, France, England, Italy, South Africa, China, and literally dozens of other countries.

You know what that means to an insurance company?

21

Nothing!

In fact, they *don't want* to insure the airplane. Period. No matter what the price. In the case of the Ju-52, there are all those passenger seats to consider. Never mind that the thing was configured for a crew of three plus seventeen passengers, and that we cut that down to a total of fourteen. Every seat must be insured. And because companies in this country don't want the insurance it means you have to shop through brokers, who go to Lloyd's of London, and — you guessed it. The price is already shooting straight up.

It wasn't always that way. Not when you could buy warbirds for only a pittance of the going price on today's market. In the old days warbirds were dirt cheap and the insurance wasn't much different. If you paid three or four thousand bucks for the whole package and you didn't carry passengers, you didn't *need* an insurance policy for anything save liability. By not paying for insurance you were really "self-insuring" the machine, and you couldn't get hurt financially even if you pranged the bird.

That isn't possible anymore. Prices have gone through the roof. Insurance has climbed faster in cost than oil when OPEC ruled the roost. Some years ago I insured the Ju-52 for a bundle. Plenty of hull insurance and liability insurance to cover just about anything. The insurance was carried in the good old U.S.A. I insured everything, and the tab came to just about $4500 a year. Dempsey Blanton Aviation Insurance of Melbourne, Florida, in the persons of Blanton and Doug Johnson, did the coverage shopping for me. They turned up an American company, big in the business, and we had years of coverage and payments without the airplane getting ever so much as a blemish. Not a ding, not a cut finger. A perfect relationship. Man, we were in, but tight.

But this same insurance company also insured a bunch of DC-3 airliners that were airliners no more. These airplanes had the seats removed and everything except the bare floor removed from the cabin, where the crew installed snap-on rings for skydivers to attach to their bodies during takeoff. That way, instead of carrying only twenty to thirty jumpers you can stuff forty or more people with all their gear into the DC-3. The Gooney Bird will carry it without too much huffing and puffing. Not *the* Gooney Bird with a full load that lost an engine at critical speed: too slow to get recovery and too low and not enough time for the jumpers to get the hell out of that thing.

They killed *everybody* in that airplane, and roughed up a lot more on the ground. There was yet another incident involving skydiver flights and an appallingly effective barrage of lawsuits that, in sum, broke the financial back of the insurance company. They went bust, folded their doors, went out of business, and just like that (snap of the exasperated fingers, please), there wasn't a single company left in the entire United States that wanted to carry insurance for *any* large or heavy iron that did this sort of thing. Well, the Ju-52 carries skydivers. The airplane is even part of the U.S. Army's Golden Knights skydiving team, as is this writer. We also do wingwalking, and, well, we fit the category of Horror for people who don't understand what's going on.

The annual insurance for the Ju-52 (because of the need to provide full protection for backers, investors, and liability) jumped from $4,500 to *$17,200!* Let me tell you, that will frost all parts of your anatomy! Then consider the cost of fuel, just the juice alone, and anything that drinks heavily of the stuff becomes regarded as a machine that annihilates fuel instead of burning it.

Why am I telling you all these terrible stories? *Because this is the warbirds game today.* Because we still feel it's the greatest way to go, and we're still in the thick of it all, and we intend to stay with it, but we must hew to the line and pay out more than ever before. In addition to the new house, swimming pool, Porsche, braces for the kids' teeth, piano, ocean cruise, and whatnot, the wife now must be prepared to see disappear into the maw of the Warbirds Cornucopia her new clothes, the family dog, the new television, and whatever other foolishness she's been hankering for.

I know, I know; out there in The Audience voices are raised in clamorous protest. We don't all want to fly a Ju-52 or a B-25! We don't all want to fly the heavy iron! There are smaller warbirds! There are many ways to save money! Why don't you tell us *that,* damn you!

Oh, I am, but you need the Big Picture, the Whole Story, the Good *and* the Bad, the Positive and the Negative, the Happy and the Sorry. The gathering of warbirds is a marvel. Flying the great warbirds is a Happening, a Great Moment in life, and it is just about everything wonderful you may conjure in your mind. And you *can* fly a warbird without gutting your fiscal well-being, but you need to know all the elements. Right away, let us get the most brooding of all questions answered, the query that lurks deep and dark within the souls of those who want the thrill of massive flailing pistons and huge props turning with unmistakable fury.

You do not need military experience to fly a warbird. There. It's out in the open. You don't need military flight training or years of wearing uniforms and hewing to the strict military line. If that were so, then probably 80 percent of all the warbirds in this country would be grounded tomorrow. So what's the big deal? The big deal is that if you do not move into a warbird with professional training, with competency, with a clear understanding of what's involved, then the odds are great that your wife will get everything she's been denied all these years when they pay off on your life insurance policy.

So hunker down just a bit and remember the rules: You need humility to fly and to operate a warbird *safely*. The bigger and tougher, the faster and more powerful the machine, the more humility. And humility is spelled many different ways, above all, *competency*.

Scratch a warbird today and likely you'll find a plumber, a doctor, an author, a professional pilot, a banker, a television broadcaster, a wholesale butcher, a mechanic, a police officer, a gas station owner, a salesman, a manufacturer, a construction boss, a restaurant owner, a cropduster, a realtor, a dentist, a housewife, a professor — or any one of dozens of other professions — grinning down at you from the cockpit.

These are people literally from next door, at your neighborhood store, in your lawyer's office, or doing your accounting, or making a cast for your busted leg — they come from every walk of life, and ordinarily there's just no way to tell them apart from the other people you know. That is, not until they hear an engine overhead, or they're heading for the airport, whatever it is that brings the gleam to their eyes, that makes their hands flash and turn in the air as they talk of their flying and of years past and of their preparations for the big event of the year. That big event is more than one moment and it could be anywhere in the country, marked off on the calendar. Wherever it is, it will be a great gathering of warbirds and an exquisitely orchestrated and thundering airshow. It could be Texas, or California, Ohio or Florida, Georgia or Nebraska, Kentucky, or, well, wherever the wings sigh down from the skies and the great aluminum warriors rumble shuddering to a halt and the men and women climb down from their machines and renew the tightest bonds of all, friends to friends.

Pray, tell, *what* is a warbird?

It is, first and foremost, a ghost. Not all warbirds join the phantom fraternity, of course, but so many of them were on the edge of extinction that the term *Ghost Squadron* came into being, applied loosely to any group of people doing everything in their power to save the great warplanes of the past that almost to the last machine had been destroyed.

The raising and resurrection of the near-phoenix is a direct outgrowth of the aftermath of the Second World War. Imagine, if you will, a sky darkened with as many as four thousand fighters and bombers, all American, on a single overwhelming mission against a few major targets in Germany. Fighters and bombers. In addition to these numbers, add in the German fighters defending their territory, and from two hundred to perhaps six hundred more aircraft are added to the total. Now bring in the decoy missions to absorb the defending fighters from the main attack, and we have British, American, French, and other aircraft involved, with numbers reaching perhaps another fifteen hundred to two thousand airplanes.

Not too long ago, if you made an extraordinary effort, you couldn't get fifty or sixty of those same airplanes, out of the nearly *seven thousand* fighters and bombers that flew combat on one day, into the air at any one time. And if you did manage to get a few dozen airborne, that total would represent *all* the warbirds of those types available anywhere in the world.

So a warbird is the ghostly remnant, or remnants, of the once great air fleets that struggled against one another in a period of time called the Second World War. It may be American, British, French, Japanese, Russian, Italian, Polish, German, Chinese, Dutch, or any other nationality involved in that fierce and far-flung struggle.

It does *not* have to be a machine that specifically participated in combat, and *in combat* is defined as an aircraft that was used to deliver ordnance in any one fashion or another, whether it be by firing machine guns, cannon, or rockets or dropping bombs or anything else.

Obviously, the combat machines are easily identified. The fighters and bombers. Less quickly identified are the patrol bombers, almost all of which were armed. Or the photographic reconnaissance planes, of any type, that were armed — or from which all armament had been stripped to decrease weight and increase performance. Suddenly we have an airplane that flew its missions in a combat zone, and was fired upon by people trying to destroy that airplane, with the pilot, or pilot and crew, of the unarmed machine relying for their survival on speed, altitude, stealth, or a combination of any of these.

Transport planes, most of which were converted commercial airliners like the famed Douglas DC-3, which became the military Gooney Bird, and was flown by nations throughout the world, are hardly considered to be combat aircraft. Yet they were in the thick of combat carrying cargo, troops, or paratroopers. Many times they had impromptu defensive armament in the form of multiple machine guns, or automatic weapons thrust through window ports; and often they were used as impromptu bombers, with the crews rolling heavy bombs out the cabin door.

How about training aircraft? We're down here to the small two-seat, open-cockpit aircraft all the way up to heavy twin-engine machines that trained gunners, bombardiers, engineers, and navigators as well as pilots. Even those that never left their home airport areas served in the military and are regarded as warbirds, even if they were not combat airplanes. But — hold on! Many training types served in multiple roles. Consider the North American AT-6 Texan, the single-engined, two-seat advanced trainer, also popular as the U.S. Navy SNJ carrier trainer, also popular as the Harvard when built in Canada, and just as well-known, if not more so, as the Wirraway when it was built in Australia and fitted out with machine guns, bombs, and rockets and rushed into combat areas where *any* kind of Allied plane was desperately needed. Or, if you want, consider the same AT-6 modified with a larger engine and special combat equipment, and heavier armament, and going forth as the A-27 attack and dive bomber. Every AT-6 and SNJ and Harvard, then, has its pedigree as a combat airplane, as well as a trainer.

Just as obvious is the fact that since the Second World War ended in August of 1945 we have let hardly a month go by without a major war *somewhere* in the world. Major wars, and even remote little wars, are fought with airplanes as well as with other weapons. In such wars, hardly any machine has seen more combat than the original, grand old AT-6 trainer. We used them in Korea in large numbers, armed with machine guns and, most important, with rockets that fired smoke warheads to identify targets for the really heavy iron loaded down with ordnance and bombs. In a bewildering list of variants, the T-6 (the post–World War II designation for the AT-6) has been used in South America and Central

America as a spotter plane, attack bomber, strafer, dive bomber, bomber escort, fighter, and general all-around basher in any kind of combat situation. The same handles apply to the T-6 variants that have fought in North Africa and Central Africa and South Africa. They have been battling enemies all across Asia, again filling a multiplicity of roles.

Well, let's get it down to the smallest of the small, the fabric-covered flivvers such as the mothlike Piper Cubs and the Aeroncas and airplanes of this class. It's difficult to imagine a ragmop of an airplane like the Cub, with its two bucket seats and putt-putt engine of 65 horsepower, as fitting into the warbird category. It's difficult only if you don't know the history of the machine, which made most of its wartime service flights as the Piper L-4, with the generic military name of Grasshopper.

As a liaison airplane it served its lowly but functional purpose of transportation, small cargo delivery, and whatever fits in the category of winged gofer — the pilot would go for this, and go for that, whatever was required. But then, since so many civilian pilots had trained successfully in the old J-3 Cub (and the L-4 was essentially the same airplane), it fell naturally into the role of primary (*very* primary) trainer for neophyte pilots.

The L-4 Cub was slow, it often flew very low, and it could go in and out of just about anywhere. That made it a natural for spotting missions and reconnaissance flights in the front-line areas, and you can't be much more of a combat airplane than when the other side is blazing away at you with everything from revolvers to 88-mm antiaircraft cannon, and they send out fighters to swat you from the sky. Of course, sometimes the people in the L-4 took along with them their own revolvers and automatic rifles and hand grenades or whatever else they could carry and still fly.

Since the L-4 could go just about anywhere, it lent itself to simple and quick modification. Many of them were altered in their fuselage layout to carry not just a pilot, but a badly wounded man on a stretcher for emergency medical evacuation from the battlefield. Chalk up one more mission category for the flivver.

Need the perfect airplane to carry your top commanding general along your mobilization areas? Over the front lines? The L-4 went to war carrying no less than General Dwight Eisenhower on surveillance and study flights of the Western Front combat areas (to say nothing of many others of lesser rank and standing).

There's little need to trumpet the role of the L-4 or its contem-

27

poraries, but I can't resist adding that the raggedy flivver was also an incredibly effective tank killer in World War II! The usual response to this statement is to consider the writer as a heavy smoker of those funny little brown cigarettes rather than one who is relating history with an accurate bent. However, if you talk to the badly mauled Allied troops who fought the Germans toe-to-toe at Cassino and other similar areas of Italy during the Big War, you will find them waxing enthusiastic about the Piper Cub in just that role of giant killer, the giants in this instance being the mighty Tiger tanks of the Wermacht.

The pilots of the L-4 Cubs mounted a triple rocket tube beneath each wing, secured carefully to the underwing struts. Each tube held a rocket approximately 4.5 inches in diameter, for a total of six rockets each with a powerful explosive charge as its warhead. No one simply charged a Tiger tank. That was suicide. One blast from the 88-mm gun of the Tiger, let alone its machine-gun fire, would literally obliterate a Cub. It would be like firing a shotgun at pointblank range at a moth. *Blooey!* It's over. So the Cub pilots would ascertain the location of the Tiger tanks, and they would start their runs not at the heavy armor, but around the flank of a mountain or swinging about the curve of a hill, and then pop into view, hold a course dead-on for the target, and fire everything they had — namely, six deadly rocket-propelled warheads. They lost a lot more Tigers than they did Cubs.

As a wrap-up, you may also list the L-4 Cub as a carrier aircraft, because it flew hundreds of missions on and off the decks of aircraft carriers. You can also list it as a wire-launched aircraft. What the hell is *that?* You won't find it in many military histories because it's barely known outside of some exclusive circles. The gimmick started when a Cub made a landing in a forward combat zone and was unable to fly out again. Everything was deeply holed, rugged ground even for a Cub. Some engineers came up with the bright idea of stringing a heavy cable from a pole high above the ground, with the other end of the cable attached to another, distant pole. Then they hung the Cub by more cables, in the form of a carrying sling, from the horizontal cable. The pilot waited until his tail was secured by yet another holding cable, then ran his engine to full power. When he waved his hand the holding cable was released. Away went the Cub, howling like an angry puppy, gaining speed swiftly. Well before reaching the other pole the pilot pulled a lever and released the carrying sling. Since he was already flying, he simply eased down a few feet to clear his tail and flew away!

From the question *what's a warbird?* we've come to the realization that virtually anything that flew in military service is honestly in the warbird category. Even if actual in-combat use can't be specified, as in the case of the ubiquitous Cub or T-6, it served as a military aircraft, and that puts it into the coveted category of warbird.

This also brings us full circle to that moment of anguish earlier in this chapter when I heard all that clamorous protest of people wanting *in* with warbirds, and wanting to know *how* to get within the inner circle when you simply don't have the scratch to buy your own winged battlewagon. There are ways, many of which are obvious from all the foregoing.

But first, everything must have a beginning, and the warbird movement — specifically the resurrection and flying of warbirds under the aegis and finances of an organization — began 'way down south, in the lower Rio Grande Valley of Texas.

Once upon a time, 'way back in 1951, a lone P-40 descended from the skies over the sleepy, remote, little town of Mercedes. Few people paid the Warhawk much attention. Remote though it might be, unheard of though it might be, Mercedes was no stranger to the roar of aircraft engines. Military bases in the area, especially during the war that had ended only six years before, had masses of iron rushing about the skies in all directions. And Mercedes itself hosted its own airstrip, something less than an international aerodrome with a runway of 2900 feet, but more than enough for the cropdusters and business planes that made Mercedes their home. The P-40 swung about the town, beat up the field, climbed out, and dumped gear and flaps, and Lloyd Nolen landed in what had been a longtime dream — his own fighter plane. Not that he was new to flying military machines. He had started flying at fifteen years old, and when the Big War busted out, the army tapped Nolen on the shoulder. They needed professional pilots as instructors in the air corps and he was one of the chosen few. Nolen pulled every trick in the book to get posted overseas, but one Lloyd Nolen meant dozens and even hundreds of trained pilots leaving his tutelage. He remained where he was in Training Command. The war ended, and Lloyd Nolen still wanted to fly fighters. No way. The U.S. Army Air Forces didn't need even instructors. Nolen went home. But the good dreams stay alive, perhaps buried, but always with their spark.

29

Six years later Nolen went to Phoenix, Arizona, plunked down fifteen hundred clams, and took the title papers to one Curtiss P-40 Warhawk fighter. He did some repair work, changed hoses, tapped this and tightened that, studied the manual, and he was off and winging his way home. It was a moment of particular satisfaction. They won't let you fly a fighter? So, you buy your own.

Rumors erupted in the Rio Grande Valley that the government was about to release a flood of North American P-51 Mustangs, mostly D models, for surplus sales to the public. And they were going to sell for a flat $1000 each. Nolen thought of more than 1500 horsepower and that huge four-bladed propeller and the laminar flow wing and he wasted no time in selling the P-40 to add to the kitty for buying some of those Mustangs.

Wrong. By 1951, the Korean War was going full blast and we weren't doing all that well, and the cry was out for ground-attack fighters. Not only did the Air Force cancel the sale of the Mustangs it was about to dump on the market, it also recalled almost every P-51D that had already reached civilian hands.

What would have been the beginning of the future Confederate Air Force went into a holding pattern for five years. The Korean War went into the history books, and the Mustangs began to trickle into the civilian market — with the price tag boosted to $2500. Lloyd Nolen and four friends each plunked down $500 and had themselves a pony with 1520 horsepower. It says something for this group that they all checked out in the Mustang and flew it regularly from the 2900-foot strip at Mercedes. I've flown that strip and for a high-performance airplane it's just this side of ghastly. Those guys were tremendous pilots (that Mustang, by the way, is still flying).

Emotions running the way they do south of the Mason-Dixon Line, a few months after the Mustang was home at Mercedes, the pilots went to the airport to find a minor change in their iron bird. Someone, never to this day identified, had carefully painted a sign beneath the stabilizer that read CONFEDERATE AIR FORCE. They looked at the sign and looked at one another, shrugged, looked again at the sign, got to like it more and more with every passing moment. On an impulse the pilots saluted one another and made the decision that the name would stay.

It was a quiet beginning on a lonely duster strip at the bottom of the country for what would become the largest and most dominant warbird organization in the world. At first it was a pleasant

Once relegated to the scrap heap in Arizona, this gleaming Curtiss P-40N Warhawk is the pride and joy of the Valiant Air Command in Florida. Seven years and $300,000 went into this resurrection. *Valiant Air Command Photo*

joke among the pilots. It was fun and, what the hell, the South had always needed its own air force. They all gave themselves the rank of colonel so that no one could ever outrank anyone else, printed up I.D. cards, and considered themselves members of the Confederate Air Force, an organization consisting of one airplane, a few pilots, and a wide open future.

By late 1958 the Confederate Air Force had doubled in size when the pilots bought a Grumman F8F Bearcat fighter. Two years later the entire air force of two planes flew off to fly their first airshow for the U.S. Navy at Kingsville Naval Air Station. Soon after that successful appearance requests began to pour in for more aerial demonstrations of the Mustang and the Bearcat. The pilots assembled for an unofficial staff meeting. They made their decision to obtain every American wartime fighter plane they could find — and were stunned to discover that the only "official policy" of the U.S. Government toward these priceless machines was to melt them down into scrap. As one indication, there wasn't a single Republic P-47 Thunderbolt, of *any* model, to be found in the entire country. Republic had built more than *fifteen thousand* of these great airplanes — and they were *all* gone! The smelters were destroying almost every last historic aircraft of the United States.

What had been essentially fun and games became a mission of urgent, almost desperate, searching for the swiftly vanishing great aircraft of American history. Nolen and his troops began gathering other pilots to the fold. They had obtained a second Bearcat for a total of three fighters, but the purchase of other military aircraft had become a race against time. The year 1961 marked the beginning of the warbird movement in the United States. The rapidly expanding ranks of the organization sent a team to Canada to bring back eight North American AT-6 (T-6) Texan trainers. Marvin L. (Lefty) Gardner, one of the most extraordinary pilots in this country, along with Joe Jones, decided to put up a bundle of cash for the group to buy every fighter they could find until they had at least one copy of each type. In May, Lefty Gardner roared into Rebel Field (they *had* to rename the Mercedes strip) with their first Vought F4U Corsair. Ten days later, Lloyd Nolen brought in the first North American B-25 Mitchell bomber. A few weeks later, John Wells went to Florida to bring back a General Motors FM-2 Wildcat. Early in June, Lefty Gardner departed Ocala, Florida, with a Curtiss P-40 Warhawk.

The Confederate Air Force was humming in more ways than one. Not only were they accepting enthusiastic, capable, and hardworking new members, they had become an incorporated entity, they had members who were putting up hard cash to meet the goals of the CAF, and their purpose had become something more than laughs. A CAF report of their search stated that some of their pilots

> went out to see what was left at the surplus disposal depots in the Arizona territory. What they saw first made these men sad, and then made them angry. They were chopping up and smelting down good airplanes by the hundreds! ... older types had long since been completely destroyed ... it was found that in the future no combat-type aircraft would be used for flying or display purposes. They were to be destroyed before leaving the base.

By 1962 the CAF colonels were learning to "dig in and to consolidate" what they had accomplished so far, and to begin to appreciate the staggering cost and complexity of maintenance. There were some memorable moments for the year, including the adoption of the first CAF Constitution and Bylaws, and the election of the first CAF General Staff. There was also the memory of a fine race among fighters at a naval air station, where the Hellcat in the race "*turned in the wrong direction* around the first pylon, creating one of the most exciting air races in CAF history." The CAF also counted 57 dues-paying members. They were on their way. They also had on hand a P-51, F8F, F6F, FM-2, P-38, P-40, and an F4U fighter and a bunch of T-6 trainers to keep the pilots on their toes.

During the following year the CAF flew its First Annual CAF Air Show, in which they could show to the world the Republic P-47 Thunderbolt found and bought in South America, and, at the airshow, in a triumphant display, they took delivery of a long-sought Bell P-63 Kingcobra. Something new had been added. CAF members in the far reaches of the country began flying their personally owned warbirds down to Texas for what would become a tremendous annual air bash. The year 1963 went into the record books for a most significant reason. By July of that year the CAF was operating twelve aircraft. That had less meaning than did the fact that sixteen CAF colonels had banded together to sponsor those aircraft by putting up hard cash to the tune of over $100,000.

There was the key. Rather than place intolerable burdens upon one man for an aircraft, or just a few men, the CAF was leaning heavily on different sources to provide the funds to attend to its aircraft, hangars, and other facilities. *The organization was the key.* Sponsorships, dues-paying members, airshows that could turn a profit that went back into aircraft purchase and maintenance, and, to no small extent, donations by those who could afford it. Add to the total a growing and meaningful dedication on the part of the members, an increasing level of cooperation from the military and other organizations, and the Confederate Air Force was off and running.

And they were the only outfit in the country who had put their name, money, time, and effort on the line. Without the CAF it seems doubtful that the warbird movement, the preservation and flying of so many warbird types, would ever have achieved the nationwide success that was to come in future years on the part of *all* organizations.

From this point on the Confederate Air Force was no longer merely a club. They had obtained so many aircraft, so many do-

33

The sartorial splendor of the Florida Wing of the Confederate Air Force visits an air force base for a rousing air show. A quiet moment along the flight line with Colonel Tom Autrey (left) and Martin Caidin as they approach their Ju-52 bomber. *Photo by Julian Leek*

nations, built major facilities, and were so well known throughout the country and the world that they had become a major force in the restoration of aircraft. But you can't run an organization without rules and at Harlingen, Texas, where the CAF now flew its flag, the order of the day was increasing control of the many by a few.

Rub pilots the wrong way and you'll find new groups springing up everywhere. By the mid-1960s the first of the powerful new pilot organizations came into being. In 1964 the National Air Races emerged from a long-hated limbo, and the desert sands echoed to the howling thunder of powerful fighters, bombers, and trainers in fierce racing competition. The stars of the show were the hottest airplanes of World War II, the same warbirds that had been rejuvenated in both aluminum and spirit by the CAF. At Reno, however, the airplanes were privately owned instead of being organization property, and therein lay the road to what would become Warbirds of America, Inc.

Warbirds wanted all the pilots to pool information, skills, and data and to supply sources of spare parts to help one another keep their machines flying. They considered joining the CAF in Texas but the general consensus was that Harlingen was the armpit of the country, and why give up anything to a faraway outfit? As aviation writer Jeff Ethell discerned, Warbirds of America came together slowly but surely, with almost all concerned aware that steady information flow from a central office to everyone else in the country was the crucial key to success. After three years of getting their act together, the Warbirds honchos sent Jerry Walbrun to see Paul Poberezny, *the* dean of aircraft resurrection, about Warbirds becoming part of the far-flung Experimental Aircraft Association.

> The courtship was successful, though not without some rough spots [Ethell explains]. Warbird owners have always been independent and hard-driving . . . There was some doubt whether they would mix with a generally more placid group. But the knot was tied, not without some tribulation, and Warbird HQ moved to Hales Corner, Wisconsin . . .
>
> The major aim of Warbirds remained flight safety. Each member owned his own aircraft separately but with the common goal of longevity. Accident reports were common features of the early newsletters, outlining the probable causes — most of them came down to pilot error. . . . Since the aircraft are individually owned and operated, Warbirds cannot form a charitable foundation such as the Confederate Air Force or Canadian Warplane Heritage to receive contributions for operation and maintenance. That everything adheres as well as it does is a testimony to the devotion, interest and camaraderie of those involved.

☆

In today's marketplace a North American P-51D Mustang in what is considered mint condition goes on the selling block for $275,000 as a nice round figure. At a recent warbird bash in Wisconsin, a Curtiss P-40E Kittyhawk, restored with years of work, piles of money, and an enormous amount of personal effort and sacrifice, sold for more than $300,000. Other special fighters carry price tags of a quarter of a million dollars on up. The prices of the once-lowly T-6, in good shape, range anywhere from $20,000 to $50,000 and higher, depending upon equipment installed in the airplane.

35

Consider, then, the most extraordinary position of the Confederate Air Force as this outfit began to assemble its aircraft from the earliest days —

☆

Date	Aircraft	Cost (Dollars)
1951	P-40 Warhawk	1,500
1957	P-51D Mustang	2,500
1959	F8F Bearcat	805
1961	T-6 Texan	800
1961	F4U Corsair	1,800
1961	FM Wildcat	3,500
1961	P-40 Warhawk	3,000
1961	P-38 Lightning	4,000
1961	F6F Hellcat	1,800
1963	P-47 Thunderbolt	8,000
1963	P-63 Kingcobra	10,000
1965	Spitfire	11,500
1965	P-40 Warhawk	12,000
1966	A-20 Havoc	1,000
1966	B-25 Mitchell	2,000
1967	B-24 Liberator	24,000
1967	B-26 Marauder	11,000
1967	B-17 Flying Fortress	35,000
1971	SB2C Helldiver	25,000
1972	PBY Catalina	40,000

☆

In the April 1983 issue of *Trade-a-Plane*, the buying bible of aircraft the world over, an antique Pitcairn PA8 Super Mailwing was on the selling block for *$175,000!*

Two Mustangs were for sale, *one at $239,000 and the other for $290,000!* These airplanes were selling in 1951 for $1,000.

If you wanted a TBM Avenger single-engined torpedo bomber the asking price was "only" $175,000.

And if your interest lay in a really hot fighter like the 3000 horsepower Goodyear F2G Corsair, all you had to do was to write out a cashier's check for *$600,000.*

Of course, your interest might be turned to the 1928 Ford 4AT B-38 that was up for sale for a tidy little price of $950,000. Not to be outdone, another Ford Tri-Motor (which also served in the old Air

Corps and is every inch a warbird) was going for a nifty $1,200,000.

Getting the true handle on aircraft costs, other than noting the dizzying upward spiral, rocketlike in that ascent, calls for someone who probably knows more about the subject than anyone else in the world. That would be a man who has spent a lifetime in purchasing, horsetrading, exhibiting, managing, restoration, resurrection, and commanding the respect of hundreds of thousands of people in the airplane business. Not an easy task, to understate a position impossible of success. Yet Paul Poberezny has accomplished all of the above and much, much more, including a reputation as one of the finest pilots in all the world, as a father who watches his youngsters carry the family name through world competitions and dazzling successes, and who more than any other person has guaranteed a majesty of historical perspective for this country through the Experimental Aircraft Association and his leadership as president. He is also chairman of the board of the EAA Air Museum Foundation. I have known Paul for many years and we have pushed some heavy air with our flying machines, and in respect to the foregoing warbirds and their costs and their place in our historical structure, I asked for his comments, which arrived by mail. I excerpt those parts most pertinent to our immediate interest:

☆

Aircraft such as these were extremely popular right after World War II and the government disposed of these machines for little or nothing. I can recall incidents where people bought such aircraft as B-17s, B-24s, B-29s at a very low price and, in draining the fuel from the aircraft, either paid for the scrap price that they paid for it or significantly toward it, in the sale of fuel.

Today, things are much different. Our government is in search of some of the very aircraft that were destroyed. But who knew or cared those years? Where are the men who made the decisions then? I can recall that during the Korean War, where we were short of airplanes and materiel, we went out and bought such aircraft as T-6s from civilians, and I myself searched surplus stores for such items as throat mikes, Mae Wests, parachutes, gloves, and clothing that were in short supply during the Korean War, and personally flew a lot of this material to Travis Air Force Base for air delivery to Korea.

Today, World War II aircraft of all types are in great demand. As the supply of these aircraft becomes less through accidents, the prices become higher. Along with this, is the great appreciation

37

being shown by the public for World War II aircraft. For example, the EAA Aviation Foundation owns the first experimental P-51 that the United States purchased back in 1940. We obtained this airplane through a trade with the National Air and Space Museum for a Northrup Alpha. The airplane was in very good condition. This aircraft we value at least between *$750 and $800 thousand.* Others have said you can't put a price on it.

Currently, we are restoring a B-25. The project has been going on for more than six years. It will undoubtedly be the best B-25 in the world. It has been completely stripped down to a bare hulk; all zinc chromate interior and exterior; removed every bit of wiring out of it; wing tanks removed; wings removed; tailgroup rebuilt; two zero time engines put on it; all accessories, hoses, landing gear overhauled; propellers overhauled; new glass and many other items including reskinning good portions of the tail and wings to take care of corrosion. I would estimate the airplane is worth approximately $350 to $400 thousand.

True, one can pick up junkers much cheaper, but several hundred thousand dollars in labor, materials, etc., will bring the price back up to an excellent, conditioned aircraft.

Our P-51D modified to a Cavalier, in its military paint, which is in excellent condition, has my own estimated value on it of some $300 thousand.

A P-38 in good condition, especially in the original condition, is worth at least $500 thousand.

A Corsair in excellent condition is worth between $300 and $350 thousand. These variances in price depend on radio equipment installed, and as we both know, it doesn't take much to spend $25,000 on radio equipment.

T-6s in the past five years have more than doubled in price, and getting spares for many of these aircraft is becoming more difficult, as many people are hanging on to them. For example, R2600 engines, which are used in the B-25 that had from three to five hundred hours, were once sold as scrap for little or nothing. How things have changed! Supply and demand has again reared its ugly head — ugly, meaning that it costs more. In fact, people are rounding up most of all the radial engines for parts or for remanufacture, as they don't make that type of equipment anymore. What good is an airframe without a powerplant?

My Twin Beech, which at one time was a drug on the market (I have an E model), was worth about $17 to $20 thousand. I've owned this one for 12 years and I wouldn't sell it for $60 thousand in its fine condition today, as you can't get that kind of comfort, long range fuel, low maintenance, etc. in any of our off-the-shelf factory-built aircraft that would cost five times as much.

☆

Paul Poberezny and I discussed a wide variety of airplanes, the fact that in the business today what was once worthless scrap and junk has suddenly attained incredible value. A good example is the Messerschmidt bf-108B *Taifun* I bought in France back in 1963 for $1500. Paul and I agreed that today the same airplane has a fair market value (which is defined by the fact that people are willing to spend that amount) of $45 to $60 thousand.

In this business of warbirds there are a number of people who are extremely wealthy. Some of them have the habit of flaunting their wealth in "rich kid fashion," and while they're usually taking a barrage of criticism for those actions, that's between them and their direct antagonists and I don't subscribe to kangaroo-court critical judgments of them, either personally or professionally. Without the generosity of these same people, with both their money and the sweat of their brows, a great many warbirds would never have been saved, rebuilt, or preserved. Paul Poberezny noted that "one of our members is donating his P-38L, which has some 1500 hours total time on it, and a 1200-hour Corsair to the Foundation."

Who can knock *that!*

Paul provides yet another look at this affair of the gathering of Warbirds:

Our own Ford Trimotor, which has been under restoration for some time now, is almost ready to go. We've had the fuselage rebuilt, using primarily new materials. We've trucked it to one of our maintenance hangars so I can keep a full-time sheetmetal man on this project until it is completed. This way I will have better control of the quality of work. . .

The Northrop P-61 is another most unusual airplane, and as you say, none are flying. I would put that machine in a class of about $350 thousand.

The Focke-Wulf FW-190, which has been rebuilt and is now complete, would be in an area of a good $400 to $450 thousand, a bit more than a P-51 in the same excellent condition, because of its rarity. I wouldn't be surprised if someone might even offer $500 thousand.

Well, you can see where the long green gets shorter as the value of the warbirds grows ever greater. Consider some of the higher prices you've just seen and then consider, now, what absolutely must be the greatest bargain ever struck in the history of warbirds. Back in the period of a few years after World War II, Paul Mantz was swinging high, wide, and handsome as a pilot flying movie stunts, tearing up air races, and locking on to some really nifty charter flying. He locked up a deal with the U.S. Government to buy — hang on to your seat — *475* warplanes that had been declared surplus. Would you believe that included in this entire air force were no fewer than 75 Boeing B-17 Flying Fortress bombers!

Total sale price for the 475 airplanes: $55,000.

And the greatest coup of all came when Mantz took title to that vast fleet of warplanes, drained the tanks of fuel, sold the fuel, and with the money received for the gasoline — paid off the entire bill of $55,000!

The New Kids
on the Block

Of all the things that make an airplane
fly, the most important is money.

SCOTT SMITH

Mike Dillon is one of the country's best warbird pilots. He's been jockeying fighters from the Big Iron of World War II to sleek jet fighters and just about everything in between, and he also has been one of the major factors contributing to the health of the warbird effort on a national basis. In 1969, on one of his many trips Mike Dillon returned to Confederate Air Force headquarters in Harlingen, Texas, to attend a three-day seminar on goals and ideals of the CAF, as well as to listen to some of the great aces and veterans of flying combat in the Big Deuce, and getting a renewed feel of what the CAF was now all about. He noted a change in attitude. Things were more serious than they had been. The cry of the CAF had always been a tongue-in-cheek *Semper Mint Julep* and was now replaced with Flying Museum. Not as much fun, perhaps, but that's the way the CAF felt, and they were getting *very* serious about the care and feeding of the growing air force under their command.

The man who had started it all, Lloyd Nolen, the dean of warbird movement in the land, laid it on the line to the seminar attendees:

> We have fulfilled the goal we had set: to collect one each of the major warplanes representing the war years, 1939 to 1945. Al-

41

though it would always be desirable to obtain duplicates, this is not now our primary goal. Most important now is to put our planes in top-notch mechanical condition and to display them in the manner they deserve.

Mike Dillon noted that when it came to maintenance of those airplanes everything wasn't quite so pristine, that the CAF was already earning "more than a little criticism" in this area. But as those on the scene noted quickly the CAF was well aware of this problem and was facing squarely what was becoming a monumental task.

When we talked with various people around the country [Lefty Gardner told the seminar], they told us it would be impossible to keep a fleet of planes this size in the air. Well, so far they've been wrong. We've had our problems — the sheer number of planes would dictate that — and it should be understood that in terms of maintenance, we've been hanging on by our fingertips. We need to get ahead, to think ahead to the times when there are no cheap engines left in the surplus yards. There will even come a time, not far away, when engine shops won't be equipped to rebuild our recip engines. If we are to continue our work in keeping these planes alive, we must now put as much effort into restoration and preparation for future maintenance as we have into acquisition.

Those were remarks from the Annual Seminar of the CAF on the Preservation of World War Two Aircraft. Just over a year later, in the November 1970 issue of *Air Progress* magazine, a thoroughly disenchanted and unhappy Mike Dillon put his byline to a damning article with the title "Don't Let Them Sabotage the Confederate Air Force." Dillon pulled no punches.

When I first visited Old Rebel Field in Mercedes, in 1964, I was appalled by the condition of the warplanes there. Though most of them flew, the P-38, the B-26, and the Hellcat were the only ones that appeared to be airworthy. Their P-40, N1228N, was particularly shabby. A year later Colonel George Walters was killed flying that same P-40 over Rebel Field.

In addition to the P-40, the CAF has also destroyed its only P-63, two F8F Bearcats, their only SBD Dauntless dive bomber, their only Hellcat, and one Mark XIV Spitfire. They have severely mauled one of the very few Martin B-26s left in the world by dropping it on its belly twice because of hydraulic problems. And three of the above-named crashes involved fatalities. On the three airports used primarily by the CAF — Rebel Field, Mercedes; Rebel

Field, Harlingen; and Brownwood, Texas — four F-51 Mustangs have crashed; three were totals with three fatalities.

Dillon also took direct aim at the manner in which the CAF maintained relationships with all the people who lived some distance from Harlingen, what Dillon labeled as "an area that smacks more of James Bond than air museums." He accused the CAF of such laxity that its members, and clearly identified as such, were implicated in illegal gun-running to El Salvador. To Dillon, the CAF was more interested in a free-wheeling public image that caught public attention than it was in protecting the good name of the CAF. Favoritism reared its ugly head, Dillon charged, and the CAF hotly denied any such attitude on its part.

> If the aim of the CAF is to promote good fellowship [Dillon demanded], why also have so many of the organization's most effective members left, disenchanted with the way it was being run? The pilot who owned the only genuine military B-26 in the museum is one of those who pulled out and took his aircraft with him. Others who have invested as much as $25,000 to $30,000 each have withdrawn for the same reasons.

There's the old saw that if you don't like the way the outfit is run — get out. As Dillon emphasized, many people did. But right or wrong, it's essential to emphasize that the CAF was and remains the most successful organization of its type in existence. People like Lloyd Nolen and Lefty Gardner created the beginning of *the* ground swell that took in the world and gave marvelous new meaning to our history and traditions.

What hacked off so many pilots was that the CAF became almost a grim business. The tongue-in-cheek war cry of *Semper Mint Julep* was discarded. No more Confederate flag. Class A uniforms! Rules, regulations, *more* restrictions. Hew to the line, toe the mark: *behave.* A group of pilots went to the big Harlingen bash to attend the CAF airshow and ran into the snarls and swamps of all the new rules. Angry words flew, middle fingers went up, and the Florida people climbed back into their planes, snarled "Screw you," and flew back to Florida to relate the sordid moments.

The uproarious response was that several hundred pilots and friends *all* raised their right hands with middle finger extended. Harlingen didn't like the upstarts from Florida, there were more acrimonious exchanges, and rising from the bubbling cauldron was the spirit of a completely new organization. The Valiant Air Command was about to be born.

☆

"I admit it's one thing to secede from the Union. But what the hell," Ted Anderson announced to the pilots, mechanics, wives, and friends gathered to rally 'round the warbird flag in Florida, "the South did it once and we can do it for them again." He scratched his beard. "Of course, it do feel a bit strange seceding from the Confederacy, of all things. But I don't think Harlingen was never really a part of Lee's army, so that makes it all right."

Pete Sherman, who flew a big and hot P-51 Mustang with a 2300 horsepower monster of an engine in his Pony, showed his impatience. "It's stupid to waste time on schoolgirl nonsense," he declared. "We've got airplanes to fly, and we need practice, cooperation, and clear heads. Let's forget all this crap about Harlingen and get down to the business at hand. The new outfit." It was good to hear those words from Pete. An old-line Air Force pilot, he was speaking for the likes of Johnny Baugh and Johnny Williams and a bunch of guys driving the heavy iron, people who wanted to get back to the business of *flying*.

So we had a big fight and named the new outfit the Valiant Air Command. We made Leo Kerwin *El Supremo*, and we went to work. It was much the same formula that characterized the Confederate Air Force during its early period of growth. True to form, the VAC quickly produced its own wings, a patch, and — *hold it right there*. It went no further than that. The feelings of the pilots, of everyone, were well known. Let's not screw around with uniforms, unnecessary rules and regulations, and self-bloated importance. Irreverence was to be upheld, and dearly.

After all, consider that the writer was voted in unanimously as Chaplain of the Valiant Air Command.

☆

Again, as a clear signal of the path to success *without* creating huge rifts among the membership, so that any organization to which you and your friends may aspire and create on your own, let me offer the comments of several top aviation writer/pilots who have covered the flying and the warbird scene from Day One.

Writing in *Air Classics*, Michael O'Leary made the incisive notations that the

Valiant Air Command is an offshoot of the old Florida Wing of the Confederate Air Force. Dissatisfied with internal CAF bickering and politics [this is O'Leary talking: MC], a number of members decided to sever ties to the original organization and step forward with a new group that would hopefully eliminate the many problems encountered in the past. The original group of twenty pilots and enthusiasts had six aircraft, and the main purpose of the VAC was to restore, preserve, and fly World War Two fighters, bombers, and trainers. The idea of eliminating many of the problems that plagued the CAF was a good one as the VAC soon grew to over 400 members who own ... World War Two machines roughly broken down as follows: fifteen P-51s, six Corsairs, eight B-25s, two Skyraiders, ten Trojans, three Bearcats, a Hellcat, a Lockheed 10, eight Stearmans, three Avengers, nine Messerschmitt 108s, 109s, and 208s, and a variety of other lighter aircraft. Members are from over twenty States and Canada.

There were other aircraft, including two Wildcats, three C-47 transports, the hulking Ju-52, a couple of P-40s, one P-38L (still under rebuild), a Beech AT-11, a mob of T-34 trainers, variants of aircraft built to "act" as Japanese fighters and bombers, a swarm of ragwings, a B-26 Invader, and a Russian Yak-11.

O'Leary offered this writer an unusual view "from the other side" when he described the Ju-52's arrival for a VAC airshow:

As Friday wore on, Warbirds began to arrive at a fast pace — Mustangs screaming overhead, Texans rumbling into the pattern and then perhaps the most curious arrival — complete with its own marching band, was Martin Caidin's Ju-52 *Iron Annie*, which entered the pattern with smoke systems pumping out acres of the white stuff and underwing speakers booming out German wartime songs that would have made any good fascist stand up and take attention. Martin has invested mega-bucks in getting the tri-motor into pristine shape and this old bird really performs — jumping off the ground in 400 feet and landing in the same distance.

What's really important here is the observation made by O'Leary (and other top national pilot/writers) as he carefully studied the manner in which the big VAC airshow was flown in Florida, not from the viewpoint of the aircraft, *but the people*. If you want the key to your own successful organization, then heed O'Leary's words:

Saturday and Sunday were spent flying and there was a lot of it — the Warbirds were in the air from the early morning until sun-

Every seat filled, the famed *Iron Annie* leads the way "down the slot" for a landing at Langley Air Force Base, where the Valiant Air Command put on an uproarious airshow for the Tactical Air Command. *Photo by Major Vern Alexander, USAF*

set, and spectators were able to see plenty of aerial activity from fairly close quarters and were allowed to examine the aircraft and talk to the pilots when they were on the ground. This is one of the big benefits of Ti-Co; the fact that the people that are paying the money to enter the airfield are actually allowed to get a real close look at the Warbirds. This, unfortunately, is not practiced at other airshows, where the public and the aircraft are kept far apart.

Ed Schnepf is the chief honcho of Challenge Publications, which among many other top, slick, and leading magazines in the business, turns out both *Air Classics* and *Air Progress* magazines. We've presented what O'Leary had to say in *Air Classics*. Schnepf also sent Budd Davisson to represent his *Air Progress* magazine in covering activities of the Valiant Air Command. Davisson went to the 1981 big air bash of warbirds in Florida and had this to say:

Having the Space Shuttle and satellites in the pattern isn't the only thing that sets the VAC show apart. There are literally dozens

46

of things that make it significantly different. Take the VAC itself, for instance. When you see the troops walking around, pounding stakes into the ground for the show line, unloading a truck load of bleachers, or climbing into a Mustang or Skyraider they look and act like plain plane-folks. That may not sound like much, unless you've hit a few of the other big warbird gatherings. Some of them are knee-deep in counterfeit colonels, uniforms, and bleached blondes with Earl Scheib tans. Little by little, the VAC troops are striking off in a different direction, which includes enjoying and preserving warbirds with an absolute minimum of pageantry and pomposity. No doubt there *is* a place for colonels and uniforms, but the folks of the VAC have decided that Titusville isn't one of them . . .

It isn't so glossy slick that it has the overall feel of commercialization that affects most of the larger airshows. It is obvious even to the newcomer that the guys and gals of the Valiant Air Command just dig the hell out of what they are doing.

The atmosphere of the show is more one of a good-sized, but still countrified, EAA show, rather than a warbird thing. It is all but impossible to separate the drivers from the drivees, the owners from the buffs. The tendency for the high rollers to look down on the *peons* and the idolatry of the Mustang/Mitchell/Etc cult wasn't there. The VAC is a totem pole with only one level. If you support the VAC, you are part of the crew, whether you fly a Tripacer, a Skyraider, or an armchair. The show benefits greatly from this type of undimensional camaraderie.

From a purely spectator point of view what really makes the VAC airshow worth hitting is the tremendous number of airplanes that you never get to see anywhere else. That part of the world seems to have some of the best kept secrets in the country.

One year later (and after sampling many of the warbird types from the left seat, and delighting the pilots with his expertise), Budd Davisson was back again, with a few more pertinent comments to hand on to the outside world. After the 1982 show he wrote:

"I figured it would fly like a T-6 or maybe a BT-13," grinned Tom Crevasse, "but I'll tell you what, this machine will bite you faster than any plane I know of." As he spoke, his fifteen-year-old daughter stood at his elbow, looking slightly out of place, as if her dad had just picked her up at the malt shop on the way to the airport. Her slightly shy image covered the fact that her dad was teaching her to fly in the Yale, and was going to solo in it on her sixteenth birthday. Was this going to be a kitten at the controls of a tiger?

Directly opposite from the BT-14 and opposite in more ways than one, Martin Caidin hulked under the equally imposing hulk of *Iron Annie*, a.k.a. the German Shepherd . . . his rare Junkers Ju-52. Caidin . . . delights in being just a little bit "different." In point of fact, as he slides down out of the flight deck of the corrugated German monstrosity he flies, he looks like a Hell's Angel gone to seed and you half expect him to unload a chopped Harley out of the back of the Junkers. You only have to hang around for a short period of time to realize that nobody has more fun in airplanes than Martin.

The opposites of the personalities at the Valiant Air Command Show are matched by the opposites in hardware. As a matter of fact, the VAC show is a very pleasing mixture of diametrically opposed machines and men (and women) that seem to dovetail together into a very tightly joined event that seems to get stronger each year. Although coming from different parts of the country and from different directions psychologically, the membership of the VAC seems to cross-weave itself into a soft and subtle fabric that somehow seems very comfortable and easy to wear, which certainly shows in their yearly air show. . .

The Titusville Hardware Show will be hard to beat. A large part of this increase in turnout and the resulting variety is the tremendous support the VAC has been getting from pilots across the country. The great warbird grapevine has passed the word that the VAC and its get-together are guaranteed good times and guaranteed good friends. As a general rule, the entire Eastern half of the United States is represented by attending airplanes. They come from as far North as Vermont and Connecticut and as far West as Texas and everything in between. . .

The question is often asked, "What is the best warbird show in the country?" and, of course, that raises a subjective question, what is "best"? It is difficult to come up with an answer, but one thing we can definitely point out is that of the shows within the United States, the VAC is by far the most enjoyable from the point of view of the participants and the spectators. It is easy-going, it is fun-loving, and at the same time does an excellent job of putting military history on parade for those who have an interest or for those who want to know what went down before. There are few, if any, personality conflicts, and those directly involved in the management of the VAC are very much aware of the problems which personalities and egos can cause within this type of movement. They have the benefit of seeing what has happened to other shows and organizations and appear to be doing their best to learn from the others' mistakes while maintaining a very high level of camaraderie and internal understanding.

☆

"Ve haff vays of makingk you fly der vay good Chermans fly, no?" Colonel Super Heine-Dog stands in for Colonel Leo Kerwin at a Valiant Air Command pilot briefing. *Photo by Russ Votoe*

One of the promises we vowed to keep when we started the Valiant Air Command was to make certain that the people who headed the organization, who were voted in by the members, would represent not only the drivers of heavy iron, and who were old-time veterans, but would clearly represent the newcomers, those too young to have flown heavy or even light military equipment in years past. The drivers of Spam Cans (Cessnas, Pipers, Beech, Aeronca, etc.) all share the Walter Mitty yearning to get their hands on the Big Stuff and drive through the sky like airborne sharks or whales. And they need to know that the guy who leads the whole group understands *their* problems. To get the new outfit on its feet we elected Leo Kerwin, accepting the fact that *El Supremo* would give everybody a hard time to make the VAC a viable organization. There are a few of us who like to work about twenty hours a day and get our sleep catch-as-catch-can. Leo Kerwin is one of those people, and there have been times when the organizational duties got a bit heavy, and a group of us would go two or three days without sleep to keep things humming properly. It's not the sort of thing we'd care to do again but we're not sorry all this took place, because it made the VAC what it is.

After Leo had served his initial term, we had a big and uproarious meeting, during which a bunch of people stood up to propose a tall drink of water named Pat Coyle as the new leader of the VAC. If Pat Coyle stands sideways you'd better have a shadow for reference to see this guy. Pat was twenty-eight years old when we launched him on his new career of headaches, problems, worries, consternation, and endless hammering as the VAC leader. So let him tell you what it was all about, and accept the fact that this is *the* blueprint for starting any outfit anywhere in the country. When I wasn't pushing the Ju-52 around the circuit for one airshow, I got Pat to mumble into a tape recorder, when *he* wasn't buried by the thousand and one chores that have to be done every hour of every airshow day.

We stood outside the command operations tent of the airshow, covered with dust and grass from taxiing fighters and bombers, swarming with people going in nine directions at once, and watched three B-25 bombers roaring down the runway in formation and lifting magically into the sky. Behind them, a bunch of Mustangs howled down the airstrip, climbing steeply into a hot sun. Pat looked at them wistfully. He felt a bit uncomfortable about putting it all down on the record, but the alternative — being tied to a Mustang prop and spun around a few dozen times — prompted him to verbalize.

"You know enough about this game," he chided. "If you work like a madman for two months before an airshow, ignore your business, try to placate your family, and do all the things that need doing, nothing will really go wrong. Nothing," he said ruefully, "that good people and a good organization can't fix quickly enough. Because the first rule in running an airshow is that things *do* go wrong. At the worst possible time, the fuel truck breaks down. Some pilots get confused about the timing of their acts. We're short a few pieces of dynamite for the pyrotechnics. The weather may give you fits. Everything wants to get done all at the same time. So the rule is you never go far from this tent, away from the phones and the radios where people know they can reach you and the rest of the staff when something really goes wrong." He looked around him at several dozen wives and girl friends, some of them pilots flying in the show at other times, working furiously. "It's a big macho world, right? Without those women we couldn't move three feet in the right direction. The guys get the glory and do their stuff in front of the crowd, and the women do most of the real work."

We turned to watch the B-25 bombers coming back, two Messerschmitts sneaking up behind and below them. Pat grinned. "You know, this was all an impossible dream not so very long ago. I mean, I grew up with my nose in magazines and glued to the TV set just to look at pictures and films of these things. I used to dream, to hope, I might just get to *see* one or some of them. And it's sad to realize that within my lifetime, I expect just about every plane here will be as extinct as the fighters and bombers from World War One are at this moment. It's incredible to be a living part of this history. I never even *saw* a real-life, honest-to-goodness warbird until November of 1976, when I went to the big open house and airshow at Cecil Field, the naval air station outside Jacksonville. And that was when I decided I had to get close to them. Just as close as I could possibly get, in fact. I went to Cecil Field and I walked slowly down the flight line, and I touched all that beautiful metal and listened with disbelief when those engines snarled and coughed and roared. My God — Cyclones and Wasps and Allisons and Merlins. What music! My whole body was hammered with sound. They had to push me out of the way of all those propellers.

"So I found out about warbirds and wondered, prayed, really, if I could get even closer. I'd heard about the Confederate Air Force, and when I heard there was a Florida Wing, man, but I was gung-ho to join this bunch. Although I was really pretty scared about mixing in with those pilots. You should have seen some of them. Faded jeans and old flight jackets and cigars and scroungy hats, mixed in with other types wearing beautiful flight suits, and gorgeous women all over the place. It was like a movie come to life in front of me. Anyway, I learned quickly there were rumbles in the state. I live in Jacksonville, not that far from where the Florida Wing headquarters was located in the Titusville area, and I went to talk to those guys. The Wing had started up in 1975, but it became so hot and so successful in the whole Southeast with its airshows and special events and its own open houses that a lot of friction came on fast with the biggies in Harlingen. I didn't know

51

much about the politics of it all, but these people looked like being pushed around was pretty stupid even to try with them. I mean, they'd run right over you. I was told to hang loose, that a lot of the pilots were really ticked off with the CAF. Sure enough, the Florida gang told the CAF where to go and how to get there, and the CAF yanked their charter in August of 1977. If this was supposed to bother them you'd never know it. They all raised their fists in the air and it was like a huge roar of *CHAAAARGE!"*

Let me make a point quite clear. I knew this story from the inside, but if it is going to have real meaning to anyone who wants to become a member of the Warbird Clan, Pat Coyle's impressions and reactions are, as I said earlier, your blueprint for the way to go.

"When the hammer fell," Pat continued, "I guess about forty of the guys, and their women, all got together for a big hoorah to work out where they were going in the future. Leo Kerwin was a dynamo and there were people around him just as explosive. I learned my first lesson there. Any one of them could have been the leader, but they *all* voted Leo in as the new commander because they also knew he was the best man for the job. In other words, the guys you'd expect to be the up-front hero types stepped back. Leo had a real good group of dedicated people. They were going to fly their airshows, *period*, and they picked this as the way to go. I was in the middle of it all as the Valiant Air Command was created, and I loved their emphasis on having the people who owned their airplane fly that same airplane in whatever show or event was going on. They also had a lot of spontaneous gatherings, and those were really wild. Talk about your impromptu airshows! Well, like I say, having the individual fly his own plane was the important thing. With the CAF, the emphasis was for the airplane to remain inside the organization and to be flown by a very chosen few, either at Harlingen or where they were delegated out to the wings and squadrons.

"I had also heard, and my new friends confirmed every bit of it, that the CAF had a high-level hierarchy. The 'in' crowd, as it were. If you owned anything less than a fighter plane they'd look down on you. You were snubbed like a second-class citizen. That is a lot of bull, as far as I'm concerned, and we had unanimous agreement on that point. Look out there at all the trainers, everything from the ragmops on up through the T-6 to the T-28s and others. The skill to fly that T-6 is even more demanding than it is to fly the

52

Mustang or a Hellcat. For God's sake, that's why pilots were trained in the T-6. It bit people. I've been in quite a few of them by now and I've got teeth marks everywhere. And as the leader of this outfit, I'll never forget what I knew even before I got near the group — that all these planes played vital roles in their own way to win a war."

Pat pointed to the throngs of people who seemed to be everywhere. "Just look at them," he said with obvious pride. "The VAC treats all its people the same, whether they're pilots or mechanics or traffic controllers or ticket-takers. Everybody who loves airplanes is welcome, and that's good enough for everybody else. Hell, when I joined this outfit I wasn't a pilot, but the guys took me up. It's tough to turn down a sad-looking puppy with his tongue resting on the wing." Pat glared at me. "*You* should know about that."

"The microphone," I urged. "Just tell it to the microphone like I'm not even here."

"Fat chance," he muttered, and then did as he was supposed to do: recalled the events. "When the guys took me up, I had a tendency to get violently ill if they did funny things when I was in the plane."

Boy! Did he ever. That's where he earned the name of *Vomit Varmint* . . .

"But since I've gotten mixed up with this bunch," Pat went on, "I worked hard at it and earned my ticket, and I can handle the controls with some sense and purpose now. I've even passed that point where I tolerate being thrown violently about the sky. Let me emphasize for the younger folk out there who may be reading this, that the first time I got into a warbird it was stinking, it was hot, it was uncomfortable, and my stomach was laying on its side and quivering like a dying dog before we ever taxied to the runway. The noise! The vibrations! But I knew I had to do it and get as close as I could. I'm a bit too young and a bit too poor for all this expensive hardware, but thanks to all these guys I get a lot of back seat, and right seat, time."

"Hold it," I broke in. "You got a lot of *left* seat command time as well by now."

That's a point *I* want to emphasize. Pat Coyle came into the outfit without ever having been *in* a warbird. The guys pushed and cajoled and helped him. He got his license in a Spam Can. He has also flown in the T-6 and the T-28, in B-25 and B-26 bombers, he's flown every position in the Ju-52, he's had some wild times in a

"Tally-ho the Airshow!" A T-6 Texan leads a low, tight formation in a salute down the runway of Patrick Air Force Base to open the 1976 airshow season in Florida. *Valiant Air Command Photo*

bunch of different types of fighters, and he'd never even *seen* a warbird until 1976. Too young and too poor, right? Look at what happened to him! And he has lots of company. *That's* what makes this outfit different . . .

I pointed to Pat Coyle's name badge. "It don't say colonel," I told him. "It don't even say corporal, or dogbreath, or something appropriate."

"Well, for sure it's not going to say colonel," Pat retorted. "I'm not the only one who feels this way. A bunch of former CAF members in this outfit came to me, as leader, and said they felt uncomfortable with the colonel idea. Sure, it was all started as fun with the CAF, I know that, but the CAF isn't so much fun anymore and the colonel name has stuck. These guys would like to see the *official* title just disappear. I agree. Let them wear any rank they want so long as they're making jokes. I've learned, for myself, anyway, that there are too many people in the world who have earned that title. I don't need the ego trip of having it simply handed to me."

Remember, this is Pat Coyle's opinion, and one of the reasons we were all so gung-ho in getting him into the commander's slot is that we wanted to know how this new generation felt about such things.

"People come to this show," Pat went on slowly, his eyes moving all the time to take in possible trouble spots, "fully expecting a great time. They have no doubts, all things being normal, that they'll leave here with that great time behind them. Not everything goes like a greased clock. These airplanes are old and the guys beat them pretty hard and every now and then one breaks down. That's the signal for the other people to ask, 'What can I do to help?'"

One VAC member we'll all remember for a long time (about every time we fly or just talk about flying) is Ken Stallings, who was killed when a biplane he was testing whipped into a violent inverted flat spin from low altitude. No time to get out. Just a few seconds at the most and the ship slammed with instant-lights-out impact into the ground. As we all do, Pat remembers Ken Stallings very closely. I feel the same way. I'd been tied up with Ken since 1976 in old Corpus Christi days, and we'd flown together many times in many different iron birds. Pat came under Ken's wing and that was one very special reason why Pat Coyle came along so fast in his flying.

"Ken was a magician in running an airshow," Pat said quietly. "It took that man a long time to pop his cork. He'd been an army flight instructor, a navy instructor, he flew with the air force, he flew helicopters and flying boats and bombers and fighters and just about anything that had wings. He had patience and understanding that was legendary. And he was a giant in building this outfit. This matter of patience and understanding is vital to any volunteer organization. The key to making this or any other volunteer outfit work is *not* the airplanes. Our growth has always been based on how we treat the members. If we take care of the people, they'll take care of us. That was a lesson Ken Stallings pounded over and over again into my head. I never forgot it. Ken also ran his airshows by the book."

Pat sighed. "And I mean *by the book*. That same nice guy, that same sweet fellow, grew long teeth and claws when it came to safety. It was all rules and all regulations, and he'd bust *anybody* out of the show who endangered anybody else. He kept warning us that there were a lot of guys in the FAA who'd like to see warbirds locked and chained to the ground forever. It would make their jobs easier. Ken had about every ticket in the book, and he was also a certified A&P. He could work on any airplane. He *knew* when a bird wasn't safe and he'd ground it in an instant.

"Remember one rule by which Ken always lived? There are a hell of a lot of good pilots, real sharp flyboys, who don't own airplanes. For whatever reason, including the one that should be spoken very loudly: They've got a family and kids and they can't afford one. So, we share. Ken wanted those people to have every opportunity to fly they could have."

Pat glared at me. "What the hell are you grinning about? *You* checked out a bunch of guys in your airplane, and someone who keeps count of such things said you've taken up more than two thousand people in the Ju-52 during our shows."

"More or less," I told him. "Look, the tape's running out. You got anything to say to those people out in the world who want to start their own warbird outfits?"

"It'll be in your book, won't it?"

I allowed as how that was possible.

"Then add only this thing," Pat tacked on. "If they get people who keep a list of things they do so they can compare how great they are to what other people do, then they don't have a chance to make it. No scorecards; *none*. At least by the person doing the job or jobs. Go at it with everything you have. Be prepared to give it your all. Get your pleasure out of *doing*. If you need to pass the hat for compliments, then stay home." He waved a hand to take in the thunder and pageantry about us.

"It's worth it all, and a hundred times more. Where else can you live all your boyhood dreams come true?"

Everything but the Flak

Don't listen to those assholes. No matter
how warm they say the temperature of
the North Atlantic may be, it's always
too damned cold.

GREG BOARD

The lookout in the submarine's conning tower shivers from the cold, flinches from wind lashing his face with icy spray, and generally curses his commander, the whole submarine, and the world in general. It is early afternoon, but ominous gloom over the North Atlantic makes it seem like the end of the world. Black clouds swirl angrily and dump icy sleet on the sub lying low in the water. What's he supposed to see in all this wretched world that he must be exposed to such misery! He faces west to escape some of the wind, hunches his shoulders, stares gloomily at thick, low fog banks, and . . .

His jaw drops. He gapes in disbelief as three great winged shapes slice the rolling edge of the fog and rush against the conning tower. He blinks his eyes and opens his mouth to scream a warning. Nothing comes from the slack jaw as the three shapes explode in size as they come closer. Four-engined bombers! It is not possible! This is *1961* and those are ancient machines and — He moans in fear as twelve engines thunder only inches over his head, then all the roar is whipsaw explosions and a terrible blast of wind and staring at rivets and the lookout shakes his paralysis and spins around to see the three Flying Fortress bombers sail around another wall of fog and *vanish*.

In the middle of the Atlantic Ocean, three B-17 bombers with machine guns roaring at wavetop level through a storm, sixteen years after the last shot of World War II was fired? Impossible! Who would ever believe him?

☆

I would. So would the other nine madmen who were aboard those Flying Dutchmen as we whipped inches above that conning tower in mid-Atlantic. It was a flight with a constant stream of minor and major mechanical difficulties that would make a gremlin delirious with joy and a strong man weep. The flight began in Arizona, with England the final destination, and the three old bombers made it notwithstanding nonstop dire predictions by our fellow pilots and aircraft owners, despite weather forecasts that should have resulted in the weathermen being garrotted until their tongues turned blue, and enough engine fires to keep a marshmallow manufacturer rich for life.

Today, in retrospect, it becomes clear we were actually part of the small group of pilots scattered throughout the world who had begun — unknowingly — what would soon be termed "the great warbird movement." It didn't start that way. Stated simply, we were to take three ancient bombers, two of which had officially been written off the register as worthless junk, fly them in formation for promotion purposes, and deliver them for the express purpose of recreating, for movie cameras, exciting combat scenes with the Flying Fortresses. The movie? *The War Lover.* Compared to the delivery flight, the exciting scenes in the movie were strictly ho-hum.

One of the two instigators of the plot was Greg Board, a rock of an Australian with a charming smile and a quiet air about him, who is disalarmingly as crazy as the Mad Hatter. He is also an unbelievably brilliant pilot, who had flown everything from soggy Brewster Buffalo fighters against laughing Japanese in Zeros, to heavy transports. Prior to this caper he had never been in a B-17.

The other plotter was his opposite number, John Crewdson, who is quickly described as taking unabashed delight in flying anything, anywhere, at any time, and in any manner that appeals to him. Columbia Pictures had contracted with these two worthies to deliver the three bombers to England. How they did it, Columbia didn't care. Which meant, simply stated, that the fixed-fee contract lent itself to outlandish methods. You see, the less money spent on the trip meant the more profit made at the close of the trip. Instru-

58

ments cost money. New radios cost money. *Everything* costs money, so the simple solution was to spend as little money as was possible. On instruments, radios, and other things generally considered necessary to the good health of machinery and warm bodies taking that machinery across the Atlantic under winter conditions.

The British aviation press, normally reticent to a fault, went bananas over the flight and arrival. They wrote of the trip that it was

> an operation not without its epic quality, with weather difficulties and engine troubles . . . They made aviation history . . . with the safe arrival, despite many vicissitudes, at Gatwick . . . The reconditioned planes were taken literally from the scrapheap. Due to tornadoes they had to touch down at Lisbon. They later made an inspiring sight, landing from formation at Gatwick, each plane touching down within a matter of minutes.

What I didn't know at the time (among *many* things I didn't know) was that I was preparing for many years of intensive activity with warbirds. When someone finally recognized that there *was* a warbird movement in the country, why, we were years ahead of most people in the game because all this time we'd been doing what they were talking about as just starting. It helps. Our delivery of the three Fortresses, even when we had everything thrown at us except flak (and that includes fighters with some very angry people aboard who were gunning for us), was adventure flying in every sense of the word. Let alone the wonder of those engines pounding away and the shudder of the wings and fuselage from some pretty violent air and the smell of old leather and oil and metal, just to look out at the other Forts in formation gave it a very special feeling, indeed. So when we took the Forts back into the skies in formation, and saw once again that there isn't another airplane in the world that even looks like the Fortress, we came to recognize, again, that nothing is as beautiful in the sky as this old girl when seen from sister ships in formation. The old bomber has a marvelous and solid touch to her controls; she's big and husky and heavy but as sweet and true in her handling characteristics as any pilot could ask, and when you took the yoke in your left hand and planted your feet on the rudder pedals, she was *yours,* and no mistake about it. It took some time to do it but you could haul the Fortress around like a fighter, damned heavy, to be sure, and without sprightly movement, but you sure could lay her over on her wing and drop her like a boulder.

Something else joined us on what probably will be the last formation flight ever made of the Flying Fortress across the ocean.

59

High above the earth, in that strange sea of haze and distance when you were drifting like a tiny mote against the backdrop of the upper world, if you listened, very carefully, then through the roar of the engines and the creaking of the airplane and the deep hard cry of the wind . . . you could hear the whisper of all those who had ever come and gone in these great fighting machines. In the deep, shadowy gloom of the fuselage, with the airplane sway- ing gently, you might almost see the phantom forms of the men. Then, drifting timelessly from wherever it is that the great battles of the skies are remembered, the ghosts would come alive.

In that half-light and gloom the turrets would seem to move and men bend to their guns. When sunlight speared the gloom and il- luminated the dust motes, you could, by squinting just so much, see behind the dust the floating wisps of smoke from the guns and see the flash of the empty shell casings as they whirled to the floor of the airplane. If you believed . . .

If you believed — and wondered where the great machines would find their final resting place, you would go to Arizona and Texas, back in 1961, and there you could find the old bombers with their weary metal bones, and when you found them, you would stand there in the dust and cry.

☆

The desert was the place both to cry and to hate the faceless bu- reaucrats and pencil-pushers who never gave the first thought to the memory of those who had fought and died in the past, or to the needs for heritage and tradition of those who would reap the past. The first time we saw the B-17s was a shock. In that desert in- tended as the last stop before a crushing machine or a smelter the wind howls mournfully and spreads a mantle of thick red dust over the world. Great skeletons rear above the dusty earth, and when the wind commands they flap and clatter and give forth a mourn- ful cry from the wind sluicing through rudders naked to their ribs. Here old wires and cables sing of death, accompanied by ailerons and flaps banging up and down in an intermittent mumble of the end. Here are the neglected bodies and ragged wings of giants that once gladdened men's hearts and mocked the forever distances be- tween continents.

Three great bombers. Once the Queens of the aerial armadas, reduced now to tattered rags and blotched metal and diseased with neglect. Plexiglas that once shone brightly in the sun was now

60

just shattered splinters. We went through the near-carcasses, brushing aside the thick cobwebs, careful of the snakes and the scorpions and the spiders.

If you know how to look past the dust and the crazed and broken Plexiglas, beyond the shredded hydraulic lines — all the signs of disease, you know if the patient can be resurrected. So Greg Board decided. Bring them back to life. He brought in the mechanical paramedics. They went through the wings and through the cabins and the cockpits, moving this and touching that, feeling the resistance of metal, sensing, testing. They saw what thunderstorms, hailstones, torrential rains had done, and when the weather gods quit, what had been done by the vandals with stones, metal bars, and hammers. They touched the seams where fabric had been and dust now swirled. They touched the dented and battered skin and shook their heads. They stared with disbelief where the airplanes had sunk slowly down until the wheels were imbedded in broken asphalt above their axles. The massive tires were so badly deteriorated you could jam fingers into the split rubber.

To get these airplanes into the air without a year of work was impossible. "How much time we got?" they asked Greg Board.

"Two weeks," he told them.

They stared in disbelief, then exploded in laughter at the joke. Board held the eyes of his chief maintenance man. "I have always said you were the best," Board told him slowly. "Do it."

The maintenance man dug deep into his experience and let the future roll swiftly through his mind. He sighed, a tremulous accompaniment to the winds. His men didn't believe what they heard. "Three weeks, Greg."

"*Two,*" Greg said, and walked away.

In the days that followed, the disbelievers and hooters slowly calmed. All bets were that these airplanes were junk. But the desert sands seemed mixed with stardust for a while, and what would become a pattern for ghostly machines all over the land was hammered across the desert by day and by night. Where there had been only clatter and moaning, there now resounded the crashing echoes of Wright Cyclone engines thundering in rising and falling echoes as the mechanics worked their magic.

Fourteen days later, Boeing B-17G, Serial Number N5232V, ran up to full power. Greg Board and John Crewdson sat in the cockpit as Greg released the brakes and they howled skyward.

One week later N5229V followed into the sky. The gear was still coming up into the wells when the Fortress staggered violently and a "horrible crash" burst through the cockpit. The complete Plexiglas nose section of the B-17 had shattered, and now a shrieking tornado blasted through the entire airplane. Greg was working frantically to control the airplane, just to *see*, when the turbosupercharger of Number Two engine "ran completely wild." He chopped the throttle in the howling maelstrom, the Fortress shaking madly through every inch. Board was moving throttles, mixtures, propeller controls, getting the flaps up, retrimming the airplane.

He made an instant decision to continue the flight 900 miles to Tucson! The wind was threatening to tear the airplane apart, but Greg knew he could do it if he did *not* fly at more than 125 mph. At any speed greater than this the compressed air could blow the entire airplane apart. He hauled back on the controls into a steep climb, unloading the Number Two engine, the increased altitude allowing its safe operation. They crawled all the way to Ryan Field. But they made it.

A few days later the third bomber was parked with the other two, and the job began not only to rebuild them for the movie, but to meet airworthiness certification standards of the FAA. Again I have to stress that all this effort, this great scrounging and the nonstop improvisation, was a harbinger of things to come. But right then and there, when we were in the midst of bringing not one but three great phoenix creatures back to life, the term *warbird* had yet to be coined.

While the elite rebuilding crews worked day and night, Board and Crewdson scoured the entire United States for parts. They rounded up equipment from Oregon to Florida, and rushed back to Arizona again and again with landing-gear retraction motors, flap-actuating motors, brake parts, dozens of instruments, control handles, tires, gun turrets, gun barrels, bomb-bay systems, control handles and levers and grips, wiring, sheet metal, hoses, Plexiglas sheets, wheels, and a list that finally included, literally, more than a thousand items.

With the exception of one propeller, *every part, every piece, every unit, everything, had been sold by the U.S. Government as junk. It wasn't even surplus; it was legally junk!*

☆

By September of 1961 we were ready for the flight. Greg Board had given John Crewdson *ten minutes'* hard training in the airplane.

That was all he needed; he'd flown everything and Greg always went with his own judgments where other pilots were concerned. When we gathered the crews together, assigning the call signs of Blue One, Two, and Three to the bombers, we had Greg Board as pilot of Blue One, yours truly as copilot, Bob Sopjes as second copilot but as navigator for the formation, and two friends who went all the way to England with us, Bill Mason and Bud Rosenthal. In Blue Two, John Crewdson was pilot and Frank Lamanuzzi was copilot, with Les Hillman as flight engineer and emergency mechanic for all three planes. Blue Three had Don Hackett as pilot and ex-RAF pilot Tim Clutterbuck in the right seat.

Some of the logistics numbers could numb the checkbook of anyone. When the Fortresses left Tucson, Arizona, each airplane held 3250 gallons of high octane (115/145) fuel in its wing tanks, long-range Tokyo wing tanks, and ugly black ferry tanks in the bomb bays. The first order of business was tracking down the leaks. While one group of crewmen patched and closed sources of leaks, the rest attended to parachutes, Mae Wests, rafts, survival kits, winter flying clothes, rations, signal flares, radios, and other goodies. When the Forts left the ground, each weighed more than 61,500 pounds, and that is gross in every sense of the word. All three airplanes ascended majestically.

Blue Two had its first fire 15 minutes after takeoff. Les Hillman crawled through the airplane to find out what was burning and passed the news up front to Crewdson and Lamanuzzi. "We've got *two* fires," he choked out through heavy smoke whirling through the bomber. He got to the first one right away; just aft of the bomb-bay bulkhead on the right side of the bomber was an amplifier. The system had shorted, and the burning wires and insulation sent acrid smoke billowing thickly through the airplane. Hillman got that one out, but the second fire wasn't so easy. The turbosupercharger of Number Three engine was blazing. Gauges in the panel were flickering crazily, and Crewdson killed all four turbos. They watched gratefully as the smoke ebbed, the flames died, and they rumbled heavily onward with diminished power. It was *so* diminished that with their heavy fuel load they couldn't climb above the mountains ahead of them. They gambled. Crewdson kicked in all four turbosuperchargers, they came to life as if they were brand new, and the bomber climbed to 11,000 feet.

They slowed down to maximum fuel efficiency, which meant 135 miles an hour. Droning into the night they got their next surprise. All the lights of Blue Two had failed. The crews discussed by radio what they would do next, but it was a short conversation. The radio equipment of Blue Three went dead and Hackett and Clutterbuck were in a void of silence. But Hackett wisely was locked into tight formation with Blue One, signal enough that he would stay there through the rest of the flight, and let Board do all his radio work for both planes.

Neat. They'd go on this way to Cincinnati, Ohio. No sweat. Until they were only 50 miles out from their destination and they crashed into a line of violent thunderstorms, one airplane without lights and the other with no radio. Cincinnati lay buried beneath a fierce electrical storm. At least they could see one another in the constant lightning as they descended. Board asked the tower to communicate with Blue Three by light-gun signals, then rolled his bomber in for a landing. On the ground he was shaken by an overwhelming roar as Blue Two thundered only scant feet overhead. Crewdson had misjudged distance and poured the coal to the engines for a go-around. "What the devil . . . I'd never landed a B-17 before in anger, and certainly I'd never landed one at night, and I just came too bloody close to Greg, and that's all there was to it. I went around . . ."

The tower was flashing signals to the radio-dead Blue Three to go around *now*. Red lights flashed and blinked like a fire engine as Hackett circled, watching more and more flashing lights in the air as airliners began to stack up like a deck of cards three miles high. Finally they gave Hackett a green light and he touched gently. It had been nine hours from takeoff to touchdown.

They had work to do. Lights for Blue Two and radio work for Blue Three *and* a new propeller for Blue One. Greg Board had fought a steady vibration all the way from Tucson. The *brand-new* propeller mounted on Blue One had its innards all screwed up and he couldn't synchronize that prop with the others. So they bought a prop right off an ancient C-47 sitting on the field and stuck it on the B-17 (it worked perfectly).

We all got together at Teterboro Airport in New Jersey and planned our departure for September 28, 1961. Al Skea of the Newark *Evening News* asked me if I was really serious about going with the mob to England. I nodded, and the B-29 pilot-turned-newsman shook his head in disbelief. "You're out of your goddamned mind." Then he sighed. "I wish I was going with you." He said he'd watch us leave at ten that morning.

He didn't. The local feds insisted we change a tire on Blue Two.

64

We changed it. We fired up. Eleven engines roared sweetly. That meant one dead engine and it was on Blue Two. A starter had died, inexplicably but with finality. We decided we'd push on with the first two Forts to Boston and wait there for Crewdson to catch up with us.

Teterboro to Boston was a great flight at 7500 feet, the Cyclones throttled back to 28 inches manifold pressure, props turning at 2050 RPM and the mixtures eased back to lean. That gave us a true airspeed of 160 knots (184 mph) and it stayed that way as we eased down for Logan Airport. We came off the power and at 135 knots I hit the gear switch, at 120 knots Greg called for flaps, we came down the slot on final at 110, crossed the fence at an even 100, and touched down at 92.

Crewdson turned up the next day. He felt better. Everything was working beautifully. But as airlines-driver Len Morgan quips to all who look without suspicion at blue skies: "A comment about how well things are going is a sure guarantee of trouble."

Blue One and Three climbed out like giant swans, on our way to Gander, Newfoundland, where we'd jump off for Europe. We circled the field as Blue Two came up like magic and Crewdson slid into formation. I stared wide-eyed at his B-17 and grabbed my mike. *"Blue Two! You're dumping your fuel!"* I looked down at a thick plume of whitish-gray pouring back from the right wing. It spelled instant disaster — the fuel spray could mix with an exhaust and Blue Two would become a gigantic fireball. The crew didn't dare bail out; the Fortress might crash into homes. They chopped power, Crewdson racked her around tight and put her down with all that weight at 140 mph, let her roll to the end as they killed the switches while they rolled. They turned off the active runway with the props standing still. A tank cap had blown off the airplane. While they refueled and found another cap we pressed on, flying north from Portland along the stunning coastline of Maine.

On and on we went, until we were over Canada. The sun disappeared behind huge, black clouds and I eased the yoke forward to stay beneath them. Sensations of speed rushed upon us as we dropped to only 200 feet in the gap between the water and the brooding clouds. We sailed by Prince Edward Island, reached Newfoundland, climbed another hundred feet, and pushed on.

Where had all the nice skies gone? We ran smack into some unforecast pressure trough and the air became like boiling rapids. It was all work as we looked for Gander, and the sight of the sprawling field was sheer delight. We climbed just high enough to make the pattern entry legal, and were merrily informed by the tower that a 60-knot gale was screaming across the airfield. It turned out to be great because the wind was straight down the runway. We touched down with a groundspeed of 40 mph. It was like landing a Cub.

It wasn't so great when we climbed out of the airplane. With that howling gale the wind-chill factor was way below zero. We hoped it wouldn't hold up Crewdson; not the cold, but that wind. As it turned out (again) our hopes were in vain.

One hour out of Boston, the ADF radio gear in Blue Two quit. Dead. *Finito.* Instead of homing equipment, it was honing time with charts and flight computers and some very precision flying by Crewdson. That went well enough, but four hours out of Boston a thick layer of clouds formed beneath the Fortress. They stared at one another: they were heading over water, there were thick clouds beneath them, and their navigation equipment was dead. Crewdson sighed, pulled the plug, and landed on Prince Edward Island. That night they failed to fix the radio-navigation gear, but were told by the weather office they'd have good VFR all the way to Gander.

In the morning they went back upstairs. The directional gyrocompass had a fit and turned belly up. They pushed on, and flew into early night. Lamanuzzi switched on the lights. The switch made a nice sound but all the lights were dead. It was darker inside the airplane than outside. Coming up on Gander with a dead ADF, a dying directional gyro, and a cockpit as dark as the Black Hole of Calcutta, Crewdson asked for a radar-controlled approach. *They landed in hurricane winds and a screaming rainstorm in the dark.*

A terrific way to start a transatlantic formation flight.

☆

The next morning found everyone trying to get all the parts of the airplanes working properly. The time spent in repairs, as well as horrible weather forecasts of stormy skies with snow, ice, sleet, fog, and severe turbulence, kept us on the ground. We set takeoff for the morning of October 3.

The night before scheduled departure one of our crew called from the terminal building to the motel where we were buried in blankets. "Get your ass over here right away! A big transport just

"A moment of grace and sweeping majesty ..." A B-17 silhouetted against the late afternoon sky as we cross by Prince Edward Island on our way to Gander. *Photo by Bill Mason*

came in from Russia and it's swarming with Russians and Cubans and Chinese and God knows what else. *Bring cameras!"*

This was 1961, and things were not pleasant between us and Cuba. The airplane was a Bristol Britannia with Cubana Airlines painted all over it, and among other passengers, it was filled with Cuban pilots newly trained in MiG jet fighters on their way home to make things even more unpleasant. It turned out (the Mounties told us) that ten such planes had come through in the past ten days. Hundreds of jet fighter pilots were swarming into Cuba. We didn't know if U.S. Intelligence had wind of it, but it sure was a hell of a story and we wanted pictures for proof. Flight 427 of Cubana and its passengers were that proof. I got chummy with the Cuban pilot, who was all smiles and gestures until he saw Bill Mason snapping pictures with startling rapidity. The *whir* and *click* of Mason's camera wiped away all smiles, and the happy visage of the pilot was replaced with that of a uniformed Cuban officer who had many things to say in angry Spanish. He made a great subject for more pictures.

The Cuban slipped away from the camera as we came under the scrutiny of a KGB agent (we learned soon enough who *he* was),

67

who loomed above everyone else like an oak tree and just as wide. People who wear gray trench coats and long black leather boots scare me, especially when I know they're carrying very heavy artillery beneath those coats. It didn't take long before the picture session brought him to a boil. We both gave him the time-honored and traditional salute with upraised fist and extended middle finger. It was a mistake. He bellowed like a bull, lowered his head, and came charging at us, waving his arms.

What I said to Mason wasn't printable then or now. Mason is a burly ex-Marine, and he grinned and said, "Take him low." At least I could cover my head as I threw my body at those booted feet. I could almost feel the kick coming. It had started, but the Russian never finished it as Mason caught him square in the jaw with his shoulder. The three of us thrashed about on the floor until the Mounties came running to break it up, hauling us away from one another. The Russian was still roaring, Mason was grinning, and I wanted desperately to get into a private room for just a little while. Two Mounties led us into a holding room to question us, while two more did the same with the mouth-foaming KGB agent. "Ten minutes, okay?" I asked the Canadian Mounties. They were very fast on their feet, these people. They nodded. "Ten minutes."

During our roll-around on the floor I'd managed to steal everything from the KGB man's body that wasn't nailed down. That included a 9-mm automatic, his wallet, but most important of all, the complete crew manifest *and passenger manifest*, listing the names of every jet pilot aboard the airliner. We photographed everything just as a Canadian official came into the room. "Finished?" he asked. I handed him the papers, wallet, and gun.

Early the next morning we finished our picture taking of the Britannia. There was our friendly KGB agent again, this time bellowing loudly as he came down the stairs of the airliner, *gun in hand*, running at our B-17. We had a machine gun in the waist and I swung it around directly at the Russian. He stopped dead in his tracks, slid the gun into a shoulder holster, and backed up to his airliner. I wonder if he ever found out that the gun was a dummy and so were all those mean-looking .50 caliber rounds. All we could have done with that "weapon" was throw it.

Later that morning we delivered all our negatives to an American pilot returning in an Apache to the States, with clear instructions for its delivery to a "certain address." It was nice to know we'd broken the story, sent proof to appropriate officials, and weeks later received prints from an "unidentified office," along with a thank-you note, from our original negatives.

☆

For a while it seemed we had better luck with the KGB than with our airplanes. We climbed wearily into the Fortresses, ready for startup and takeoff, waiting for Blue Two to complete refueling. A lovely 707 jetliner taxied along the ramp, turning for the terminal with a blast of power *that blew all the fuel caps of Blue Two to a fare-thee-well.* It took an hour with everybody from all three bombers scouring the weeds and frozen ground, to find the caps. We finally made it into the air, and Mason and I crawled into the back fuselage to get some sleep (which we'd missed during our friendly games with the KGB).

We had slept all of five minutes when Rosenthal woke us with swift kicks. I went forward where Board said, "You know those big flaps in the wings? They went down very nicely for takeoff, but now they won't come back up again . . ." A glance at the airspeed dial showed we were 50 mph under normal cruise. Bob Sopjes sat glumly in the right seat. He and Greg would stay up front while Mason and I would try to bring up the flaps manually. If we succeeded, we were on our way to the Azores. If we failed, Greg Board would plant the Fortress at St. John's. We were at 62,000 pounds and the other B-17s were having fits staying slow enough to remain in formation.

Mason and I dragged cargo and spares from their lash-down positions to get at the airplane floor directly behind the aft bulkhead of the bomb bay. An up-limit switch had jammed and locked the flaps in place. The airplane wanted only to climb, and cruise speed was a hollow laugh.

We pried off the floor panels. We had to use a heavy pinch bar because everything was stuck from years of disuse. Below us we saw the curving bottom of the Fortress, the structural ribs exposed, and finally a faded sign that identified an opening as the manual emergency flap-retraction system. Now all we had to do was get the emergency crank handle into the ridged groove, crank it until it worked, and bring up the flaps. Nothing to it.

Except that our emergency crank handle was made for a B-24 bomber and we were in a B-17. So we gave it a try with large, heavy-duty pliers. For more than an hour we traded off work, squeezing the pliers and getting fractional movement each time.

Our hands were badly cut and bleeding, but we got the flaps up 10 degrees. Only 5 more to go! We did it finally, with blood spattered rather sloppily about our clothes, and I staggered back to the cockpit. "The sonofabitching flaps are up," I snarled.

"You did a fine job," Greg Board told me with a smile, and pulled *back* on the power.

"What the hell are you doing!" I think I screamed at him.

He smiled a serpent's smile. "Hackett just lost all his radios. We're landing."

We put in at St. John's, very carefully at better than 60,000 pounds, and spent the night soaking our hands in salt water in a hotel that was 135 years old. At least the whiskey was good.

☆

Once again the weather gods chuckled and chortled. The meteorologists promised us good weather and the weather gods rattled their bones. "Blue skies," they said from the met office, and we emerged from the mess hall early in the morning to look to the northeast, where the sky was an angry black with cloud walls twisting and writhing as they rolled toward us. To the north and the east it was the same. If we didn't get off *in minutes* we'd be socked in for days, possibly a week or more. We scrambled for the airplanes. Hands flew, ramming primers in and out, adjusting knobs, switches, and controls with blurred speed. We fired up and ran up the engines for all checks as we taxied.

As Greg swung onto the runway the edge of the storm passed the opposite boundary of the airport. We were in rain during the take-off run, with the other Fortresses rolling right behind us. Hackett took off in rain so heavy he let Clutterbuck guide him down the runway while he shifted automatically to flying on the gauges as they lifted off. We all stayed low to get away from the boiling clouds, and finally we were at the edge of that storm front with clear skies before us. The three bombers leveled at 1000 feet in a loose Vee formation.

Now the hours went by slowly, the formation drifting lazily between a thousand and two thousand feet, depending on the vagaries of clouds. Bob Sopjes remained down in the nose of Blue One, performing his navigational magic to find our one navigational checkpoint in midocean, a small vessel between Newfoundland and the Azores. Sopjes brought us directly over the vessel. "Directly" means within one eighth of a mile and 28 seconds within pre-takeoff estimates!

"What the hell am I doing here?" Martin Caidin (left), Bob Sopjes (center), and Les Hillman, worn out and frustrated after the unplanned landing at St. John's, ponder their evil ways that brought them to the "middle of nowhere." *Photo by Bill Mason*

Things were going *too* well. The airplanes had been flying beautifully and that was cause for a higher pucker factor. Sure enough; 30 minutes after crossing the checkpoint vessel a haze thickened before us and soon we were in the midst of black and ominous clouds. Oh, forecast of light scattered clouds — where are you!

Blue One did all the navigating and the other bombers stayed tight on us. They *had* to. With the fast-growing storm before us we talked about climbing over the weather, but the clouds might top out at 25,000 feet for all we knew, so that was out. We went down to 400 feet and bored straight into the worsening weather. Everyone cinched seat belts and shoulder harnesses. Blue Two and Three tucked in tighter than newlyweds in a cold bed.

Board called Crewdson and Hackett for altimeter readouts. It was lousy. We showed 380 feet, Crewdson had 440, and Hackett stared at 290. "Let's go down and get some accurate readings," Board told the others, and all three bombers went to wavetop height to reset their altimeters so we'd all read the same. The ocean became a blur whipping before us. This was no time to falter; one mistake and it was smashing into the ocean. I set the altimeter at 10 feet. Greg said to make it 8 feet, and then we eased back to the stupendous height of 200 feet. Crewdson called in and

71

politely asked us to hold exactly where we were. Seconds later a joyous *"Wheeee!"* burst over our headphones and a dark shape hurtled beneath our airplane.

Crewdson's Fortress streaked beneath us, skimming the waves, and then he lifted up on one wing, soaring beautifully to just beneath the clouds. The Fort poised on one wing, slid back, and locked into formation. "Where's Blue Three?" Greg asked. We found out soon enough. He looked out his side window at a closeup view of a B-17 wingtip. "Back off," Greg growled, and immediately the Fortress locked into position 150 feet away. *Then* came another call from Hackett's plane. Clutterbuck was on the radio. "John, would you please hold your position?" he asked politely. *Too* politely, for moments later the Fortress with Hackett and Clutterbuck screamed *between* the other two bombers. Hackett skidded neatly between us, shot ahead, zoomed and banked to fall beautifully off to his left, and came around through the bottom half of a curve — precisely in formation.

That was the end of the fun and games, for soon we were in serious formation at 100 feet, racing just beneath the clouds. And then the good things left us. We couldn't draw fuel from our outer right wing tanks, and before long Blue One felt as if the right wing was made of lead. We had to feed more and more trim into the airplane to hold up the right wing, which now had a nasty tendency to drop below level flight. The trim could do only so much, for after a while the airplane develops a yaw and presents a slight sideways effect to the wind coming across the wings and past the fuselage. We took turns at the controls, each of us nursing our arms as we maintained left aileron pressure and nudged the rudder to keep aligned for true flight.

It could have been worse. The clouds even eased upward a bit and visibility improved, and Santa Maria in the Azores hove into view. It was no easy landing for Greg Board, with 514 gallons (3084 pounds!) jammed all the way out in his right wing. He brought her down with the control yoke *all* the way over to the left and standing on right rudder to gain maximum deflection of the right aileron.

☆

I guess the KGB has friends everywhere. After a great stop in Santa Maria to unplug our Tokyo tanks, bathe, get shaves and haircuts, eat and drink to gluttony, we fired up for the nonstop flight to England. Everything went fine and we were rolling, when shouts brought Greg Board to kill the engines immediately. *Someone at the last moment before we climbed aboard had opened all the fuel tank caps in the bomb bay.* Full acceleration would have dumped that fuel into the bomb bay, making a howling fire a distinct possibility and making fuel starvation a certainty. We taxied back, went over all the bombers with a fine-toothed comb, found a few other nasty surprises, and finally took off.

Beautiful weather. Everything hummed and purred. *Too* good. Sure enough, directly ahead of us, a solid wall of dark clouds. They also had all the signs of being just the opening play of a big, mean, and very dangerous storm. Fifteen minutes after we penetrated the clouds we were in trouble.

We drifted through deep caverns of gloom, rode a worsening turbulence that went from mild shocks to hammerlike blows. Some storms *feel* evil; this one had all the feelings. We were forced down to 200 feet and this time there weren't any fun and games. The height didn't bother us for we could fly across the ocean at 50 feet. But patches of fog rolling across the water made us pretty damned uptight. We went from light showers to the real frog-stranglers you usually find at the bottom of powerful thunderstorms and visibility went down to a cat's whisker. Becoming separated now could prove fatal to Blue Two and Three because they were totally dependent upon us for navigation.

The sea became frustrating. It went from periods of calm to sudden white fury, foam whipped by unexpected hurricanelike gusts. And we were forced down steadily by the clouds until we went all the way down to 10 feet, adjusted all the altimeters, and managed to get back to 120 feet with the high tails in clouds. And still that damned ceiling kept coming down.

Fifty feet. The clouds dropped about us right down to the water. Scattered fog became thick walls rolling all about us. We weren't flying airplanes over an ocean but were trapped in a bizarre labyrinth of darkness and shadows and sudden light. We pounded just above the waves. The man in the left seat of each plane kept his eyes glued *totally* to flying. Screw the gauges! He didn't dare to look at them. In each right seat the copilot attended to power and other details and *told* the pilot anything he needed to know, which was, when you think about it, damned little.

It was much worse for Blue Two and Three than for us in the lead bomber. They *had* to stay in exact formation whenever we

73

plunged through fog. As we burst through gray mist they held position strictly by instruments until we broke free and were again flying eyeball. And the whole time they had to fight the wild roller-coaster and shock effects of the turbulence hurled back by our propellers. They pounded into the swirling wake vortex from the wingtips. Flying this kind of formation was a bitch. The pilots were inching the throttles back and forth, while the copilots kept almost constantly adjusting the propeller RPM.

We flashed through corridors of clouds on which strobelike light and darkness flickered, and pale silvery light glowed between the cloudy walls. Every so often we rushed into an area over which the clouds hung like a huge dome. At the edge of penetration the clouds were only 50 feet above the water, then rose in a great curving arch until, many miles away, they reached sky that was clear for hundreds of feet. Far to the other side, the clouds arched down. It was like racing through a cave and rapidly running out of space.

We had hoped to reach Bordeaux, France, a change from our original plans, for we all felt we'd earned a "night for ourselves" and had rented the entire floor of a brothel. We gave that up as impossible, for there was no way to fly any sensible course, but just to keep pounding in an easterly direction. If we flew toward Bordeaux it meant plunging into a wall of blackness. More and more we were pushed south of our original course. The haphazard dodging gave us a flight of unpredictable weaving and careening, and we were more concerned with remaining airborne and together than with holding a set course. As Don Hackett spelled it out, "We were groping our way like half-blind men through the light and dark spots on the deck, and the front of the airplane picking up spray from the ocean."

How lightly he says this! Our flying became all precision eyeball work as we skimmed the ocean with salt spray splattering the windshield. In Blue Two, Hillman left the nose because a minor crack in the Plexiglas showered him with sea water and coated everything with a salty grit. In our own airplane, the space left open at the bottom of the bomb bay to dispose of gasoline fumes was working in reverse. Sea water was sucked by the propellers and whirling passage of the bomber into the bomb bay and hurled back into the fuselage.

Up front in Blue One, Bob Sopjes did everything possible to guide us toward Lisbon, Portugal. No matter how we dodged and ran a broken course, he kept bringing us back to what must take

74

us to Lisbon. If we ever got any altitude the ADF might home in for us. But for the moment, it was staying on the deck. Finally, a great wall of fog obscured all visibility ahead and to the left. An opening yawned at the far right of the fog bank, and we eased toward this space. Blue Three sliced through the edge of the fog bank as we came around; immediately beyond were great rolling patches of fog, and we began to weave through them.

Almost before we could see it, a shape loomed ahead of us in the water. There wasn't even time to shout a warning. We saw a black shape, curving metal, and then an upraised white face and a darker space for an open mouth as we thundered almost along the very top of a submarine conning tower.

Whew . . .

Twenty minutes later the cloud deck had lifted enough for us to climb to 100 feet. Not much, but infinitely better than sucking water into the bomb bays! Another twenty minutes passed, and we eased upward to the terrific height of 200 feet. Things were looking better.

And then it all came unglued. One of the artificial horizons in Blue Two tumbled and lay like a dead roach in the panel. That left only one, and that's a thin margin in that kind of weather. To top it off, it was now dusk, and darkness was settling in with a vengeance. Crewdson had a violent headache from staring for hours at the flashing beacon of our bomber. It's a sort of fixation blindness. "Instead of one light," John explained, "I found myself seeing at least eight lights flashing and blinking in front of me. That's when I feared the possible onset of vertigo — the complete loss of reference as to what's up or down. Things got to such a state I told Frank to get on the controls with me and to do absolutely nothing but keep his eyes locked on the instruments. At any moment I knew the fixation could give me trouble and if we went into instrument conditions I would never make the transition from staring at that bloody light to our own panel. If we went into fog or clouds, Frank was to take over."

A lucky break: we hit an area free of clouds. In a flash Sopjes was taking a star fix, whirling computers, scribbling numbers, and going back to his computers. Minutes later clouds again covered the sky, but Sopjes grinned hugely. "We're two hours out of Lisbon," he announced.

We had another reprieve for a while. The airplanes droned on sweetly, we were out of the strong turbulence, we cruised at 400 feet, and then in Blue Two things started going to hell in a hand-basket. The gauges for the number two engine of Blue Two picked up a St. Vitus dance, everything from a jiggle to a twitch. In Blue One I was glad to leave the right seat and give the controls to Sopjes, who now gave Board a badly needed stretch of his own. I climbed back in the fuselage, draped myself over a tire, and fell asleep. It was another of those five-minute naps; Mason shook me awake. "Trouble," he said tersely. I went forward. We weren't in trouble. But Blue Two was foundering in it.

The needle of the carburetor air-temperature gauge for engine number two slammed way over against the peg, showing 100°C. This was warning enough of a fire in the carburetor. But nothing showed in the detection system; yet. Then the cylinder head temp gauge showed steadily rising temperatures and that left no doubts they had real problems. Immediately Lamanuzzi cut the throttle and feathered the propeller, pulled the mixture control to OFF, mags to OFF, cowl flaps CLOSED. They pressed on with three engines, Crewdson advancing power on all three to keep up with the other bombers.

Everything settled down — for a few moments. Then a brilliant shower of blazing sparks poured back from the feathered engine. Now they had that damned fire, all right. Lamanuzzi pulled the toggles to release carbon dioxide fire bottles in the wing to smother the blaze. *It didn't work.* Sparks still poured from the engine, and then a tongue of flame appeared. Crewdson, his eyes still glued to Blue One, ordered parachutes on and his crew ready for immediate bailout. If they went, he'd climb first for every bit of height he could gain, but it still meant jerking the D-ring on those chutes the instant they left the plane. Les Hillman yanked open the escape hatch.

We couldn't believe it. *The fire began to go out.* Flames diminished and then winked out. The sparks still showered back, but they also lessened. Crewdson was having fits with his vision while all this was going on. Lamanuzzi was monitoring the gauges; Hillman was down below at the hatch. He looked forward through the nose Plexiglas and his blood froze. He spun around to the crawlway and shouted at the top of his voice: *"Look out! You're going to hit Blue One!"*

Lamanuzzi snapped up his head and saw the towering tail of our airplane filling the windshield . . .

Moments before all this I was on my way back through the narrow catwalk of the bomb bay. We were transferring fuel and Greg wanted the main transfer system of the bomb-bay tanks shifted to pump fuel into the wing tanks. The controls were directly behind the bomb-bay bulkhead. Just back of me was the Plexiglas sheet that gave me a view up and to each side of the fuselage. I looked out and, like Hillman, felt the blood freeze inside me. Filling the sky off our right wing was this huge shape, sparks spraying from an engine, *plunging straight at us.* I had just enough time to get one foot raised over the bulkhead beam with my head and shoulders in the cockpit and shout, *"Dive! Dive it!"*

Reacting with pure instinct, Greg slammed forward on the yoke. Blue One lurched wildly and went down like a stone. Crewdson was already tramping rudder and hauling back on the yoke in Blue Two. His Fortress thundered over and across us bare inches from our airplane. Almost immediately, Greg was pulling up and, with that dark ocean scant feet beneath us, he did so with a vengeance. As we came back up violently, the sudden motion threw me off balance and my right knee slammed down on the hard edge of the bulkhead. Talk about seeing sparks all your own! I felt the bone going; I had torn the cartilage messily and chipped off a chunk of kneecap.

But the view of Blue Two skimming over us safely, sparks and all, was worth it. After all, a midair collision can screw up your whole day . . .

Things were just getting warmed up. The oil-pressure needles on *three out of the four engines* of Blue Three were swinging wildly, and Hackett didn't know whether or not all three would quit or burn or what. Clutterbuck had already moved their parachutes within instant reach. Hackett eased off power on two engines, nursed the third, and crooned the fourth into singing sweetly.

This went on for another hour. Crewdson's bum engine continued to spray sparks intermittently, and the oil pressure on his number one engine began to fluctuate up and down. Hackett and Clutterbuck played nursemaid to their three faltering engines. Bill Mason sopped up blood from my knee and fashioned an emergency bandage and gave me a long swig from the whiskey bottle.

We hung in and Lisbon came into view far ahead. We could actually *see* into the night. The clouds had thinned and we went upstairs to 1200 feet. We went to 1500 to let Crewdson land first. But John, with one dead engine and one faltering, poured the coal to his Fortress to go around because Hackett was breathing down his neck. "I couldn't help pounding down the stretch on top of John," Hackett explained. "Hell, engines were going out all over the place.

My oil pressure went completely to hell on those three engines and we had to cut 'em back completely or risk all three burning at the same time . . ." In fact, Hackett came in to land at night with only one engine going at full power. He hauled the B-17 around in a fighter approach and brought her down beautifully, even as Clutterbuck was feathering three propellers.

Crewdson came around to land and a second engine died at the worst instant. They landed hard and the impact ruptured the oil tank of number one, sending a gusher of oil down the runway. Greg hugged the opposite side of the runway when we landed.

We'd made it.

☆

We read an interesting newspaper story of our arrival:

> The arrival of three Boeing B-17G Flying Fortresses at Lisbon, Portugal, stirred local police to a froth and landed the planes' crews in custody . . . The charge was gun running and starting a war. Interiors of the three Forts were crammed with machine guns and ammunition boxes. Exteriors bristled with gun turrets and bomb racks.

We were more interested in the fact that the engines of Blue One hadn't so much as twitched the entire flight. Blue Two and Three had been pummeled mercilessly as they throttled back and forth almost constantly, and had their propeller pitch changed just as often. We were convinced that had we flown economy cruise, as planned, we would have made the flight without all that mess with the engines, sparks and fires and all.

And I wouldn't have had a busted knee.

Anyway, the Portuguese secret police had a lot of questions, and before long we were all ensconced in a convoy of black limos, surrounded by very large and beefy men with very large guns. We drove along a narrow, cobblestoned street, stopped in deep shadows, climbed out of the cars to see machine guns covering us from different angles, and were all directed to a building with lots of people with lots of submachine guns. It is a long and a most fascinating story, but not for these pages; suffice to say we were the guests of the Portuguese secret police and of Interpol and they were *very* curious. They were also baffled and disbelieving, then incredulous, and finally hysterical with laughter. So were we — when we got out of jail.

☆

78

Just released from the dungeons of the Portuguese secret police, the B-17 crews work with unrestrained alacrity to practice the time-honored maneuver of "Fill 'er up and let's get the hell out of here." *Photo by Martin Caidin*

On the morning of October 8, Lisbon Tower cleared us for an unbroken takeoff, during which all three Fortresses would be permitted to roll one behind the other in unbroken procession, and no other traffic permitted near us until we were on our way. It went beautifully, we stayed low until we crossed the coastline, and in tight formation we wheeled northward along the coast. And then we were back in among the clouds, and starting our familiar descent toward the ocean. At 200 feet through patches of clouds and shafts of brilliant sunshine, we bored on. Portugal slipped beneath us and we sailed along the coast of Spain. The clouds went still lower and we were right back in those same damned conditions we had struggled through to reach Lisbon. But ahead of us it went zero-zero as a solid wall of fog smeared the ocean surface. We circled in a great open area. Greg Board looked at me. "I, we, are *not* going back. I have had enough."

We called Blue Two and Three, we set our power and slipped into a long trail formation and began a spiraling ascent into a world of incredible beauty. The clouds were dazzling white, the sky overhead an impossibly deep blue, and there was music in the air as the three Fortresses rose higher and higher until we leveled off at 14,000 feet, sliding like tiny motes through fantastic ravines and gorges of billowing white clouds. At the edge of France, we sailed over the edge of the cloud front; then there were no clouds and France lay beneath us. Crewdson and Hackett eased gently into tight, precision formation, and we began a long descent to 500 feet, a ghost flight out of history. The news of our passage was passed on by excited villagers, and hurried phone calls brought thousands of people into the streets of towns and villages to wave wildly to us as we roared overhead. Then we were over the English Channel and we climbed lazily to 1000 feet.

We brought them down to Gatwick and exactly at five P.M. rubber squeaked on English concrete. Long before this moment John Crewdson had promised to deliver the three bombers for filming the morning of October 9. We were exactly on schedule.

☆

It had been a most exciting period. Early in 1960 I lived with and flew with the Air Force Thunderbirds jet aerobatic team. During the summer months, with Jim Yarnell loaded down with cameras, we toured America in a spanking-new Beech Debonair, covering 55,000 miles in 320 hours of hard and marvelous flight. There was more flying in between, and then the saga of the Flying Fortresses, during which so many things happened it became an ultimate adventure of its own special kind. Months later, John Crewdson brought one of the old Fortresses back to the United States and we joined in for a terrific get-together in a jaunt across the country. It wouldn't have been right without *something* going wrong. This time the old girl flew beautifully, but we ran into a howling sandstorm from which there was no escape. We couldn't land because visibility was zero-zero. We couldn't turn back because there were other storms behind us. We couldn't stay in the stuff because it would have sandblasted the Plexiglas and eaten the props and engines alive. The only thing to do was to go up, and we climbed steadily along the edges of the storm until we could get above the gritty mess.

Twenty-two thousand feet and no oxygen. Interesting; very interesting. We took turns at the controls, gasping in the thin air, watching each other carefully for signs of hypoxia and the sillies that precede unconsciousness. Then we were beyond the storm and started down, *fast*. It seems there's never a quiet moment.

I learned enough from all the foregoing to start qualifying as something of an authority with the old warbirds. In the very near future I would be back in the skies over the Atlantic, but in another kind of bomber, and headed for some more hysterical flying, and I'd end up with a couple of Messerschmitts and totally committed to this wonderful nonsense of resurrecting the past.

That "other kind of bomber" was a twin-engined North American B-25J Mitchell, and again I flew right seat as copilot, and again — you guessed it! — there was Greg Board in the left seat, and we were on our way into a new world of flight, the kind of stuff from which dreams are to be found and adventure is to be written.

Me and
My Messerschmitt

What can go wrong *will* go wrong. And
what is already wrong is bound to get worse.

Murphy

I have never *really* enjoyed flying over long, wide, deep, and very wet oceans, and I know of few other kinds. I enjoy it even less when my pilot is sound asleep in the left seat, we're in a B-25J at 14,000 feet, Greenland somewhere beneath us and to our left, and we are bucking our way fiercely through a screaming snowstorm.

In July, yet.

After spending a few months flying with the Thunderbirds, criss-crossing the entire continental United States in a Debonair, and embarking on all manner of mind-bending with the Fortresses (to mention only a few variations on a flying theme), I was ripe for the call from Greg. "You and I," he announced, "are taking a Mitchell to England. They're shooting a movie there, *633 Squadron*, at Bovingdon, and they need the airplane for a camera ship. We might just get in some good flying there. They'll be using Mosquitos, Messerschmitts, the whole lot."

The B-25 was in fairly good shape. Compared to the B-17s we'd taken across the Big Drink, it was pristine. Compared to what it *should* have been prior to leaping across the North Atlantic, it was enough to turn your insurance agent into a quivering wreck. The airplane had one especially bad habit (among others). The inboard wing tank on the port side leaked like a sieve when it was full. The trick, then, when flying at less than maximum range was not to fill that tank to capacity, and to use the bomb-bay fuel cells to full advantage. But when we needed *all* the fuel we could carry, the procedure was to have everything ready to go, the fuel crew ready to pounce on the airplane, and the instant the tanks were full and dripping, fire her up and *GO*. Whatever that sounds like, it worked. I know, I know; it was *not* the way to do it.

Neither, for that matter, was the lack of preparation for crossing the Atlantic Ocean with less than mandatory emergency survival equipment. Greg and I landed in Boston without Mae Wests in the airplane. Not that he'd forgotten them; it's just that we were once again on one of those schedules to "get there on the time set in the contract." Greg figured we'd buy the Mae Wests in Boston.

Wrong. Nobody had any for sale. Nobody had any for sale in all of New England. So we called friends, and Eastern Airlines saved the day for us by loaning us several spanking-new life preservers. Aha, we were ready to launch, right? *Wrong.* Both of us had forgotten signal flares, and when you land in Canada to overfly the Big Water, they don't let you out without inspecting your emergency survival gear, and signal equipment is either in the airplane or you're grounded. We were taking off from Goose Bay, and that meant Royal Canadian Air Force, and they are very sticky about this sort of thing. We scoured Boston, found a fireworks factory, and bought all sorts of fireworks, most especially Roman candles and stick-balanced skyrockets. The Canadian inspector who studied the Roman candles had a face reflecting inner turmoil of monumental depth. He'd never seen these, they weren't in the book, but they *were* pyrotechnic signal devices, and we were waved off.

Why do I mention all this about a B-25 when this chapter is about Messerschmitts? First, because it was a rather silly way to go and I bring it to your attention as how *not* to do these things. We got away with it. Obviously; I'm still here after all these years, but that doesn't make it any smarter, and since then I have *refused* a number of flights across the ocean because I found the equipment less than satisfactory in terms of safety. One such aircraft, which should have been condemned rather than simply being grounded, did make it across the Atlantic, but came in for a landing in the form of a blazing torch, and its crew *just* managed to escape being roasted alive. Not the way to go, not at all.

I should have paid more attention to other details (which I have since learned to do in a most assiduous fashion). Not until we were in the midst of a long on-the-gauges session did I learn that the artificial horizon on the right panel showed a 10-degree bank to the right when the airplane was in level flight. That meant little when we were eyeballing things or Greg was flying on the gauges from the left seat. But when he decided to have a long siesta in the left seat and the world vanished in clouds and snow, I faced three hours of solid instrument flight with that heeled-over horizon. It went well enough, but I leaned like a drunken sailor when we finally landed. Oh, that gimmicky fuel system? We took off from Goose Bay, overflew Greenland, and landed finally in Iceland (with enough fuel aboard to have continued nonstop to France). So it worked, but it was still *not* the way to do things.

If ever you have the opportunity to make this kind of flight, and it is a lovely way to enjoy the world, do at least two things (among many others) before you flip the starter switches. Find out where everything is in the cockpit and what it does, and even before you do that, *read the damned manual.* We didn't do either. The gods were good to us.

In the snowstorm at 14,000 feet, before Greg went into his deep sleep, we had a problem. The engines were icing up. Lots of rumbling and coughing and shaking.

"Put on carb heat," Greg mumbled into the intercom.

"You put it on," I told him.

"Why me?"

"I don't know where they are."

"I don't know, either. I thought you knew."

"I thought *you* knew."

"Jesus, where's the manual?"

"I thought you had it."

"I thought —" He scrambled from his seat. "Never mind. It's in the back."

You really *don't* crawl into the fuselage, the aft section, anyway, of your B-25 when the bomb bays are crammed with fuel tanks, and just about everything you're carrying in the way of survival gear, food, beer, parachutes, and personal goodies is jammed atop the tanks. Greg finally managed to find the aircraft manuals, climbed back into his seat with a look of triumph, opened the covers, and watched the pages crumble into powdery dust in his hands. He didn't say a word. He tossed the remains over his shoulder in a fine spray of ancient debris, and we set about moving everything we couldn't identify until we found the carb heat and brought succor to the complaining engines.

We finally did get to Bovingdon, after spending a night in Iceland and completing our flight in absolutely horrendous and typical English weather. Greg and I got a room at a pub in a nearby town, and we needed much attention to wending our way through the delightful, charming old place with *very low* passageways by the doors. After the third or fourth bashing of skulls against unmoving beams we *always* ducked when moving from one room to another.

Bovingdon was a paradise of the old warbirds. There were Mosquito bombers everywhere, and bunches of Messerschmitt bf-108B *Taifun* fighter-trainers. Few planes I have ever flown offer more crispness and satisfaction at the controls than the 108. The models used in the film were painted up as Me-109E fighters, the rear windows painted black. Not good enough to convince the purist, to be sure, but the purist doesn't shell out the long green to make a movie. Without being responsible for *anything*, he just sits at home and whines that everything isn't perfect. Keep that in mind when you're in the warbird game and some asshole carps that you've got a number painted in the wrong place.

At first glance you knew that to fly the 108 you had to be something of a magician. At least, until you learned some of its idiosyncracies. The gear had a width of 4 feet 10 inches. Another way to spell that out is "built-in crosswind." It's like tippy-toeing whenever you're on the ground, and there are many old pros who have been startled by the 108 whipping into a tight groundloop with little or no warning. But like almost all flying machines the trick is to learn *that* airplane, and it will be good to you.

I managed to drag myself away from the first 108 I saw, because all I wanted to do was to fly that little sucker as soon as I could, but not without protesting. Then I realized we were having a grand old home week. Tim Clutterbuck was there, and John Crewdson and Les Hillman, and with Greg and me coming in with the B-25 it really was the old gang. I was introduced to a newcomer in the crowd, John R. Hawke, known to his old flying mates as Jeff, ruddy-cheeked and barrel-chested and one of God's chosen when it came to flying iron beasties with wings on them. John had been the chief aerobatic instructor of the Royal Air Force; he flew anything and everything, and had almost been shot down when flying a Hawker Hunter jet fighter, by a Turkish F-100 Super Sabre, while John was very busy trying to shoot down (a futile exercise, he soon learned) a black-winged U-2 cruising far above his maximum ceiling.

All that was behind him now; he'd traded in his active commission for a reserve slot with the RAF. In his midtwenties, he figured (correctly) that if he wished to taste some of the wine offered by the more challenging moments of life, the way to do it was to get right down there among them. Crewdson had brought along the young bucko of a pilot, and after we met Hawke — a prophetic meeting that spawned quite an adventurous friendship — the grins we shared grew ever wider. John Hawke had also stepped down from English Electric Lightning and other supersonic jet fighters to fit his bulky frame (he was also the heavyweight boxing champ of the RAF) into the Messerschmitt; by the time I arrived at Bovingdon he was as much at home in the 108 as he had been in a Hunter. I sat in the airplane with him, learning the controls, getting the feel of it. Hawke held out his right hand, palm up, and shrugged. "Shall we?" I slapped skin. "Damned right. Let's do it."

If there is one thing for which the Messerschmitt bf-108B was intended, it's *fun flying*. It is a spectacular machine with crisp and superbly light controls. It flies like a fighter, yet it carries four people with dual controls in the front seats. It saw heavy service with the Luftwaffe as a fighter-trainer, but was also used as a liaison, utility, and small airliner craft. It appeared on the European scene in the early 1930s and promptly stole accolades from every pilot who took it into the air.

Where else can you get a small four-seater that is perfect as a touring aircraft, that is fully aerobatic, an excellent instrument machine, cruises on spit for gas with its 240-hp engine, and, after landing, folds its wings and can be towed home to your garage! *That's* why the gear is so narrow; it's exactly the same as the German automobile, and fits neatly into the ruts made by its towing auto. Very, very neat.

And it *looks* mean. Painted up with the wartime fighter insignia it damned well poses as a fighter, which is why it was so successful as an ersatz fighter plane in so many movies. The gear is retractable through a manual system. Pump a handle back and forth 96 times (48 each way) and the gear is up. Turn the handle to lock the ratchet mechanism, and it's secure. Turn it the opposite way, the locking mechanism is released, and 96 fast strokes and the gear is down and locked. Seem like too much work? We could get that gear up and down just about as fast as a power system, and ours had a lot less mechanical nonsense to go wrong.

The 108B served another purpose, as the nucleus of what would become the famed Me-109 fighter. Indeed, the first of that line, the Me-109V1 (V stands for Versuchs, or experimental), flew with a Rolls-Royce Kestrel engine of some 650 hp, which is not all that much greater than the higher-powered 108 series with 400 hp.

Our ships in *633 Squadron* flew with 230/240-hp Renault engines, since during the war the Germans moved their 108 production line out of Schweinfurt and Regensburg to French factories. Little matter; they were made on German machines and any difference in performance turned out to be nonexistent. What you really had to look out for in this ship, I repeat, was its tendency to ground loop because of that narrow gear.

Hawke checked me out quickly in the 108B. I learned to *always* make my takeoffs in the same manner. As the throttle goes forward, so does the right foot. Not soon after, not one second after, but simultaneously, or you're going to see that nose whipping sideways along the horizon. As soon as you get about 30 mph, the stick goes forward to bring up the tail and get better effect with the rudder. Keep in that full right rudder until you're in the air. If you have your crosswind from the left, you go to right brake to keep the tail from swinging to the right. Just tap it in, no more than you need, in small bursts of brake pressure. You'll be flying quickly enough and everything settles down.

After learning the airplane, and running riot in footloose-and-not-so-fancy fun aerobatics, I was into the swing of things with the film. I followed John Hawke through some passes in which we attacked the British "wartime" field. How terrific to fly this way! We came down low, "shooting up" airplanes, people, petrol lorries, hangars; anything and everything. When we landed, Hawke got chewed out for not flying low enough. It wasn't realistic, complained the director.

We went back into the air. John's only words — through grimly clenched teeth — were: "Follow me." Lead on, John!

When we came around this time, I was flying behind and to John's right, and I watched his Messerschmitt slide right to the ground. Or so it seemed. His prop couldn't have been more than two or three inches from the grass. He said to follow him, right? So we had two daisy-cutting 108s ripping the field. Ahead of us people were hurling themselves prone, and we had to ease up to clear their bodies with the props. When we crossed the field, I discovered two very large hangars directly before us, and not enough time to clear them with pulling up. All this sort of thinking takes place in a split second; your body is moving even before you consciously work out the details between your ears. If the damned hangar doors had been open we'd simply have flown through them, but they were closed. John settled for the small space between the two buildings, snapping over into an almost vertical bank and flashing between the buildings with one wingtip pointing straight up at the sky. I followed in the same maneuver, but I did have a better view than John!

When we landed, the director *and* the producer and a bunch of other people were screaming curses at the top of their lungs. John held up his middle finger, murmured, "Bloody twits," and we went off to find a cool beer in a land of warmish brew.

☆

It was an old British gentleman who gave me my first clue as to what we might do with this airplane if I brought some of them back to the States. The purists would grumble about the difference between a fighter-trainer and a fighter, but I've already expressed my opinion of purists who talk out of both sides of their mouths and never put their money where their mouths are to be found, all adribble with nonsense. I was walking down the main street of the English town near the airfield, when Board and Hawke came roaring overhead, barely clearing church steeples and with engines howling. There was no way to miss the iron crosses and swastikas. A crusty, mustached old Englishman stopped, undoubtedly remembering 1940 and the London blitz. To him, time had simply snapped back to yesteryear. He looked up at the two German airplanes and shook his fist at the sky. "Bloody Nazi buggers," he muttered indignantly, and stalked off.

Well, if we could get this sort of reaction in England, in 1963, what could we do with these same 108s back in the States! We flew for several more days, Messerschmitts and Mosquitos and the B-25 having a field day in the sky. And then there was a big party in Paris and we all flew over, and the party lasted for three days. I recall only the first few hours. Everything else is a sodden blank. When I emerged from it all, hanging across a gun turret on the way back to Bovingdon, I tried desperately to sort out what had happened. I found out that night when going through my checkbook. I'd bought two Messerschmitts, one for Greg and the other for myself. In the next few days, I finished my flying in the film, whether I liked it or not. The home office was screaming about the endless research trip and it was a fast trip back to New York. I arranged for John Hawke to fly the little bird from England to Zahns Airport on Long Island, outside New York City.

Now, preparations for such a flight demand just that: preparations. Since the 108 had been manufactured in France, Hawke would fly back there in the airplane to pick up as many spare parts for the airplane as it was possible to find. The lessons of the B-17s in our formation jaunt across the Atlantic remained strong in my mind. *Get everything while you can.* That's the rule, the law, the commandment. So I gave John a couple of signed blank checks, he bid me a bleary farewell as I walked into a sweptwing whale of BOAC, and as I lofted for the long and sleepy flight back to the States, he was on his way to France.

Dear reader, consider all you will now discover as sometimes tantamount to necessity in refurbishing, supplying, and rebuilding your own warbird. It forms another memorable chapter in many such sagas . . .

John brought the Messerschmitt down at Toussous de Noble. As people came tumbling out of buildings to watch the Luftwaffe fighter, John blithely taxied up to the tower and parked in the most conspicuous area of the whole field.

"The hostility of the French government officials was rather distressing," he explained later. "A huge, fat customs official trundled up, huffing and puffing like a pregnant elephant, trying to terrorize me with a glare he'd been practicing for thirty years. He shouted quite a bit, too."

John speaks a sort of mongrelized French. His natural joviality as he tore the French language to shreds left the customs agent one step short of rage. The madder he got the more his corpulent frame shuddered, the greater the shudder the higher the heave of his ponderous belly, and the wider became Hawke's grin until he burst out in contemptuous laughter. This led the customs man to threaten arrest if Hawke did not march at once with him to confront the airport commandant. That worthy stood a literal six feet eight inches and stood forth as a heavier and stockier imitation of Charles de Gaulle. Somewhere through the argument with the commandant, a red-faced, wide-eyed Frenchman burst into the office to scream about a German fighter that had invaded the field.

In the ensuing uproar fingers swerved and trembled and steadied in their point at John. The swastikas painted on the tail assumed proportions of an international incident, and John had grisly visions of a guillotine blade going *thwack!* into the back of his neck. There *were* a few problems. The airplane lacked a registration number; they told John this was a heinous crime. The ownership papers had been forgotten in England. Hawke dug through his pockets to produce papers that identified him as being with the French *navy*.

"You are in the naval arm, *m'sieu?*" the commandant asked.

Hawke shook his head. "No."

"No?"

"No."

"Then, *m'sieu* . . . these papers?"

Hawke shrugged. Someone accused him of being a spy. The commandant rubbed his nose and agreed this was possible.

John Hawke groaned. They accused him of being a spy for the French navy. He groaned again and shook his head.

"You are a pirate of the air!" the commandant shouted.

"Blah," Hawke said.

"Who owns this machine?"

"Caidin."

"And what is a Caidin?"

"He's an American. Martin Caidin. That's his name, you dolt."

"Where is he?"

"In America, you twit. Where else?"

"Where is the ownership! You are an Englishman, you say, carrying French navy papers, flying a German fighter plane that is unregistered and owned by an American who is four thousand miles away?"

John smiled. "I say, that *is* rather brilliant."

"Shoot him!" the commandant roared. Windows shook. "Crap," John said, and simply walked from the office. He continued walking back to the airplane, the spare parts forgotten, climbed into the cockpit, and was about to start the engine when a crowd of shouting, gesticulating officials and gendarmes descended upon him.

"You cannot take off!" they cried.

John smiled sweetly. "Oh, but I can and I am going to."

An official waved a pistol at him. A *big* pistol. "I will shoot!" he screamed.

"Shoot and be damned." Hawke pulled the air starter, the blades spun and the engine roared, and he rolled away. The official stared, the gun sagged, and John took off straight ahead, down the taxiway.

It wasn't over yet. All the way back to England he kept a sharp lookout for French fighters. He needn't have bothered. They had no desire to fly into the thick fog that covered the Channel and swallowed the Messerschmitt. Hawke began to sweat. He was over England and he couldn't see a thing. He groped blindly in the mists when a hole opened and he dove at full speed for a concrete runway beneath him, turning tightly and banging the airplane down on an abandoned wartime strip. Safe!

An hour later, an agitated farmer dragged a British customs official to the strip. They stared in disbelief at the Messerschmitt. "My God, man," the official cried, "don't you even know the war's long over!"

John couldn't resist. He jumped down from the wing and snapped to attention. The crack of his clicking heels rang out in the foggy gloom. "*Jawohl!* I vish to zurrender!" he bellowed.

This wasn't the end. A drunken Englishman pedaling his way unsteadily home from his local pub caught sight of the 108 as he wove down a nearby road. He was overwhelmed with patriotic fervor. An hour later, the local police dragged him away from the side of the hangar — where he'd been trying unsuccessfully to set the concrete afire.

At long, long last, John in my airplane, accompanied by his fiancée, Jean, in the front seat, and a 55-gallon drum in the rear seat for extra range, departed England on the way to the States. The second 108 had Francis Freeman and a photographer in front. They would all have good reason to regret the trip. First of all, they were quite insane. No one would try, if he were sane, to cross the North Atlantic in the middle of winter storms, flying against the prevailing winds, in tiny, single-engine planes. This crowd *did*.

While they were preparing to leave Scotland, a volcano exploded beneath the sea south of Iceland. A blazing volcano is a marvelous sight at night, hurling house-sized boulders into the air and generating violent electrical storms that present a huge guiding light in the sky for single-engine Messerschmitts. The night *my* Messerschmitt showed up, John was using the volcano as a navigational beacon, but he seemed to be far off course and heading north. Jean pointed out this little error to him. He pointed at the blazing lights in the sky. She pointed to the compass. They passed

91

Messerschmitt bf-108B, F-BFYX (to become N108U) with John and Jean Hawke at the controls passing by a very dead volcano of Iceland. *Photo by Robin Carruthers*

their estimated time of arrival for Iceland, when John realized two things. The volcano *had gone out*, and the lights in the sky he was following were the aurora. He turned immediately to pick up a new heading for Iceland and began calling their tower. All his radios picked *that* moment to fail. They came in to land at Reykjavik with the engine running on fumes.

They made the next leg to Greenland with a promise of good weather. Oh, believer in miracles! The winds were doing *100 miles an hour*. Guided by an unseen radio voice, they spiraled down from 14,000 feet in thick clouds, slipping hazardously through a huge cavern of frozen fjords. They landed, stopped, and felt the airplane blowing sideways across the flight line until ground crewmen, hanging on to heavy trucks, snagged them with ropes.

But this trip was far from over. Remember the *second* 108? Keep your notebook handy on all the thrills of bringing your own warbird home from a distant shore. We'll let Francis Freeman tell it in his own words —

———————— ☆ ————————

This was one hell of a way to spend Christmas. The world was a blinding white. The white was snow coming at me at nearly 200 miles an hour. It came out of the air in a white mass, past the blur of the propeller, and at the last instant the blast of air sent it curving sharply over the canopy. Through the snow I saw something even worse, the dark and menacing green of Davis Strait, water so cold it freezes a man to death in minutes. All this time I was huddled in the cramped cockpit, my body wrapped in an immersion suit and a Mae West, a life raft shoved against my back, flying on instruments at only 200 feet, with another Messerschmitt tucked in so close to me it was almost shoving me off course. And there was no heater in this bloody thing! I was too cold even to be scared, and common sense said I should have been terrified.

My earphones crackled with a voice from the outside world. "VU, this is TWA Seven-Oh-Three relay from Ocean Station Bravo. Your position on radar at fifteen-forty-three Zulu is two hundred twenty degrees true at eleven nautical miles. They would like your flight details, please."

It was wonderful, the crew of a huge four-engine airliner taking the trouble to help us out. I called back to them. "Roger, Seven-Oh-Three. Copied okay. This is F-BGVU, in company with F-BFYX. Messerschmitt One-Oh-Eight aircraft, from Narssarssuaq bound for Goose Bay, and we are estimating fifty-four fifty-five north fifty-six fifteen west at seventeen-oh-one Zulu. Over."

TWA 703 paused a moment. A pregnant pause. "Uh, roger, VU. Would you, ah, say again your type of aircraft, please? Over."

"Roger, Seven-Oh-Three. A Messerschmitt. Repeat, Mess-er-schmitt. A Mess-er-schmitt One-Oh-Eight. Over."

"Roger, VU. That's what we thought you said. Are you *armed?*"

What the hell was I doing on this crazy flight, anyway? Here we were in an airplane designed thirty years before and everybody believed we were armed to the teeth. The most dangerous thing we had with us was an old toothbrush. But each leg of the trip — England, Scotland, Iceland, and Greenland — had already provided enough hazards to last any sane human being a lifetime. But maybe I wasn't sane because, after all, I was a pilot on an insane flight. For almost a month, four of us had coaxed two unwilling monsters — ancient Messerschmitt bf-108s — toward their final destination in the United States. It had not been a flight or even a series of flights, but a series of *fights*. We were struggling against 100-to-1 odds, but so far we had managed to stave off disaster. Then we were on the last, long, overwater hop.

Spread over my passenger seat in a loose and jumbled mess was

Robin Carruthers, a balding British photographer who came along as a cameraman and who, between cranking his cameras, repeated incessantly his woes and laments about the whole nutty affair. On top of all this, I found myself at 200 feet steaming along barely above that killing water, in a blinding snowstorm, and a couple of airline drivers were asking us if we were armed! The sense of insanity took a firmer hold on me. I was still babbling to myself when Hawke's voice came across the radio: "Francis, let's get the hell above this stuff."

I eased back gently on the stick and the two planes climbed steadily through the white curtain. These were the moments when I was so grateful to have Hawke off my wing. His formation flying was unbelievably precise; in fact, this was the man who trained the world-renowned British jet aerobatic team, the Firebirds, to do all their special routines in their 1600-mph Lightning fighters.

We bored steadily upward in tight formation, and at 6000 feet we burst away from the smothering snow into that miraculous world of the airman. The transition was breathtaking. The sun glinted brilliantly off the windscreen, sparkling on the melting ice.

Moments like this made everything worthwhile. The tension of scraping our way just over the waves left us almost at once. Just below, the clouds whipped by to give us an impression of tremendous speed. Even with the subzero temperatures outside the cockpit, the sun poured its warmth over us beneath the glass. We were able to relax for a few moments and study the world of sun-washed clouds: a panorama of rolling hills and gentle valleys.

Our tiny formation continued westward. John, barely ten yards away, duplicated my every control movement as I wove around the cloud tops. I could see the cloud layers ahead of us thickening. Too soon we'd be again enveloped in that icy cloak. Every few moments I glanced around the panel to check the instruments. Soon I would have to glue my eyes to the blind-flying panel and the engine instruments. As usual, Robin was worried. As usual, he looked it. He was glaring straight ahead at the approaching clouds. In line with his gaze was the oil-pressure gauge, which was flickering.

My God — *it was flickering!* What a hell of a time for an engine to start going to pieces under me! We were still three hundred miles from nowhere. I groaned; I knew this couldn't be happening to me. And as for Robin, I knew he hadn't yet discovered the flickering light; otherwise he'd be trying to climb out of the airplane. That wasn't such a bad idea. My kingdom for a parachute! Naturally, we didn't have any.

I tried to talk trouble away. It must be the gauge, not the engine. I watched the pressure going down, and right at that moment came the blasted clouds. I called John and told him the neat little disaster we had on our hands. We agreed the only thing to do was to press on, hoping the engine would stay together until we reached land.

Jean kept her eyes glued to us and finally used her radio mike. "Francis, there's a slick of oil trailing from the cowling."

I groaned again as John slid in for a closer look. "You've got thick black oil coming out from the engine," he said calmly. "It's trailing slowly along the belly. The wind is carrying it away from the tail."

No more funsies. We were in deep trouble. The only thing in our favor was that despite the clouds we could see for five hundred feet, and that helped John in holding formation. I called him on the radio. "John, let's get out of this stuff. We could start icing up, and I'd hate to carry the extra weight. Besides, we might get a tailwind up there."

We clawed upward through the thinning air. At 9000 feet my airplane flew like a sluggish brick. No question but that I was steadily losing power. I eased forward on the stick to build my speed up to normal cruise. It was a slow and painful process, and bitter cold had again invaded the cockpit. Without our immersion survival suits we would have frozen solid.

I couldn't get my eyeball off that oil-pressure gauge. We were down to less than half the normal reading. I really wondered if we were going to make it. Mentally, I had accepted the fact that we were going to ditch, and the prospect scared hell out of me. I called Gander, got through, and requested an interception by a rescue plane. At 1701 Zulu I reported my position to Goose Bay in Labrador. Now there was a chance that we might just squeeze to some sort of safety. We were only forty miles from the Labrador coast, and Goose Bay reported a rescue plane was on its way to escort us in. We'd never make it *that* far; not two hundred miles.

The oil pressure went down to zero.

I kept crooning to the engine, imploring it to keep going, to keep turning.

The engine exploded.

So did Robin. He threw his hands wildly into the air, fluttering like a great wounded bird and cast a look of utter anguish through the window to John in the other plane. To hell with Robin! The engine shuddered violently in its mounts and rattled the airplane. It wasn't at all funny with smoke and acrid fumes pouring into the cockpit. All you need to do is to get that biting taste of burning oil and a hot engine and your heart tries to stop. Robin was ready to die.

I banged the magneto switches to OFF, seized the HF mike, and shouted *"MAYDAY! MAYDAY!"* to Goose Bay. By now we were dropping toward the sea, John staying tight with us, helpless and frustrated because he couldn't come to our aid. In as long as it takes to tell this we dropped a thousand feet. I had my hands full and my mind was jammed with everything that had to be done swiftly. Through the smoke and the shaking airplane, Robin was yelling and carrying on something fierce, wanting to know what to do when we ditched. "Just undo your belt," I snapped, "throw out the dinghy, and step into it." His eyes were pure agony.

My eyes were also burning from the fumes, but the cockpit had begun to clear. I flicked the switches back on and tried the engine. Hell, what was there to lose? *It started!* Not really, because it shook and rattled and roared madly and tried to shake the airplane to pieces, but it spun the prop enough so that we could barely maintain our altitude. Someone seemed to wave a wand, for abruptly we slid from the clouds and I shouted. For joy, I'm certain. There, far ahead of us but clearly visible, was the frozen coast of Labrador.

We had a stretch of fifteen miles to cover. The way the engine threatened to tear itself from the mounts I was really worried that we might not make it. And even if we did make the coast, and then managed to survive an emergency landing, surviving in this wintry hell would test us to the quick. We were down to 6000 feet. We'd already lost 3000 and the engine was now shaking so violently I was afraid it would really tear things loose from the airplane. In the cabin everything that wasn't tied down danced in the air, and we were taking a severe physical beating as well.

The moments dragged on, and I begged that engine to keep running, and then — the coast of Labrador slid beneath the nose. Thank God we wouldn't have to ditch in that savage water. Yet I still had to land without crumpling up this crippled machine in a flaming ball, and I damned well knew we weren't out of this yet.

We were being offered one miracle after another. Buildings! I saw them clearly in the snow, casting long shadows before the low polar sun. There appeared to be a long stretch of level ice between two islands close to the buildings. We saw no sign of life and really didn't care. Down there lay salvation.

John's voice came into my headset. "Francis, I have those buildings in sight. Keep all the height you can. Keep that engine going as long as you dare. I'll go down and have a look."

John peeled off. The Messerschmitt racked over into a vertical turn and went partially over on her back. Within seconds the airplane was a bright speck, racing just over the surface as John whipped along the ice, examining it carefully. He shot past the buildings, came around in a swooping reversal of course, and again raced past the buildings.

"It looks pretty good," he called, relief clear in his voice. I watched the tiny winged shape darting up and down the channel between the islands. John had just pulled up into a swift, steep zoom to rejoin me when a terrific blast rattled my teeth and blurred the outside world. The engine had exploded with even more violence than before. Thick smoke boiled outward and our power ebbed away like a punctured balloon. We dropped earthward.

I was ready for anything, especially a burst of flames from the shattered engine. John reported the snow looked fairly firm, and I gambled on a wheels-down landing. If I managed to avoid hitting anything I could still prevent damage to the aircraft, and damned if I didn't want to still deliver this thing to Greg Board in Arizona. At three thousand feet the wind whistled past us with a shrill cry. I remembered I had a long trailing aerial for our HF antenna and I was busy as hell winding this in. Then there was the chore of pumping down the gear. It takes the manual system about ninety fast fore-and-aft strokes to get it down and locked. I was pumping like mad until it dropped in place.

The altimeter unwound like a falling rock. I came around in a descending rectangular pattern, and as I did so I switched off the magnetos, shut down the fuel flow, and killed the electrical and all other systems. I was all set for the landing when I received another shock. Robin had lost his fear, emerged from his funk, and was actually filming the whole thing!

We had a crosswind blowing at a right angle to our flight path, and this didn't make me happy. I glanced to the side, my eyebrows lifting. There was the other Messerschmitt, locked in tight, staying with me all the way. My airplane slipped across a slight rise and I felt the wheels brush into the level snow. We touched only lightly, still with speed, and were buffeted by the crosswind of better than 25 miles an hour. Now the speed fell off rapidly and the wheels dug

Francis Freeman in his last visit to Greg Board's bf-108B just before it broke up and sank through the icy slush of Pirate's Cove in Canada — "a lousy way to cross the Atlantic." *Photo by Robin Carruthers*

deeper into snow. As the tail started to drop the left wing started to lift and we ballooned into the air. Damn! For several yards we floated along. The next time we touched, I came back firmly on the stick and all three wheels settled into the snow. For several seconds we had a running battle between the crosswind and the drag of snow. I never thought I'd *like* snow, but it kept us running straight and began to drag us to a halt. We heard snow scraping and pounding as the wings slapped into the drifts, the airplane shuddering and lurching easily.

Abruptly we plowed into a deep drift right alongside a jetty and jerked to a halt. Utter silence. *We'd made it!*

I ripped off my safety belt, unlatched the hood, and clambered onto the wing as quickly as I could. John came roaring overhead, banking steeply to look at us. Behind me there was a great thrashing as Robin fumbled and stumbled to get out of the cabin. He tumbled off the wing, floundering wildly through the snow like a bull moose in heat, waving and shouting hoarsely to John.

"You bloody idiot!" I shouted at him. "Get the hell onto that jetty before the plane goes down!" I plowed my way through the snow, followed by that bull-mooselike thrashing behind me, and clambered onto the frail wooden jetty. Above me John screamed by at low altitude for another look; I waved to him. His wings rocked in reply; he held up a thumb and tore out for Goose Bay.

The huts we saw would provide us some shelter. People knew where we were. But this was no time to stop thinking. We had several cans of fruit and four days' emergency rations in the airplane, and we could get water by melting snow. But I had to get those supplies *fast*. Robin helped by whipping off his gloves to take pictures. The wind took quick care of him, turning his fingers icy blue and half-freezing his camera. I ignored him, working my way very carefully back to the plane to unload survival gear. I didn't like what I saw. Behind me, in the wheel tracks gouged in the snow, I saw water seeping in. Apparently there was more slush than ice beneath us; the sea here was probably only half-frozen because of the swift channel currents. I walked only in the immediate vicinity of the plane, where the slush was holding my weight quite well. We just managed to get out our gear before sinking through that slush into the water . . .

———————— ☆ ————————

Now *that's* a delivery flight. But it wasn't quite over. The Canadians flew by, dropping radios (all of which failed to work). A rescue plane came in to land but the wind was too violent and darkness was coming in fast, so the Otter peeled off, ready to come back the next day. A four-engined transport dropped them a large sled with food and clothing, and it fell to the east of the Messerschmitt. Freeman tried to get to the supplies and one foot crashed through the ice into numbing water. He barely made it to shore. He fought his way to a small house where Carruthers (the photographer) wisely had started a fire to keep them alive. An hour later they also had boiling water, open cans of fruit, and their survival rations. The night didn't look so bleak.

For a while. The cold was utterly brutal despite the fire, despite their immersion suits and their winter clothing. They nearly froze to death while choking on smoke and fumes in the room from the fire. They settled finally into a fitful sleep, only to be awakened — frozen and miserable, but totally alert — by the howling of wolves rushing closer, and then snuffling about the smashed door to the little house. That gave them an hour of agonized waiting as they pushed against the splintered door. The wolves finally left, Robin found a bottle of whisky in their gear, and they drank the night through without bothering to sleep.

A helicopter picked them up in the morning.

But the problems of delivering a military aircraft were far from over, and what happened subsequent to Freeman's crash landing in the snow happened to John Hawke in *my* airplane. It also provides an excellent "warning program" for anyone who may become involved in bringing ex-military aircraft into the United States. Keep in mind, always, that what you know and understand and appreciate about a warbird may be alien to those lofty figures in official niches who must sign and/or rubber-stamp the permissions papers you need to bring your machine into the country. What happened to John Hawke in France is, admittedly, not your usual delivery flight or even a short hop to pick up spares. But it reflects on the official mentality, and it must *always* be considered.

Now picture the situation in Labrador. Freeman and Carruthers have just crashed on the ice and emerged unhurt. Canadian rescue planes reached them immediately and Canadian officials were continuing efforts to pick them up the next day. The mayday call had flashed to the entire area. With all this going on, John Hawke and his fiancée raced to a landing at Goose Bay. A warm welcome was going to be something of a thrill after *this* flight, for sure.

Well, it wasn't quite like that. No sooner had John cut the switches and thrown open the canopy than "a little man in a curling cap, who fancied himself a cousin of Napoleon, came rushing up to us, screaming quite incoherently. Jean and I were dazed by his performance. He howled and shrieked and carried on in a completely demented manner, which became all the more worrisome when two Canadian frontier guards joined him. They didn't have the foggiest idea of what was going on. All they could see were the German markings on the Messerschmitt."

After a while, reason doesn't work. Explanations don't matter. Courtesy is ignored. So you try something else. John had already learned that his own considerable bulk, stentorian voice, and bristling angry dark beard can often communicate better than normal words; he finally threw back his head and roared. Everyone stared at him. He continued roaring, eyes glaring, beard bristling, climbed down from the wing, pushed aside the rifles of the frontier guards, stormed up to the little man, pushed his nose against the official's nose (and John has quite a nose), and bellowed. Most of what he said was unintelligible, but since nothing else had worked,

100

he bellowed all the louder. Two things happened. The little man shrank back, both cowed and impressed, and several female moose wandered to the edge of the forest to investigate what they probably believed to be a magnificent mating call. All the bombast, however, did result in specifics.

Despite all the careful paperwork that had preceded the flight, the Canadian official with the Bonaparte complex charged John Hawke — and me, indirectly, as the owner of the aircraft — with illegally entering Canada, violating several air defense zones, landing illegally at a military airbase, flying a German military airplane, and violating some obscure but frightening regulations. Nothing John said, or showed in his paperwork, had any noticeable effect. He went back to bellowing. He might as well be arrested, since that would result in charges in writing, and he would contact the British government, *and* the Royal Air Force, and me, and whoever else he needed to bring pressure into the now very disagreeable situation. By a stroke of good fortune, all this proved unnecessary. An officer of the Royal Canadian Air Force entered the picture. He stared at the diminutive bf-108B that had just crossed the killer North Atlantic, shook his head with understanding, went into the office where the bellowing continued unabated, and *ordered* the customs official from the room. "Into a moving propeller, I would think," John murmured.

But the RCAF and its officers extended to John and Jean full courtesies, which John described as "quite splendid, to say the least," approved the paperwork, and cleared the airplane to continue to the United States — where things fell apart again.

Getting the idea? Officials must make problems, stir up a broth, muddy the waters, whatever, or they diminish the justification for their very existence. If everyone in official business were efficient we could do away with nine out of every ten officials in the whole world. To prevent such a commendable prospect from becoming reality, they have developed the fine art of nitpicking to a mind-shattering science.

John flew the 108 across the border and down to Burlington, Vermont, where he cleared customs. At least, he *tried* to get through U.S. Customs. We had taken *every* requirement under consideration and, the night before John arrived, had cleared the airplane with the customs office, and had the fee paid by a local broker. Everything was in order.

Wrong. What a way to greet guests from England. By midmorning, the local broker gave it the old-fashioned try by "jacking up the cost of his fee." He refused to release the airplane unless we paid out considerably more money than the figure agreed upon previously. *Get your dollars and cents in writing.* I don't care *whom* you know; get it on paper and signed by all concerned. We hadn't done this because of the vagaries of schedules, and now they were trying to stick it to us. In fact, the broker insisted upon cash. No checks; nothing but the long green.

Scummy people like this are found everywhere in the world, and we knew what to do. I called a legal beagle friend, and he called the office of the governor of Vermont, and the word was passed quickly to the broker that he was about to be arrested for violating his bond. The broker turned pale and Hawke burst out laughing as the broker begged Hawke's permission to pay the fee and release the airplane at once.

But it wasn't so easy with the Loch Ness Monster, as Hawke immediately named the U.S. Customs agent. John Hawke is a big man and he stared at a physical giant who was literally seven feet tall and a yard wide, but, as John stressed, he was just "a big pudding of a man." The pudding alleged that the Messerschmitt was a deadly weapon, that Hawke was in violation of the something-or-other Munitions Act, that a machine gun was clearly visible on the aircraft to prove his point, and, customs was going to impound the airplane. Furthermore, insisted the pudding, all the aircraft papers were illegal, and whatever papers we didn't have in the airplane were (obviously) the ones that should have been there, although no one identified any missing papers.

The upshot of all this bantering back and forth was another phone call to me in New York. We kept bringing in attorneys and government officials *we knew* on extension lines until it seemed we were holding a telephonic meeting of the United Nations. Now, I want to get something absolutely clear. Most, almost all, of our dealing with U.S. Customs is fast, courteous, efficient, all the things you want, especially if you've done the preliminary paperwork in the proper manner. *This* asshole was a whole new breed. He insisted he worked for the State Department (he didn't; he worked for the U.S. Treasury). He stated loudly he didn't give a damn about the Federal Aviation Agency. He refused to accept the papers sent to us by the FAA, and he chose to dismiss the identification papers signed by an American vice-consul in Europe that legally cleared the aircraft for entrance into the United States.

The airplane was released when the people to whom we spoke in Washington *ordered* this official immediately to release the aircraft and to have no further dealings with us.

John and Jean landed at Zahns Airport on Long Island, New York, at 4:30 P.M. on January 19, 1964. More than fifty newsmen from local and national newspapers, and a pleasant mob of television news crews, were on hand to greet them on arrival. I missed most of the press conference. After all, the moment belonged to John and Jean, and I was hunkered down in the cockpit, touching everything and making plans for the immediate future.

Because the best was yet to come.

6

Pig Flight

This aircraft is flown by a superior pilot.
A superior pilot is one who stays out of
trouble by using superior judgment to
avoid situations that might require the
use of his superior skill. You may exclude
Martin Caidin from this list.

MAJOR KARL VON STRASSER

You just can't pass up the rare moments. We drifted eastward toward New York at 8500 feet, JFK airport sprawling hugely before us and with huge sweptwing ironmongers all over the place. Very upsetting, so the right thing to do is to call approach control, tell them who and where you are and where you're going. At this altitude you don't need to do this, but it's a matter of courtesy (TCAs were still in the future), and it is one of *those* moments.

"Ah, Kennedy Approach, dis ist Messerschmitt Von-Oh-Eighdt-Onkle. Ofer."

"Aircraft calling Kennedy Approach, say again your identification." Naturally, in that tumultuous sky, those words were blurted out in machine-gun fashion. But not ours.

"Rocher, JFK Approach. Dis ist Messerschmitt Von-Oh-Eighdt-Onkle, twenty-fife milez vest uf you. Ve are at eighdt-fife-zero-zero. Ofer."

"Uh, roger that, and you're coming in just a bit garbled. Did you say *Messerschmitt* Von — One-Oh-Eight-Uncle? Over."

"Ja, Kennedy! Dot izz gorredkt vrom Messerschmitt Von-Oh-Eighdt-Onkle. Ve are now bassingk twenty milez vest, der heading

104

izz niner-zero degrees, undt ve are now komingk down zru zevven thousandt feets. Ofer."

"Um, ah, roger that, and your destination, One-Oh-Eight-Uncle?"

"Kennedy, ve are komingk down to make der landing at Zahns, and ve bassingk ofer you. Ofer."

There was always a pause at this moment. We knew by now they had us on radar. "Umm, say, ah, Messerschmitt Von — I mean, *One*-Oh-Eight-Uncle, whoever you are, you are cleared through. Just please go away . . ."

We had a few weeks of this before I yielded to the smarts of this business and grounded 108U for a mandatory teardown and IRAN — Inspect and Repair As Necessary. In fact, I should have grounded the airplane immediately. But the siren call to fly this machine was so great I pushed aside common sense for a while and got a good taste of the bird. I also had the chance to repay someone who had brought me along in my own flying. Ed Lyons, one of the owners of Zahns Airport and one of the true grand old masters of the flying game, had never had the chance to fly something like the 108B. What an opportunity. Ed had chewed on me merrily for years as I went from one new rating to another, and now I was providing the airplane and the know-how to return the favor. After checking out Lyons we moved the Messerschmitt across the field to the Center Airmotive Corporation for the tear-down and checkout.

Center Airmotive was owned and run by Lord Malcolm Douglas-Hamilton, a former Group Captain of the Royal Air Force, and he was acquainted on an intimate basis with aircraft such as our bf-108B. There was only one way to IRAN an aircraft as far as he was concerned: the *right* way. They cleared a section of the main hangar and 108U went up on jacks and blocks. We had already translated the French manuals into English, as well as the charts, graphs, drawings, and diagrams, and we knew what we were dealing with.

In such a program you assign different people to different tasks. One group attended to the powerplant section. They removed the Ratier propeller and system and overhauled it until it was like new. They went into the innards of the engine, probing, checking, and adjusting everything. Little by little they accumulated a shopping list. They wanted new gaskets, valves, springs, pieces here and there with which they would reassemble the engine so that if

105

it might not be as good as new, it would be damned close. The key was to find anything and everything that needed work and especially items and pieces that needed replacement. As the shopping list was given to us for all these parts and pieces, which could not be obtained in the United States, we typed them up and gave a copy to one of our many friends who made the round trip between New York and Paris as a matter of course. Airline captains and engineers would land in Paris and be off as quickly as they could to the Nord factory for aircraft parts and to the Renault plant for engine parts. Our rule was to buy three of anything we needed in order to lay in a good supply of extra parts. It's the only way. You will *always* find a need for more parts than you order, even if you get everything you want the first time around.

We had a flow of parts from France to JFK Airport to Zahns Airport that resembled a wartime supply line. We even changed Plexiglas panels. We bought new tires, tubes, brake systems, even cowl fasteners. After all, 108U had been around a long time and plain old wear-and-tear had taken its toll. Where there was the slightest question of metal corrosion, we replaced those areas with new sheet metal. We got all new hoses, lines, belts, and similar systems. We went into the wings and through every inch of the fuselage. We scoured out every drop of oil and patch of grease and redid everything. We removed bolts and tested them for strength. We x-rayed, used dye-penetration, Magnaflux, and other tests to determine the strength and reliability of what we couldn't determine through eyeball and experience.

I have one overriding rule whenever rebuilding a machine such as Messerschmitt N108U: *Replace every wire in the airplane.* No excuses, no breaking the rule. Tear out every wire and put in new, mark it properly and draw up all new electrical schematics. You can never tell when the old wires are going to go. You can eyeball them from now till hell freezes over and you may always be on the edge of a failure. Every plane has a level of reliability that is always in direct proportion to the dependability of its electrical systems, and there is simply no shortcut when it comes to wiring. We didn't leave so much as a shred of old wire, and when this particular job was done, we *knew* what we had and that we could depend on the new systems.

Talk of new systems was almost cause for acute fiscal distress, because the new systems I had in mind were all new gauges and instruments, and new avionics. Once again we are involved in that

106

The intrepid John R. Hawke, pilot extraordinary, former RAF ace, infamous roustabout of Las Vegas, and old flying buddy of Martin Caidin, checks out the roaring engine of N108U at Zahns Airport. *Photo by Howard Levy*

area of authenticity for a resurrected warbird, and I stand strong on this subject. The purists — those same moaners and harpers who bleat plaintively from the sidelines — will tell you that to be a pristine rebuild, the warbird should have the old parts and systems of the original. Easier said than done, friends, when you can't get the original tires because the factory was bombed into rubble and no one ever made new parts. On this same basis, you dare not stick new antennae on your machine because the types of antennae didn't exist in the old days, especially VHF and other modern systems, and therefore you're really not perfect.

You can carry this sort of nonsense — and it is stupid — to ridiculous extremes. Should we burn the old gasoline? Should we scour the rubble heaps of the world for original spark plugs? Or insist on original paint? Or refuse to use new Plexiglas or Lexan? Insist on the ancient seat belts and shoulder harnesses because they're authentic (and liable to rot and break)? So the question poses itself: Where do you draw the line?

You draw the line where safety is at issue.

That's it. No ifs, ands, or buts. You put things on your airplane that are reliable and safe. If you're talking about functioning parts, *you do not compromise safety.* Those who do sooner or later pay the terrible, ultimate price of a failure or a fatal crash because the old system, tremendously authentic, finally gave up the ghost, or just did not fit into the demands of modern flight and the air traffic control system.

Until this time, when I rolled the 108 into the confines of its hangar for IRAN, I had been flying with the European system of instruments. I didn't like it one bit. Oh, sure, it's easy to paint green lines, yellow lines, and red lines on your gauges to let you know when you're operating in the safe, caution, or dangerous areas. But that's a lousy way to do things, and the information those gauges give you is never up to the capability of better gauges telling you how this thing is whirring and ticking. European metric systems don't hack it with me *in this country.*

Sure, it's easy enough to paint the dials and the glass. You can figure things out, too. It's easy to land the 108B at 100 kilometers per hour. I know I'm doing 62 miles per hour when it reads 100 kph. *But why bother?* There's altitude in meters instead of feet, and you've always got to convert in your head. Your vertical speed is measured in meters per second, and that kind of conversion demands time and attention away from other things, and when you get it down to precision flying the chances for error are magnified enormously. If you're going to putt-putt in severe clear weather and daylight only, you don't need much more than a piece of string tacked onto the airplane for yaw, if you need even that (and you don't).

I changed all those instruments. I kept the air-bottle systems of the airplane because they *are* a special characteristic of the 108B. When starting this airplane I made sure the air pressure in the bottles was up where it belonged, she was primed, the brakes locked, mixture set, throttle cracked, then just pull the handle, and like *that*, the air bottles spun that prop into an instant blur and she was running. We charged the bottles in flight through ram pressure. What if those systems failed or I forgot to set all the little doodads and gidgies? Well, you can always get air pressure, at an airport or a roadside garage (and I've had to do both). In fact, the air-bottle system of starting is far superior, in cold weather, to the notoriously unreliable small battery.

108

But I went to American flight gauges. Airspeed, needle-and-ball, vertical speed (rate of climb and/or descent), altimeter; the whole ball of wax. I yielded to only one instrument because it was working so beautifully; the original French artificial horizon. We checked it out, found out we couldn't check it out properly, and sent off to France for a spanking-new model of the same type. My engine gauges now read in familiar terms and I wasn't trying constantly to do mental gymnastics when I should have been flying the airplane.

Let me add one more point. When you remove a foreign gauge that's starting to sound like an old coffee grinder, or it's begun to twitch on you, how do you get the damn thing overhauled, and tagged, and properly certified? *You don't.* There's the rub. Our instrument shops simply lack the equipment to test these gauges. Most shops don't want a thing to do with them and they'll refuse to work on them, because if "something happens" and you roll the airplane up in a ball and perhaps do in some good people, *that shop can be sued.* No matter that they disclaimed all responsibility for anything. They're right on the firing line when something like this happens. So if you insist on keeping the old gauges, you're begging for trouble.

Next came the avionics. The French antennae were worthless for us. So were their radios. We put in all Narco VHF equipment. We used VOR and localizer and glideslope and three-marker beacon and ADF and all the systems and radios that were intended to fit right in with *our* communications and navigation systems. We didn't keep so much as a screw from the old panel. It was *all* new, and it was also a very comforting feeling to know you could handle it all in a sweeping glance and know what you were dealing with. When all the shop work was completed, John and I took the 108B out for her test trials, and that bird sang as sweetly as any airplane I'd ever known. I would have liked more power than the 230 hp we were getting from the Renault 6Q10 engine, and I know the prop could have been more efficient, but the system checked out so perfectly we stayed with the originals. So long as the engine ran well and I had plenty of parts to keep it running that way, I didn't care where it came from.

However, if I had my druthers, I would have gone for an American engine and prop system . . .

When we finished the checkouts we figured it was time to do a real number on the airplane. The FAA had an office right on Zahns

Airport, and from the beginning, from opening the first panel, we followed a system that always pays off in spades. We went to the FAA and told them what we were doing. We laid out all our plans, told them how we were going to do things, where we'd get our parts, showed them the translated service manuals, and invited them to come over any time and sit in on the work. We asked that they perform their inspections as we went along, while the airplane was stripped as naked as the day it was being assembled. We wanted them to poke and pry and question. That way, not only were we on top of all requirements with the FAA, but we also had their experience to benefit us. They made some suggestions; we studied them, found they were excellent, and followed them. When we were all done, the final inspection was cursory. They were able to sign off N108U as being as close to perfect as they could want.

But Ed Lyons had a creased forehead and a frown. He didn't like the pilot's operating manual, or flight manual, or whatever you want to call that handy-dandy handbook the pilot uses to know his airplane and operate its systems. We had translated the French pilot manual and it simply wasn't that worthwhile. Lyons didn't insist we write a whole new book, but he sure alluded to it. "You two maniacs want to fly that thing more than you do anything else," he reminded us unnecessarily, "so why not go the whole route? Do your own flight tests and determine all your performance parameters by yourselves. Run it through the typewriter, bring it to me, I'll sign it off as the *proper* handbook and you can make as many copies as you want. By the way, I'll have the first one, if you don't mind."

We did just that. Years later we discovered that anywhere the Messerschmitt bf-108B might be found, everybody was furiously making copies of that flight manual that we did together. Paul Perret is a pilot who's flown a very wide variety of aircraft, and one day had the opportunity to fly NX108V, another 108B owned by a friend of ours, Lee Dufrechou. When Paul wrote a detailed report of his familiarization flight in NX108V, there we were —

——————————— ☆ ———————————

The flight characteristics of the 108 are exceptional. Martin Caidin, the owner of Messerschmitt N108U, and John Hawke cite the aircraft for its "sensitivity, sureness, and swift and positive response to the controls that have consistently delighted pilots." They say it is a "thoroughbred all the way." According to these experts, "it has no characteristics to surprise the pilot and, despite its outstanding performance, is much more a safer and better handling machine than any other production aircraft in the world." This non-expert, who has flown too many types of aircraft to recall, can only fully concur with their learned observations . . . Performance data on the Dufrechou Me-108B was something that I did not have an opportunity to personally measure. Caidin says that his bf-108B cruised at an indicated airspeed of 155 mph, and that the level flight speed at 5000 feet is 190 mph at a weight of 3000 pounds, and it cruises around 160 mph true airspeed, burning about fourteen gallons of gas per hour. The Dufrechous concur with Caidin's performance figures. Of all the aircraft I have ever flown, or have flown in, one that I will never forget is the Me-108. It's the finest classic airplane this pilot has ever flown.

———————— ☆ ————————

Well, thank *you*, Paul Perret.

☆

You get wild notions sometimes. I got one. I decided it would be real neat to start out at Jones Beach on the south shore of Long Island, head due east along the shoreline, *and barrel roll the airplane the entire length of Long Island.* That would be about a hundred miles of barrel rolling. N108U went through barrel rolls as most airplanes just cruise through the air. Nose down, power remaining at cruise, let her pick up speed to about 180 indicated, up with the nose to about 30 degrees, and start her into the roll. She came around just as pretty as you could ask for and in perfect position and speed to renew the maneuver.

Why did I want to do this? Hey, here's this fabulous airplane and a crystal blue sky and all that shoreline and who cares? I wanted to do it. I went up to 5500 feet and rolled — literally — down the tubular slot to the east. I got through 32 consecutive rolls, I felt terrific, the airplane was a marvel, and as I came out of the thirty-second roll, I threw up all over the front of the cockpit.

I don't know why. I never felt the first discomfort, the first sign of nausea or anything except tremendous pleasure at what was happening. Maybe it's like watching one TV set with the sound off and listening to another TV set with the picture blank and the sound on a different channel. I don't know. I do know I spent all that night cleaning up one splattered cockpit.

We flew N108U throughout the United States. We had no special place to go and that meant everywhere was a special place. We soared above the Rockies and wandered across the midsection of the country. Almost everywhere we went we flew impromptu air-shows and performed for the press. We were more than surprised at some of the attention we received; we were still getting the fore-warning of the warbird movement to sweep the nation.

Not all the landings were as graceful as I would have wanted. We flew a long and hard session one day with a lot of turbulence and, unhappily, a prop seal that began to leak and to throw a fine spray of oil across the windshield. That's not *too* bad in daylight, but at night it turns the world into an LSD trip of wavering and blurry lights. I landed at McCarran Field, wanting that long run-way ahead of me because of the almost blind approach. I was hold-ing her off as best I could, groping for the ground, and slammed into the propwash of something big in the dark and it was at the worst possible moment. The 108 soared, a gentle lofting that spilled away the airspeed and brought the automatic slats along the leading edges of the wing to slam forward as I let her loft into the stall. Power, stick forward! Get airspeed! I sure did, slamming her against the runway like some ham-handed dolt, and even as she bounced again I knew I could get into an oscillating stumble down that long runway. *Think* is often much better than *react*. More power, hold her steady, let her *fly*, ease off gently on the power, stick back, that's it, don't let her land, guide yourself by the runway lights to the side, don't let her land, and blind, she settled by herself a hell of a lot better than I was doing.

We almost flew into a killer situation at El Paso. We had N108U loaded to the gills and beyond. Full fuel and oil, John and I in the front seat and Jean in the back, along with massive piles of bag-gage, food, and lots of good whisky. Mayhap we were a bit *too* mas-sive in the weight department. We got to the field later than planned. We were also in the midst of a scorching heat wave. The temperature stood at something over 120°F. I looked at the air-plane and then at the sky and back to the thermometer and thought of the field elevation at 4000 feet. John taxied out to the end of the runway, with 7000 feet of concrete stretching before us. Before he could take the active I called the tower. "November One-Oh-Eight wants to delay takeoff," I called. John and I talked about it.

"I don't think we'll get off this runway," I said.

He looked at me as if I were crazy. "That's seven thousand feet out there, jocko," he rebuked me gently.

"I know," I said, still unhappy. "And the outside temp reads one hundred and twenty, right?"

"Right," he said, nodding.

"And that's *in the shade*," I reminded him.

"Oh," he said quietly, thinking that it was a hell of a lot hotter in the sun and the day was cloudless. He picked up the mike. "El Paso Tower, One-Oh-Eight prefers your longer runway," he called.

"Ro-*ger*," came the response. "Good thinking." They taxied us to the end of the runway that stretched 12,000 feet ahead of us. "Take it," John said. "I want to watch this."

We rolled. And rolled, and rolled. It took forever to get the tail up. When we did, 108U still had all the zap of a dying camel. Faster and faster we went, well over takeoff speed. We passed the marker at 7000 feet and I eased back on the stick, not expecting her to fly. She didn't. She settled back as if she were weary. John's eyebrows went up. "My, oh my," he said quietly. I let her build even more speed and eased back on the stick at 9000 feet down the runway, and she eased into the air, the wings solid with all her speed.

Obviously, we would never have made it using the 7000-foot runway. Moral: *always* take the best situation when there's any compromise with your conditions. The old saw still prevails: You can't use the runway behind you, the sky above you, or the fuel that's still in the truck. *And know your density altitude.*

One of the greatest assets of the bf-108B, despite its sleek lines and desire to keep flying no matter what, was the ability to put the airplane down into a short field. You could fly this thing along the edge of a stall all day and night, without benefit of an airspeed indicator, because of those Handley-Page slats on the wing leading edges. As the airplane slowed to just above stall, the changing airflow caused the slats to bang forward, alter the camber of the wing, and instantly increase lift. (Look at any modern jetliner in takeoff or landing configuration and you'll see those same slats.) Now, no airplane can *sustain* a true vertical turn because, since the lift is perpendicular to the wing, lift is then being exerted sideways, or level with the horizon, rather than against downward-pulling gravity. The 108, because of those automatic slats, could be reefed into a vertical turn (and held there with both arms holding the stick full back) and as the airplane shuddered into the stall, the slat boomed out, and increased lift. So the vertical turn *could* be performed, with the wings rocking gently while perpendicular to the ground, and the slats going BANG! BANG! BANG! as you held the turn.

Now, all this lent itself to excellent slow flight, such as is needed to get into tight fields on the ground. And no incident in N108U will ever match that of late 1964 when John, Jean, and I were en route from New York to Florida. We had hit strong headwinds on the way and were squeezing our fuel pretty tightly. Fifteen minutes out from our en route airport the engine coughed and sputtered. We'd purposely let the main tanks run to the bottom, and I switched to the reserve standpipe, a tubular fuel cell behind the cabin that gave us 45 minutes additional flying time. Everything was taking place right on schedule.

Except that when the engine quit it didn't start up again. Later we confirmed that a huge air bubble, about the size of a tennis ball, had formed in the standpipe and blocked off fuel flow. Whatever the reason, there was silence and then only the sighing of the wind. We also had a marvelous view of the West Virginia mountains into which we were descending in that same silence. The only field in sight lay between two small mountains, and to get there I'd have to do a few nifty turns, roll her out with the gear already down (this is when you love a manual system, old friends), and drop her in with enough room to roll free and *not* impact the fence on the opposite side of the field. There was really no way other than to follow this procedure. John got out a few mayday calls before we shut her down, switching fuel flow to OFF to drain whatever might remain in the lines, pulling the mixture to idle cutoff, and killing all electrical power. Let me not make this more than it was; the wind was fine and the turning, twisting descent was duck soup for this airplane. I concentrated on the flying and John took care of the gear and then I rolled down 48 degrees of flap.

"What in the hell is on the field?" John squinted ahead, I squinted, and behind us, Jean laughed. *"Pigs!"* she cried. "The bloody field is full of bloody pigs!"

She was right. It was so ridiculous the cabin rang with shared laughter, and then I cut it off as I rolled onto a very short final, held the nose down, and let her drop with the stick coming back. She touched down on three points onto a very soggy surface and rolled only a short distance.

"Well, that was convenient," John noted. "I wonder what slowed us so neatly?"

114

I knew. I hated it, but I knew. "Pigshit," I told him.

"Bah," he said, opening the canopy and climbing down off the wing into an ankle-deep deposit of — you guessed it. The stench was horrendous. The sight of a few hundred porkers staring at us wasn't all that much better.

On the way down we had been watched by hundreds of people. Now, it's 1964, the war's long over, and here comes a German fighter out of the sky *in dead silence.* We waited by the airplane for twenty minutes or so until the first sign of non-pig life appeared.

Over a nearby rise came about a hundred people armed with pitchforks, axes, poles, and more than a few shotguns and hunting rifles, moving cautiously toward us as if we'd burst through some diaphragm separating us from their world in some Twilight Zone. John climbed back onto the wing, strewing pig effluvium across that shiny surface, waiting until his audience was close by. He stood erect, eyes glaring, and pointed a finger at a youngster in the front row. "You!" he bellowed. "Vhere in Vest Chermany are ve?"

The boy stammered. "B-but, s-suh . . . y'all is in Wes' *Virginnyia.*"

John lifted both hands upward, rolling his eyes to the heavens, beseeching some invisible deity. "You haff done zis to us again!" he cried. "Ve vill neffer reach Valhalla!"

The crowd fled. Ten minutes later it returned behind a jeep. Driving the jeep was an old-timer with crow's feet on each side of his eyes and I knew we'd found a friend. He was also a U.S. marshal. "Wal, what's it all about, fellers?" he said with a wide grin.

He was an old P-47 fighter pilot, and we all talked the same language. They got us the highest-octane auto fuel they could find and we filled the tanks about one-third full to keep down our weight. With the help of some local youngsters, John and I dragged the airplane back to the fence we had crossed on the way in. We fired up and the crowd, now grown to about 500 souls, cheered heartily from the side. I held the stick full back and applied the power slowly and steadily. The tail came up and the nose went down and she didn't move. I chopped the power. "Too much weight," John grunted. "I'll go outside and push to get her started. Now, when she gets moving, for God's sake *don't stop.* Bring her around in a wide circle to your right and I'll run alongside and jump onto the wing and I'll climb aboard while you're still running. That way you can come out of the circle any time you're ready and we'll take off."

"You're crazy," I told him. Jean rolled her eyes. John climbed

115

"A winged arrow in motion ..." Martin Caidin brings his sleek Messerschmitt down to the deck in a high-speed pass to do some fine-honed "propeller grass-cutting." *Photo by Bill Mason*

down, I felt the tail moving and he banged his hand on the stabilizer. I brought in the power and she started to roll, and I got her going pretty good and brought in about 15 degrees of flaps and heard Jean yell, "Start turning!"

Man, what a way to fly. I brought in right rudder and started a wide circling turn and sure enough, there was John running full tilt in a spray of mud and pig dump, coming in toward us like a circus acrobat about to jump onto a horse running in a tight circle. He thundered toward us and hurled himself onto the wing, grabbed a handhold as Jean stood and held the canopy hatch open. Suddenly John pumped his fist up and down and I took the signal to mean full power. I held the stick back and poured the coal to her, and for a timeless instant I saw a look of total astonishment on John's face. He hung poised *in space* as the prop blast loosened his hold and instantly he was gone. Jean shrieked, I kept turning and came around to see John sprawled, spread-eagled in you-guessed-it. He came erect slowly, the stuff dripping from his eyebrows and nose and beard, shaking his fist. Jean was in complete hysterics and 500 people applauded madly.

I came around again, running her as slowly as I could and watching John make his mad circus dash for the airplane. Again he hurled himself onto the wing and managed to get his upper body into the cockpit. The stench was ghastly. Jean had him by the belt and was hauling with all her might as John struggled to get into the airplane against the wind. "Goddammit, don't stop, you bloody nit!" he roared. I kept circling, there was a thud and he flopped into the airplane, face on the floorboards, rump in the air and feet against Jean in the back seat. She slammed the canopy shut and cried, "GO! GO!" I went, coming out of the turn and adding power steadily, the slats whapping away out on the wings, and then we had flying speed and I pumped up the gear and twisted down a valley as John slowly came upright and Jean and I gasped for air. We flew to the nearest airport, a large commercial field with luxury facilities for general aviation. I taxied to the ramp and shut her down and John opened the canopy on his side, and somewhat more urgently I did the same on my side. A greeting hostess in tight sweater and miniskirt came be-bopping up to the plane to bid us welcome. She stopped downwind, her face turned white and she fled in horror.

First we hosed down John.

Then we hosed down the airplane.

Then we sprayed it with about fifty bucks' worth of perfume. It didn't help that much.

☆

After six hundred hours of some of the greatest flying in my life, the engine began to give up the ghost. John announced we had a cracked block. We'd been based at Merritt Island Airport in Florida near Cape Canaveral, still a grass strip, when we got the bad news. It was time to sell the bird. John performed a few minor miracles with the engine. I think he glued it together. "It'll last forty hours and not a minute more," he announced.

A week later we had our customer. For many reasons he shall remain nameless in these pages, but he wanted that airplane and he wanted it badly. We told him about the engine. "Forty hours and it's a goner," we told him. "You buy it, you sign a piece of paper that these are the terms."

We gave him a flight. He drove a big airliner for a living, but he was hopelessly in love with the 108. He checked out neatly and flew off to the northland. Months later we again saw N108U. At

117

thirty hours of flight, the new owner grounded her. By then he was ready for his big step up with the airplane. He removed the engine, modified the engine mounts and connections, and installed a 400-hp Lycoming engine along with a new three-bladed prop. As great as I'd known this airplane to be, he had turned her into a *real* tiger. Her rate and angle of climb were phenomenal. She could fly or flit as the pilot wanted. He put on airshows on a regular basis. One day he came out of a loop much too close to the ground and pulled up through tree branches. Green sprayed everywhere, but the bird kept right on going and landed safely with only a few dents and scratches. God, what an airplane.

The saga of N108U ended one night when a fire swept through a large hangar. There was no hope of containing the blaze. Along with twenty other planes, the little Messerschmitt was consumed.

7

208 and
The Ultimate 108

Let's get the hell out of here!

DEE DEE CAIDIN
(after she crashed in a
Messerschmitt bf-108B)

There were other Messerschmitts after the fiery demise of N108U. I flew other 108s in California and down in Texas, in Florida and in Wisconsin, but it was never really the same. So I'm an incurable romantic when it comes to my own planes I've nursed through resurrection. I've got lots of company.

It took my wife to accomplish in a Messerschmitt bf-108B what I always managed to elude. *Crashing.* If she could rearrange events in time, Dee Dee would gladly hand over all the honors to me. It was 1976 and a gang of us were at Harlingen, Texas, on the ramp of the Confederate Air Force, working day and night to get a giant collection of weary old metal bones, my ancient Junkers Ju-52, into condition to fly her home. Terry Ritter had been in the Texas wastelands for weeks, performing large and small miracles as the moment demanded, and when we got the call that he had all three engines "burning and turning," we hied off to the deep southland.

During the period of test flights with the creaking old monster, we had the opportunity to take breaks in a wide variety of different warbirds. Walt Wooten taxied up in Messerschmitt bf-108B,

N40FF, and invited everyone for a flight. I waved off the invitation, but Dee Dee and Terry were gone in a flash, Dee Dee to try her hand at the controls from the right seat, and Terry's great bulk occupying the back seat of the airplane. Off they went in a great spur-of-the-moment adventure, racing low over the wide Texas fields, Wooten's mastery at the controls evident in the crisp feel and response as they made mock attacks and played tag with cottony low clouds.

Dee Dee took the controls, timorous at first because even the word Messerschmitt was foreign to her world. Quickly the marvelous feel of the little airplane allayed her overcaution, and she blended in with power and swift flight. Five hundred feet over long-reaching farms they turned and sped and then the engine quit.

Just like .. *that*. One moment it ran beautifully, the propeller a quicksilver shadow. The next it was as devoid of life as a rock, and in that same instant Wooten's hand flew to the stick and his feet planted firmly on the rudder pedals and he did all the things one is supposed to do when the ground is only scant seconds away. But life would not return to that balky Renault because a great air bubble (as happens in the 108, it happens) had appeared like some monstrous virus in a fuel line and that was all she wrote. Walt Wooten picked out a cotton field, made his decision to leave the gear in its wells rather than to jab those legs into freshly plowed land, and brought her down neatly.

They headed straight for a row of trees, but Walt hadn't quit flying when he touched down. Rather, he had calculated it most carefully and once they felt the earth hammering in hard rippling jabs beneath them he had the rudder tramped full over and the little Messerschmitt was turning as it slid on the fresh wet earth and then it was over, they were stopped, the switches were all off, the hatches flew open, and Dee Dee yelled, "Let's get the hell out of here!" They went out fast and Dee Dee stood looking in disbelief at the airplane when two big men grabbed her beneath her arms and literally ran away with her. Just in case. But Walt had done it as perfectly as might be expected, and even from a safe distance the Messerschmitt only sighed and crinkled gently as it cooled off.

They brought the airplane home on the back of a pickup truck, which wasn't as bad as it sounds, because the wings fold very neatly and buttressed in with a bunch of two-by-fours, they had the airplane standing on her gear that afternoon. Ten days and a lot of sheet-metal work later N40FF was back in the air, not even bothered with her recent dismaying descent into a Texas cotton field.

Some years later I took the controls of that same airplane. Doc Leo Kerwin and I had sashayed about a good part of the country in his Skylane, a comfortable old slipper of an airplane if ever there was one, and our winged travels brought us gently to light in the outskirts of Austin, Texas. There was the same 108 that had briefly but firmly spanged onto unpaved Texas countryside. Taking the lithe machine back into the air was fun, and it also launched Kerwin onto a longtime adventure with the basic bf-108 design that is even just now approaching its zenith in what is justifiably billed as the "Ultimate 108." That engineering caper lay some time in the future as we took the little bird aloft over Texas, and the one flight that stands out among the others was made with an old astronaut friend (who must in these pages remain nameless and obscure, for the good reason that what we did might be considered as less than dignified NASA protocol, and he is still driving that sweptwing whale of a Shuttle spacecraft).

Suffice to say that said astronaut, sans silvery suit and wearing an old baseball cap rather than a globular pressure helmet, was requested to pay an aerial visit to a local shindig then under boisterous way. A huge barbecue and country swing was undergoing transformation to near hysteria as we approached.

"They didn't say we should announce our arrival, did they?" asked UA (Unidentified Astronaut).

"Nope," I obliged.

"We'd ruin it for them if we just circled, wouldn't we?"

"Reckon."

UA studied the immediate countryside. "Big field of wheat or something to the east of the barbecue," he observed.

"Uh huh."

"Put your hand on the stick, if you please," UA bid me.

I catch on fast. "You got it."

We came out of the wheat field, or whatever that tall grass was, with the engine wide open and the prop screaming in flat pitch and pounced onto the huge parking lot and open bays of the barbecue festival. Just like we'd been asked, of course, but I tell you straight, all we could see in that parking lot was a small sea of asses and elbows. We didn't make any turns but kept going on the deck. You can't get aircraft numbers that way.

121

And why both pilots on the sticks in the front seat? Well, friend, the truth, now, the plain old truth is that if he's asked who was flying, he points to me and says, "Him." And if I'm asked who was flying I point to UA and say, "Him." You can't have *two* pilots in command of an aircraft. That's the *law*. You can find only *one* pilot in violation of something. And since there just ain't no way, *no way*, to tell which one of us was telling the truth, or both, or if both of us was lying, well, it's no case.

☆

Well, the people running that barbecue were true to their word. No one ever complained about that whistling approach through the tall grass to burst out across the parking lot to present various bony and fleshy parts of anatomy to the sky. A couple of years later, with that little Messerschmitt relegated to a fond memory in a far part of the country from where we hang out and dip wingtips into the high blue, I was again in a Messerschmitt, only this time we had something completely new.

Old N108U, the first Messerschmitt I'd owned in the States, was apparently the first model of its kind to make it on the warbird scene, followed by now, of course, by a small *staffel* of 108s of various models being rushed to the United States. The long and short of it is that N108U was the forerunner of the small but growing pack to follow. Now, it's the *in* thing to have a 108, and they're appearing on the scene with Renault engines, with German engines, and with American engines adapted to the superb wings and fuselage of the fifty-year-old German touring marvel. After all, where else can you find a small, fully aerobatic, excellent cross-country, economical, four-place warbird with all the pizzazz of the 108?

Down in Fort Lauderdale, of all places!

☆

Ray Martin, he of the tall, broad-shouldered frame and wicked mustache and sharp eyes, was on the phone at a barbaric six A.M. "It's here! *It's here!*" he cried, sounding like a Viking who has either just run off with a pigtailed buxom blonde, or killed her husband for the fun of it. "My Messerschmitt! It's here!"

"What the hell are you talking about?" I managed the question in a half whine and snarl. I figured Ray was either drunk or crazy. I knew the disposition of every bf-108B in the entire country, and

Ray Martin was *not* on that exclusive list. But he wasn't crazy. We'd been flying for years, and he knew how to find the ground when he ran out of fuel; that sort of thing. He wanted me to fly the Ju-52 down to Executive Airport at Fort Lauderdale to see his prize catch. Whatever it might be, I thought as I dropped the phone back onto its cradle.

I made the flight the same day. I hadn't planned to but the tone in Ray's voice forbode all manner of strange beasties. I parked *Iron Annie*, shut her down, and was dragged off to a hangar by Ray, who looked about him furtively before opening a huge lock on the hangar door. "Close your eyes," he insisted. "Okay, okay," I humored him. By now I figured it was all a practical joke, that he'd bought a T-6 or something and painted it up in German markings. The hangar door clanged shut behind me. "Now!" Ray shouted.

Eyes squeezed shut I asked, "Now what?"

"Look at it!" he screamed.

"I can't look at it! You told me to keep my eyes closed!"

"Open your goddamned eyes!"

It was the first Messerschmitt *Me-208* I'd ever seen. And it was beautiful. From the cockpit back it was an old friend, the bf-108B. But the cowling was different, the wings were stuck onto the fuselage with a startling upward dihedral, and it rested on tricycle gear. I walked around the airplane, making mental notes of all manner of stupendous work to be done, and admiring the lines of the machine. I climbed into the cockpit. Mostly the same as the 108 but with obvious changes, such as the gear handle that was a power system rather than the ratchet twist-and-pump-like-hell of the 108.

And I knew this airplane. Not by experience but by reputation. Only two had been built during World War II. The Germans were in a huge program to develop a wholly new fighter plane out of the old Me-109 line. They figured they'd gone as far as engineering changes would allow with the Me-109G fighter, and they'd screamed at Willi Messerschmitt for a big performance boost in a new design that could use much of the old machine tools. Willi came up with the Me-309, a brute of a single-engine fighter that was intended to wax even the best of the Mustangs. It also had a tricycle gear, and to train pilots for what was a radical departure in German fighter design, Willi told his people to modify the bf-108 into a new design. Thus was born the tricycle-gear Me-208 as the trainer for the tricycle-gear Me-309 fighter. In every basic principle it followed the 108. The main differences were visible in the tricycle gear and the upswept wings for inherent stability. Gone were the automatic slats; they simply weren't needed, and simplicity of design (that spells out *fast production*) called for a noncomplicated wing.

They stuck the same basic engine onto the fuselage, the Renault 6Q10B, an inverted six-banger with dual carburetors churning out 240 hp and driving the familiar Ratier-Figeac electric controllable-pitch propeller. With the gear up, the two airplanes, 108 and 208, had basically the same performance, with a top speed of about 190 mph, a sensible cruise between 160 and 170 mph, a landing speed of 62 mph. In really wicked tight turns the 208 simply wouldn't hack it with the 108 because of the lighter wing loading of the 108 and those handy-dandy automatic slats that provided instant increased camber when you needed it creeping along the edge of a stall. In that respect the 108 was still to be preferred, but the 208 made it up with the feel of a really solid Cadillac. Think of the 108 as a hot Pontiac and then climb into an equal-performing but more luxurious-feeling Caddy, and you've got the basic pilot reaction to the two airplanes. Of course, where the 108 was a dicey little bitch with its tightwad narrow gear, the huge widespread stance and nose wheel of the 208 made this airplane shamefully pleasant to lift off and plant back on the ground. Which, in a crosswind and in the dark and with oil from that misbegotten French propeller all over your windshield, is a friendly item not to be ignored.

There was another not-so-visible change within the machine. The 108B provides marvelous legroom and stretch for the pilots up front, with the *geshtunker* passengers crammed into the rear seat. The people watching from the back row never complain because just flying in the 108 is such a joy *and* a rarity. For whatever reason possessed these people when they redesigned the basic 108 into the 208 they reversed this situation, and the pilots are crammed into the front seats with the once-lowly passengers now spreading out loosely with bratwurst and beer parties in the more capacious rear. Lest you feel this is overly restrictive, *I'm* comfortable up front, and if it's hardly spacious, it presents no problem to the six-foot-three-inch hulk of Ray Martin.

Much of the 208 is hauntingly familiar once you're in the left seat, and as the reader may imagine, the moment I determined the 208 was airworthy (before it was to be torn down and have all sorts of things done to its innards) we pushed it from the hangar and

Winged steeds of history, as beautiful now as when they were created in the "old days" of aviation: Ray Martin's Me-208 stands before the huge Ju-52 bomber flown by Martin Caidin. *Asgard Flite Photo*

did the walkaround and I was clambering into the airplane. Ray had been driving the Ju-52 at every opportunity and now it was my turn, b'gum! I liked what I found with the conventional control sticks and left-hand throttles for both front-seat drivers, and to my left against the fuselage there were the familiar trim and flap wheels. We went through the drill and again the hauntingly familiar sensations stayed with me, à la 108B, through the pneumatic starting with the air bottle, the same instrument panel, the switches that seem to have been stolen from a German army telephone switchboard, the mag switch that looks like an antique knife-type system (and is precisely that), and, well, it was a matter of mostly familiar and some slightly changed.

The air bottle zapped the prop around into a blur faster than you can think of its happening, and there came the first big change as the 208 bobbed forward slightly on the nose gear. *That* was different. I'd always looked at blue sky directly ahead of me in a Messerschmitt and now the world stretched forward like looking from the cockpit of a high-legged Comanche. We taxied out, easy as pie compared to the 108, went through the runup, and rolled onto the active. What a dream. We were at 2900 pounds, I rechecked the prop position for takeoff and eased in throttle and right rudder at

the same time, and the 208 lived up to its reputation as a pneumatic baby carriage. None of the super-care you need in the 108.
Ease it on, press lightly with the right foot, the world waits for you;
and at 100 clicks (100 kilometers to equal just over 62 mph) I came
back on the stick and we brought up the gear and adjusted for
climb and there we were at 132 mph and launching upward at just
over 900 fpm.

What is there to say except that the airplane's feel is solid, comfortable, luxurious, that it responds immediately to control input,
that it has no surprises, and after a few minutes in this machine
you *know* the airplane. We took it up to seven thousand and played
around with steep turns, and held up the nose and came off the
power until she sort of gently wallowed into the buffet and unless
you were kicking the ball out of center to some gross distance she
simply fell through when the break came. If you manhandled her
and let her slide and slew when she stalled, she fell off on one wing
and did everything but smack you in the shins trying to straighten
out on her own. A dream!

After a bunch of this and some of that, wheeling around the sky,
the natural happened. Never even planned it; not really. We let her
sing along and the nose went down until she showed 180 on the
needle and up with the nose to 30 degrees above the horizon and
full left rudder and the stick full over to the left and let her come
around and as the world rolled the other way, stick forward a bit
and let her keep right on rolling, and back again with the stick and
she slides around the inside of that big barrel in the sky as though
it was programmed into her controls. We came out of the barrel
roll with shamefully little effort and let the speed build again and
brought her into a loop and she soared up and around as pretty as
a bird, slight forward stick as she came through the top and slowly
off with the power and down we came, half-rolling left and right
for the fun of it.

Well, then it was time for some formation work. We got a friend
of ours to come up with an Aztec so Ray could work in close to the
other bird. At this juncture we traded seats and he sat in the left
seat and it was all business as he rode different formation positions, especially directly beneath and aft of the Aztec's right wing.
There was a method to this madness, because Ray and I were already planning many months of tight formation and airshow work
together, and I wanted to see what he had to do and how it felt
in *this* airplane before he would start inching up to the Ju-52 in

126

air that would often be bumpy and tricky at our airshow performances.

When we finished playing, Ray took his new fun machine home and with a long sigh of "it's just got to be done," grounded the Me-208 and began dismantling the lovely little bird.

This wasn't a case of rebuilding the airplane. Ray had bought the 208 in one of those storybook finds wherein the former owner had kept it hangared in some godforsaken small airport, polished and repolished, oiled and greased and serviced the airplane, and then for some unknown but personally pressing reason, made the decision to divest himself of his pride and joy. That background is compellingly poetic but insufficient unto itself to be *that* certain of uninterrupted longevity over the coming years. Having had no small experience with dismantling and inspecting the innards of a few German aircraft I was drafted by Ray to yield all books, papers, photographs, records, and *anything* that would let him know his new bird. He disconnected lines and checked them all for wear, reliability, and pressure seals. He tore out electrical wiring and replaced it with new. He went through the wings and found to his delight (and good fortune) not a speck of corrosion anywhere. He burrowed and inspected, poked and pried, tested and x-rayed and Magnafluxed and did dye-penetration tests and anything else necessary to peer within even hard metal. He scraped with his penknife and tapped and scratched and measured and studied. He redid the interior with XP-400A to allay any corrosion that might suddenly decide to take root in the airplane in its new home at Executive Airport, uncomfortably high in salt content in its air. He replaced radios, tested instruments, did everything to bother and knobble his machine until he had no questions left.

And then he proceeded to fly the hell out of it. We flew together up and down the East Coast of the United States, and the Ju-52 and Me-208 became a familiar pair. Ray learned to ease upward from below after I'd heard the now-familiar words: "Hold her steady. We're below and to your right and coming up." Light and airy and as comfortable as a swallow, he'd bring in that 208 until the two machines seemed welded together, and then he'd call out, "Let's smoke 'em," and we'd turn on the smoke generators, the two planes pouring out three streams of the thick white stuff. We developed combat routines for the airshows where the Ju-52 would mix it up with American fighters and then, beset with howling Mustangs and Corsairs and Wildcats and Sea Furies and Thunderbolts and Bearcats and Kingcobras and Spitfires and Lord knows what else, we would be appropriately shot down, gunners blazing away as we fell toward convenient tree lines, Ray in the 208 weaving a protective cordon about us and shooting down a few Mustangs or whatever in the obligatory kills for the crowd, before the 208 took a final devastating blast in its own innards, to fall stricken from the heavens.

When we drove the big Ju-52 down to the deck for the really low passes, it has been said we have come back with green stuff on the tires. Fast brushes with grass and foliage, it has so been reported. During such runs down the field before thousands of people, I became accustomed to Ray Martin in the 208 and Jack Kehoe in his T-6 calling out: "Hold her steady, baby . . ." And as low as I'd bring that Ju-52 (which is a low-wing airplane), holding her as rocksteady as I could, I became accustomed to Kehoe's pale blue-and-gray T-6 screaming beneath the left wing, and Martin's Messerschmitt bursting ahead of us from beneath the right wing. I don't think they had two inches to spare from either aircraft, and it was a hairy but exciting maneuver.

Finally there came the airshow when something had to give. That's a gentle way of saying "accident." But it's really difficult to brand an incident as an accident, and if this is getting confusing then let me explain by saying that when something goes wrong, if no one is hurt, if no one did anything stupid, and if the repairs are less than monstrous, it's an incident. It happened finally at a great airbash of the Valiant Air Command. Peter Lert of *Air Progress* magazine was riding with me in *Iron Annie* and we had just completed an hour of very hard flying and were coming home to roost. We called in to Ray to land ahead of us with the 208 so we could stop the Ju-52 short and hold up the tail and "walk" her slowly before the crowd. It all went well, but then Peter Lert was stabbing the air with his hand and pointing and there, disbelieving to all of us, was the Messerschmitt slowly collapsing to the runway with its left wingtip against the ground and the right wingtip angling into the sky. But there had been no crash! No accident!

The whole thing had happened so slowly we couldn't believe what we were seeing. As Peter Lert put it:

No actual crash had occurred; a forty-year-old downlock in the gear system had simply become disinterested in further cooperation, and while the over-center geometry of the gear legs prevented them from folding during a straight roll-out, as soon as Ray

The first of the few ... Ray Martin's sleek Me-208 slices across the In-
dian River of central Florida during tight formation airshow work.
Photo by Ken Lindsley

put even a slight side-load on the gear — in this case, a taxi turn
at a sedate walking speed — the left main gear and nose gear
started to fold. The process was slow enough to allow Ray to get
all power off, so that by the time the propeller contacted the concrete, it was turning only fast enough to damage itself, rather than
the engine as well. The only other casualties were some minor
dents in the bottom of the cowling and the large pitot tube ...

We got the 208 onto its gear, corrected the problem with the
downlock, and quickly towed the Messerschmitt to a hangar. Now
came a rush trip in a Baron to my home field to pick up a spare
prop assembly. Then came some more parts slung into Ray's helicopter and Ray went to work with a bemused Peter Lert watching
the operation. It was interesting, because this was an electric
rather than a hydraulic prop. As Peter described one of the great
moments in learning the idiosyncrasies of foreign machines:

We set to work: Off came the cowling; off came the old prop, complete with the slip-ring-and-brushes arrangement that got elec-
tricity to the motor in the hub. How nice to pull a controllable
prop and not be greeted by a gush of oil from the shaft! Off came
the motor with its magnetic brake and gear train. Off came the
blade-retaining rings, using an improvised spanner. Off came the

129

"Getting down there among it" is the key to keeping your warbird flying. Ray Martin adjusts the brakes of his Me-208 as he "warms up" for an airshow performance. *Asgard Flite Photo*

blades, one by one — and out onto the hangar floor came about three million bb-sized ball bearings that had held the blade in the hub. Oh well . . . perhaps Martin Caidin still has a spare prop around? I think he did, in fact . . .

Peter was right. I did, it was flown to Ray, and the next day the 208 was back in the air and Ray Martin was back in his element with his pocket-sized winged Cadillac.

Peter Lert, aside from being a marvelous pilot and one of the best aviation writers in the world, is also (like the rest of us) a dreamer. And he dreams of what? "Ah," he says with a smile, "it's long been a dream of mine to find a really clean, really strong -108 or -208 airframe, then graft on one of those old 650-hp inverted V-12 Rangers . . . The result would be a real 'pocket rocket,' even if you couldn't safely use more than 400 of the available 600 hp at sea level. At altitude, cruise speeds might nudge past 250 mph . . . A seductive daydream indeed, and rumor has it that someone is doing it."

Peter was *so* right — and it was taking place only ten miles from where he watched those three million bb-sized bearings bouncing across the hangar floor. A bit to the southeast and across the wide river along the Florida coastline, ensconced in his private hangar, Doc Kerwin — he of the old slipper of a Skylane with which we'd lazed our way around the States — was hard at work making that dream come true.

The Ultimate 108

It isn't finished.

Neither the rest of this chapter nor The Ultimate 108. But it (the 108) has been under all-new modification, redesign, and construction now for several years, and we're getting closer and closer to another kind of ultimate moment — the first test flight — so we can bring you an inside-the-hangar look at one of the most fascinating warbird redesign-rebuild projects in the country. Or, for that matter, the world.

The words are best related by Dr. Leo Kerwin II of Cape Canaveral, Florida, who wore the gold crown as El Supremo and Virtuous Leader of the former Florida Wing of the Confederate Air Force and the Valiant Air Command that arose from those ashes. As mentioned earlier, El Supremo and I have bandied about this land in various types of metal-winged creatures, but when it comes to the truly innovative and bizarre, we yield to the originator. And now, in the words of the inimitable bone-crusher himself —

——————————— ☆ ———————————

For me, the implementation and Germanation (the pun is clearly intended) of the Messerschmitt mystique began at San Marcos, Texas. The date of 21st September 1975 was duly recorded in my logbook as a familiarization flight in N40FF, a cherished entry as it was not only my initial exposure to the Messerschmitt bf-108B, but took place in the rather overpowering company of Joe Engle, X-15 pilot and astronaut, and Martin Caidin, who fills various capacities as a bf-108B owner, a pilot of accumulating decades, and a spinner of filmy bionic tales. The recollection of that flight is as clear to me today as the very first time in my own past when the first truly lovely maiden ever nodded shyly, lowered her eyes, and whispered, "Yes," to me.

Forget the girl; it's the airplane that really crowds the memory banks. That sleek little Messerschmitt did exactly, and everything, it was asked to do, and with the utmost precision. To spread icing on the coveted cake, it did all this with minimal control input and, as surprising as anything else, it put out this performance with only modest power available. Yet it performed like no other machine, before or since, in its category.

Five years later, the date now the 16th of March in 1980, the sleek little Messerschmitt again slipped into my life. To all those who aspire to the Clan Warbird, who entertain Walter Mitty dreams of hurtling through the skies on wings of steel and engines of great thunder, heed the progression of events as I know them both intimately and painfully. For often the warbird fever will slip beneath the skin in a rash unnoticed on its arrival and affecting both body and brain before it may be diagnosed, let alone cured.

We begin with a commercial fisherman who, through good fortune and mountains of fish compelled to hurl themselves into his nets, amassed a not-inconsiderable bank account. This enabled him to satisfy an old dream of becoming an Ace of the Skies. He learned to fly, passed all the appropriate tests, was blessed by his priest, and obtained his pilot's license from an uncaring FAA. The moment the neat little paper was tucked securely within his wallet amidst bank deposit slips he fell prey to the guiles of the bf-108B. He saw one fly. It flew like an angel. His heart soared and his bank account thumped mightily, and he began Making Plans.

Enter another player in this stage play. An airline captain who journeyed frequently to Europe, wandering through the French countryside, discovered not one, not two, but *three* bf-108Bs that could be bought for scrubby old francs. He snatched up his prizes and shipped them to the United States. There they were hidden from view in a decrepit old hangar where they were certified by the FAA, bolted together in an approximately correct fashion, and then splashed liberally with paint to resemble former Nazi warbirds. The eager fisherman was shown these aircraft and promptly made himself the Catch of the Day. He wrote a big check with big numbers to the airline captain, who had made good on his entire investment with but this one sale. The airline jock had the bread and for the price of a bunch of fish the fisherman-turned-pilot had his Walter Mitty warbird.

To those of you who are somewhat acquainted with pilot training in the 1970 and 1980 period, newcomers to the fold were generally brought into the flying game in meatloaf Spam Cans. The trainers were of docile disposition resting atop wide-stanced tricycle gear. They had marginal power and padded seats, operated from long and wide concrete runways, and were essentially intended to be idiot-proof. Our fledgling birdman with expensive fish odor moved from this cloistered world to the bf-108B and found himself overwhelmed. With suddenly acquired wisdom he looked wide-eyed and with no minor trepidation at a narrow-geared taildragger that had extraordinarily sensitive controls, minimal crosswind component, laughable brakes, unusual instrument layout — expressed in such brain-numbers as meters, kilometers, and hpz — to say nothing of air-pressure starting, manually retractable gear, electric propeller, manual flaps, and other nuances that brought tears of frustration to his eyes. Being inclined to enjoy for as long as possible the good life all his fishmongering had brought him, he moved the bf-108B into an expensive hangar. There he proudly and *safely* admired his new toy. Every now and then he ran up the engine and flew Walter Mitty adventures with the security of the machine chained heavily to the concrete. He then shut down the machine and slunk home.

We now follow our progression from the airline captain-become-investor to the fisherman-become-pilot to, of all things, a flying gynecologist. The latter was good friends both with the fisherman pilot whose airplane had become a ground-loving monument and with this writer, who is also a chiropractor. The gynecologist, lifting his eyes from pubic distraction, brought the chiropractor to the fisherman. They spoke gingerly about flying, narrowing the conversation down to the nub of the matter. The fisherman wanted his 108B in the air but was damned if he'd kill himself. The chiropractor also wanted to fly the 108B but was damned if he'd pay for it when so rich an opportunity was now apparent. The two struck up a deal. The fisherman would permit the chiropractor to fly his Messerschmitt at various warbird air bashes. That way the 108B would be exposed to possible purchasers of this type of aircraft, and the fisherman might get back his money and spend it lavishly on a small armchair of an airplane. The chiropractor would have a blast flying an airplane he loved and for which he didn't have to pay. Because the chiropractor was responsible for producing about a dozen major airshows every year, featuring the pilots and warbirds of the Valiant Air Command, the deal was about as perfect for all concerned as one might concoct. It was, if not a marriage, at least an arrangement, made in heaven.

That, then, was the progression from airline captain to fisherman to gynecologist to chiropractor.

133

I am tempted to continue this refrain with the standard opening of the mystery writer who proffers, "It was a cold, dark, and rainy night." That's poetic, but the truth is always more believable and, in the case of flying airplanes such as the 108B, almost always more terrifying. Because the reality of the situation simply had to be faced. The years between initial construction of the little Messerschmitt and the moment I climbed into the left seat had not been terribly kind to this machine. It had flown as a trainer with a French Air Force academy. It had then been passed on to a civilian flying school. Neither of these two careers is recommended for *any* airplane. After the many years of ham-handed abuse, the French students being no better than ours, the machine was placed on the block. It had stayed there for many years when it was discovered by the treasure-hunting airline captain, who performed minimum mechanical surgery and maximum painting and then sold it to the enthusiastic fisherman.

The airplane was all there, anyway. Well, *almost* all there when I first saw it. At various times the landing gear doors had been blown off the machine (a common problem to pilots who like to exceed the redline). The airplane had been parked on Cape Cod and, essentially, was hangared right in the middle of the Atlantic Ocean. Nasty questions by yours truly discovered that it had been hangared for only a short while and for most of its time on Cape Cod left exposed to the elements.

Colonel Bob Casey, retired from the U.S. Air Force after an incredible lifetime of military flying in every type of aircraft imaginable, went with me to inspect the 108B. We use Casey shamelessly to protect ourselves from things we don't know about warbirds. It keeps us alive and our insurance writers happy. We went to the airplane to inspect it, check it out, and bring it down to Florida. Bear in mind that the last time I'd flown something like this with my grinning astronaut and maniacal writer friends had been five years in the past. And the last time Colonel Bob Casey had flown this type of airplane was Never. Usually he was shooting at Messerschmitts.

I brought Casey along (1) for ballast and (2) because his experience in anything with wings gave us the only real chance of getting from Cape Cod to Florida — alive. Many people rely on Lloyds of London for their insurance. I rely on Bob Casey.

So there we were. The temperature was 25°F. The wind howled at 30 knots at a 70-degree angle across the runway. The landing

134

gear was unspeakably narrow. The airspeed indicator had died and most other instruments were clinically near death. What instruments still gurgled and twitched were in French, German, or Arabic, and we could read none of them. But the engine turned over, belched smoke with enthusiasm, and ran with surprisingly little vibration and with good sound. We taxied, and laughed hysterically at the brakes while the wind shook us frighteningly. We did a mag check, and the engine didn't fall from its mounts. The runway was clear. The only obstacle to flight was the ocean. Go for it! On the runway, pointed in the right direction, stick full back, right rudder all the way forward, and the tail comes up immediately — and in that wind our takeoff run was only *five* seconds!

We crabbed into the wind, hand-pumped the gear, climbed steadily. The engine still sounded good. Instruments were twitching. Maybe some of them would even work; maybe. Eight minutes later we were at 9000 feet, still circling the airport (insurance!), and then headed for home, a long, long way south. We made our first landing into another 30-knot wind but this time it was straight down the runway. Hey, the radio is sputtering! It worked sometimes. The airspeed *felt* good; we didn't trust the gauge. We came down on final and flared looking to each side of the airplane, certainly not straight ahead because the sun directly into the crazed windshield obliterated everything in that direction. Hey, *hey!* We only bounced twice and we landed. We congratulated one another on being down alive. This same scenario continued down the eastern coastline of the country, and finally the airport on Merritt Island hove into sight. This was a nice thing to see, because we arrived in the dark just as the cockpit began to fill with acrid, pungent, and choking smoke. We had no instrument panel lights, which could have shown us our dead and unreliable instruments (it just feels better to have the lights). The landing light beneath the wing was also dead. The runway lights were as bright as a hooded candle under a blanket. Obviously, we made it. Here we are in these pages.

Within two days we had the Thing back in the air to fly an airshow over Cocoa Beach and at Ti-Co Airport. Sick as was this machine, burdened with failures and problems to be overcome, it was still a dream, and we flitted through clouds of T-6s and T-28s and P-51s with grinning abandon. My God, could this airplane maneuver!

Events became prosaic, and my world filled with skinned knuck-

135

les, oil, grease, wrenches, screwdrivers, and all the things one does to bring an airplane back into proper flying condition. The first rule of staying alive with a warbird is to take *nothing* for granted. We installed a new windshield, rebuilt the brakes, began to understand the foreign instruments and brought them back to life, checked the lines and tubes and hoses and wires and the connections and interconnections, scraped and sawed and rubbed and buffed and cleaned and alienated ourselves from the rest of the world. Hey, there was this big airshow coming up at Patrick Air Force Base and we were going to fly the 108B there, right?

That meant getting the bird out of the bang-and-thump shop and back into the air so I could practice. There's only one way to do razzle-dazzle things with an airplane and that is getting to know the bird and there's only way-one to do that: fly it. I also wanted a lot more proficiency in landing this bandy-legged dude and hied off for a long session of touch-and-go landings. For the first approaches I left the gear down and flew the thing with those appendages grumbling in the airstream. That's easier than going through 96 strokes *every* time when you're doing bumps and grinds in the circuit. On what was intended to be the final circuit before climbing higher for some air work, I raised the gear. Oh, pride! A photographer stood by the runway, anxious to get a shot of the 108B in clean configuration. Hey, why not?

I made a high-speed pass down the runway, climbed out and circled and then, as an afterthought, decided to put one more touch-and-go into the bank, but this time using full flaps. At the appropriate airspeed and in the right place in the pattern I began churning the big wheel to my left to bring down the flaps, at the same time cranking in trim, a neat little arrangement that was prevalent on many German aircraft of the thirties era. As you roll in flaps the trim compensates automatically for the change in pitch.

The final approach was picture-perfect. Wind right down the runway, weather beautiful. I pulled power completely off, and felt that as I flared I was a tad low. That thought didn't last long, since my attention went from idle mental chatter to the attention-riveting sight of propeller tips curling and the unmistakable sound of fast-moving metal grinding against concrete.

That landing had been set up as picture-perfect and it remained that way. Directly in the center of the runway, minimum rollout with the gear still nestled comfortably in the wheel wells. I could go on for several pages rationalizing why this *faux pas* occurred, but it all boils down to simple stupidity. Well, after some 5000 hours of flying, everybody should be allowed one "Oh, shit!"

But Willi Messerschmitt, who designed this little bird, must have kept in mind ham-hands like me when he sketched his lines. There's an armor-plated cover over the fuel tank sump, strategically placed on the bottom of the aircraft. This built-in skid took *all* the abrasion that normally would have worn through the belly, *if* the duralumin of the airframe skin had contacted the runway. Except for some paint removed from the armor plating and the curled prop tips there was no other damage. We found a new prop, searched the engine for shaft damage (none!), and embarked on some major and minor repairs — and we were back in the air in time to fly in the Valiant Air Command show at Patrick Air Force Base.

You may be assured that through this period I became acquainted, intimately, with the innermost workings of this remarkable aircraft. That belly landing convinced me. You guessed it. I bought the airplane. Like so many before me, I was hooked.

The airshow came off with our characteristic verve, thunder, precision, and crowd plaudits, and now that possession meant something new to me, I hangared the bird at Merritt Island (where Caidin had kept his airplane, N108U, back in the Dark Ages of flight) to prepare for a long list of minor modifications. I would upgrade the radios, instruments, redo the paint job — the ultimately countless things you discover when you mix in liberal doses of pride with possession. To my rescue came Colonel Ward Duncan, USAF Retired, with 25 years of priceless experience in airframes, engines, instruments, and other equipment of military aircraft. Not only was Duncan the Prize Catch of all time for me, but he had also been Chief of Maintenance at Edwards Air Force Base in California. Now, Edwards is the mecca for experimental aircraft work. It is where trail-blazing and experimental aircraft systems are everyday events.

Ward Duncan brought mountains of joy to my life when he "volunteered," after bent-knee pleading on my part, to oversee the "minor modifications." I found quickly that a "fast run-through" doesn't exist in the minds of people like Duncan. There is only one way to do something. You guessed it. The right way.

His idea of "minor modifications" began with the blood-chilling phrase of "this damn engine has got to go." It did. It flat *went*. It wasn't *that* bad an engine and it got some Band-Aid treatment and it's been flying on another 108 ever since it departed Merritt Island.

But *my* airplane came quickly to be known as Goering's Revenge. Ever since we removed the Renault engine, the 108B has been sitting in my hangar on custom-made jacks. And it really hasn't been a bf-108B for a very long time. The clue to what's been happening is that term, *custom-made jacks*. Because Duncan got the old gleam in his eye, threw his caution and my checkbook to the winds, and decided to build us the *ultimate* 108.

In the process of locking the bird onto its gold-plated jacks, we completely gutted the airplane (that made Caidin happy; he's a fiend for gutting airplanes). We removed *every* Nazi-inspired nut and bolt and screw. And the whole time we were planning not only the removal and the rebuilding, but severe modifications to the entire design. That really is the crux of all this.

When we made our decision to send the engine off to Texas and be reborn in another aircraft, I had been thinking in terms of an engine that would deliver between 400 and 500 hp and that would be converted from a V-8 automobile powerplant. Such designs have done yeoman work with aircraft and, being experimental, we could hang anything on the 108. But then I went deeper into the history of this surprising little bird and found that Uncle Willi Messerschmitt was way ahead of us, and that was way back then. He had hung a 400-hp inverted V-12 Hirth engine on one of his aircraft and turned it into a howler. I relayed this information to Ward Duncan, who smiled, snapped his fingers, grinned hugely, and exclaimed: "Let's put in a Ranger engine!"

I didn't believe what I was hearing. The only Ranger with which I was familiar had six cylinders and was an inverted in-line engine and it went back into World War II history. I knew it had approximately the same power and configuration of the engine we were replacing, but I didn't see any advantage to the Ranger. Other than that it was an American engine and used, more or less, standard parts. But why the big deal and all the toothy enthusiasm of Ward Duncan?

It was research time and Duncan dropped massive tomes into my lap. He stabbed at the books and commanded, "Read." I read. Oh, my! The Ranger the colonel had in mind was nothing I knew. No potboiler, this. The exact model was the SGV-770-C1B-11. What did that mean? Everything! It was a supercharged engine, was geared, and went on the description page as a 12-cylinder, air-cooled, inverted-V powerplant. When I put down the books I knew what Ward Duncan had planned all this time. That Ranger was made for the Messerschmitt; made-to-order is more like it.

It was an airplane engine; that was vital. The original German powerplant had been an inverted V-8, so the shape of the firewall bulkhead was already properly proportioned. Friends and fellow pilots, let me tell you that is *everything*. It reduces an impossible task — impossible in dollars, effort, time, and engineering, so to speak — into common sense. It would still cost in dollars, effort, time, and engineering, but it would all be within reason.

There would be no increase in frontal area due to the fact that the German Argus V-8 had 90 degrees between its cylinders, while this Ranger had only 60 degrees between the cylinders. That fact, along with the horsepower increase, evoked visions of fighter performance for the 108, which was already a super-performer with only 240 hp. The Ranger would boost me from that 240 all the way to 520 hp! And the Ranger was tried-and-true and had, in fact, powered the experimental Bell XP-77 fighters in World War II.

People like Ward Duncan never play all the cards of their poker hands on the table. The venerable ace-up-the-sleeve is always there, and Duncan watched me ride the roller coaster of knee-jerk exultation to the concept of the Ranger engine to the harsh reality of "where the hell are we going to find one of *those* things in today's world?" He let me soar and plummet and then announced, "Leo, I can't bear to see a grown many cry, dammit. Now, cheer up, will you? I've got *two* of those engines. Or at least I know where to get them."

And he did! He had actually found two of those engines that their owner absolutely *had* to sell. These are the moments when you believe in the Tooth Fairy and whatever other minor deities may be around, because both those engines were brand new and still in the original crates from the manufacturer! We made phone calls immediately to lock up the deal, and soon the engines were en route to Florida from Minnesota along with an engine overhaul stand thrown in for good measure.

Now, those of you new to this game who will be whistling at our great fortune and the expected haste with which we "must have" thrown that engine onto the mounts of the 108B, let me assure you that those experienced at this game knew we were really just getting started. Despite the fact that we had a marriage of engine-and-

139

airframe made in heaven, it takes a great deal more to bring off the marriage than simple metal bashing and cutting. It is an enormous task that involves much metal work, realignment of airframe, beefing up of structure, rerouting of subsystems and connections, rebuilding the cowl to adapt to the engine, and keeping the most meticulous of records as to every pound and ounce and where they go.

The tour de force required to translate this machine from its inverted in-line 6-cylinder French engine of 240 hp to the new inverted in-line 12-cylinder American engine of 520 hp was calculated to take more than a year, and we won't cut a day from our estimates. Note that the French engine is an inverted *in-line* 6-cylinder; the American replacement is the inverted *V* of 12 cylinders, and the mass and inertia are only distant cousins. To be sure, it took only a quick cry of "Let's do it!" to commit us to the project, but that's simply the first blurt in what takes forever and evermore because you're really starting from Square One.

You have a new engine, see? That means a new engine mount, and that means a new firewall and a few hundred vital small changes to accompany the vital major changes. It also meant converting the four-seat 108B, with the four seats two-by-two in a cabin, into a three-place configuration. We moved the engine itself approximately 9.5 inches back into the cockpit and eliminated one front seat. This was absolutely necessary to keep the weight as close as possible to the original, but more important than weight was balance, that old devil *center of gravity*. We now have the pilot seated directly in the cabin center, *à la* fighter style. In effect the pilot is straddling the engine, the rudder pedals mounted one on each side of the great mass of the engine, something resembling the arrangement in a Formula racing car. The rear seat for two occupants remains standard. It's like being taken for a joyride by a pilot-for-hire.

The firewall itself is truly a work of art. Through precision measurements and the most meticulous bending, Ward Duncan *created* a one-piece stainless steel firewall, which also adds immeasurably to the structural strength and integrity of the entire system. In order to handle the torsional loads the cockpit area was beefed up with .063-T6 aircraft aluminum, extending from the firewall along the sides of the attaching points of engine-airframe, for a distance of 10 feet. Aluminum of the same thickness was then bent and attached to the upper longeron on the inside of the cockpit from the firewall to the door post. This aluminum was bent into channel form to further strengthen the area, which gives a feeling of massiveness and strength to the aircraft that would gladden the heart of anyone who's ever done a wingover to rush for the earth far below.

The engine itself, while fitting superbly into the configuration of the airplane, still gave us headaches that for a while defied solution. There were even moments when I began to yearn for that old French six-banger with its dual carbs and its own host of problems. But with dreams of a Super 108 coming ever closer, the moments passed quickly enough. Stated simply, we had to produce an entirely new engine mount compatible to both the engine *and* the fuselage. Much easier said than done. The mount itself, the end result of calculations and vast recalculations and metal bending, took a year all unto itself. But Ward Duncan relied on every ounce of his own vast experience, and what he produced is already a legend among the warbird crowd.

The mount is stronger by several factors than anything needed to meet FAA specifications. Let's face it: if the mount fails in flight the FAA inspectors will simply fill out a report while my own conclusions will be unable to be voiced aloud. So we bent far, far back in our reach not just for structural integrity, but a mount with the solid feel of a rock called Gibraltar. The mount will support the engine under full loads in *any* direction and in any attitude. Because of its design and construction, it can take loads far greater than can be borne by any other part of the aircraft structure. It's terrific insurance. It reduces the pucker factor. It's that Cadillac feeling instead of cockleshell vulnerability.

For the past several months, and for some months to come, there will be a custom-designed and fabricated oil tank with a built-in oil cooler. With proper ducting this will also serve as the cabin heater. Gone is that wicked little electric prop from France; rats to the Ratier. In its place is a Hartzell three-bladed constant-speed prop, with the spinner right off the nose of the R-985 radial engine mounted to the Beech 18. When all engine modifications are completed, we'll go over everything with the obligatory fine-toothed comb. We've already figured that to maintain the proper CG range we'll move the battery and its systems toward the tail, along with oxygen bottles and monitoring and flow systems, for high-altitude operations.

I've said it before, but I'll repeat that every inch and stitch of wiring is being replaced. *All* instruments are new and of the latest design, along with a literal fortune in communications and navigation systems. Finally, or maybe not so finally, there will be gear warning horns, flaps, recorded announcements, and any other little hints and jolts Colonel Duncan thinks are necessary to remind yours truly to "Get that gear down!" at the proper moment. The gear itself will be actuated through a new electrical system, but we'll retain the old handgrip crank method as a manual safety backup.

There always emerges *the* question: "When's it gonna fly, huh, Leo, huh, huh?" In the spring of 1983 we look forward to at least another year and perhaps more. I like the feel of the summer of 1984 as a good bet.

The second question also has a familiar ring: "How fast will it fly, Doc?" The truth is we really do *not* know. Offering more in response than the grunt-and-shrug, then based upon drag coefficients, wing loading, power ratio, and many other factors that emerged from tests with the first experimental Me-109 fighters (the Me-109V1 flew with a 650-hp Rolls-Royce Kestrel engine), we estimate our *cruising* speed to be in the neighborhood of 275 *knots* at 20,000 feet. Our top speed will be some 290 knots, give or take a few knots for being less than perfect. I estimate our fuel burn at low altitude, based upon specifications of the engine manufacturer, to be about 25 to 30 gallons per hour. But at high altitudes we can drop that to about 18 gallons per hour.

"Hey, how about the rate of climb?" We really hesitate to say, but it sure will be on the order of jet performance. The wingspan is two feet greater than the Me-109V series, and since we are considerably lighter, and our paint and finishing will be slicker, and our propeller far more efficient than the old two-bladed hammers of the experimental ships back in the thirties, I should be able — literally — to hang her on that prop.

So if you see a black-crossed fighter clawing her way vertically into the sky sometime in 1984 and afterward, let's hear your applause.

You'll be watching us.

———————— ☆ ————————

Ragtime!

If it ain't broke, don't fix it;
if it ain't fixed, don't fly it.

LEN MORGAN

There's more warbirds out there that are invisible than all the warbirds ever showed up to fly at the fancy shows." Eddie Keyes scrunched up his eyes, weathered at the corners like crow's feet from decades of flying everything from one-lung flivvers to thundering military transports in Burmese jungles. Keyes was more than a pilot; he was a sliver of aviation itself, and if he wasn't recognized as were many others famed for their deeds, it was because he was like a cornerstone in a foundation. It's there, it holds up the building, but you never really see it. But there were a few of us who had known and flown with, and been taught by, Eddie Keyes from what seemed like Day One, in aviation.

There was also an unwritten rule that followed this man wherever he went. Eddie never spoke unless he had something to say that had some meaning to it. And because his years were long and his experience endless, and he had that rare habit of thinking through what he said before anyone else would know his thoughts, we always listened to this Old Master of the game of flight.

"All over this country there's a forest of the littlest warbirds. I've seen many of them flying," Keyes went on, "but mostly they're tied down in old barns, behind farmhouses, or even in rows along isolated grass strips. Just about everywhere. Hundreds of them. Most likely even thousands. They're the little old ragwings, most of them. Some have aluminum skin. But they were all military ships doing a military job, and that's the meat of it. I flew the Gooney Bird in Burma and China and a bunch of other places, but I also flew the grasshoppers, the fabric machines, in those same countries. I was shot at by the Japanese in airplanes built by Piper and by Aeronca and Stinson, to name just a few."

A forest of the littlest warbirds. Interesting. And, above all, promising. "If ever we're going to get a warbird movement going that means something real deep, then we've got to include the little fellers," Keyes said. We recognized the sharp gleam in his eyes. He hadn't quite finished.

"There's another point to make. You take any hundred people and you sort them out into different groups and out of that whole hundred you got maybe two or three people who can afford to own and fly the heavy iron. And you know what? You better be sure those hundred people are all avid warbird fans. If you take an average hundred people from all walks of life, maybe one or two of them can fly.

"So you can see the problem. The people who own, operate, and drive the heavy iron are only a tiny part of all the other people who own and fly airplanes, but within their reach. That's the key. For every man with heavy iron there are hundreds with the flivvers, the grasshoppers, to whom anywhere from forty to two hundred horsepower is their kind of flying, and the birds with the real big engines are sorta over the horizon from their reality."

So we began the search. Were they really warbirds? Well, we know the ragwings performed yeoman service throughout the world in all kinds of missions, everything from carrying the mail to hauling wounded out of tiny strips, to spotting for artillery or even slamming rocket shells into German tanks. But how many were there? Or, how many had there been? *And how many were left?*

Oh, my. They were like locusts. You couldn't see them because they were in different guise now, with fancy new paint jobs and big identification numbers painted on them. Or their paint had faded and they were largely nondescript and, as Eddie Keyes had said wistfully, they were behind the barns and hangars and on isolated strips, their fabric worn and weathered, often hanging in tatters, and their color and numbers faded to a ghostly shadow by a relentless sun, aided by wind and rain and cold and the inevitable vandals that seem to attack anything just because it's *there*.

Who remembered, or could identify, the ancient Taylorcraft L-2 with 65 hp? When decked out in olive drab and flat white stars there was no question but that the machine was there for training, observation, utility, liaison, and any other work that might be dredged up for a rookie in wings. The little liaison planes were often the KP sufferers among the elite heavy iron. If not exactly held in contempt or disrepute, they received, at best, little attention from the press. It *was* difficult to wax eloquent about hauling beer or a fat major to an advanced field when the war was churning out heroic deeds, massive bombing raids, and new keen-of-eye aces with every passing hour.

Earlier in these pages we went through the drill of placing the flivver warriors in their true perspective. They are, simply, part and parcel of the entire warbird scene. Now we reach the new issue: Do these dumpy, clattering, fabric, skittish putt-putts also capture the public attention and stoke its imagination? How do they stand up in thrills and *oohs* and *ahhs* against the gleaming Mustangs and the deep-roaring Fortresses and all that heavy metal tearing apart the sky?

You'd be amazed, friend, just as we were the first time we decided to introduce the ragwings as a major package of a warbirds airshow. Not dribbling them onto the scene to fill time and space while we were jockeying warbirds from one slot to another, but as a major presentation unto their own gentle wings. We brought fifteen of them together; some had fabric covering their wing ribs and some, like Luscombes, had metal, but they were one and the same. And we had the pilots fly a loose gaggle, not the kind of KEEP-IT-IN-THERE-TIGHT! formation the big boys like to show off with. The ragwing pilots got so much into what they were doing they began to weave in and about themselves through the sky. Being low and slow, *they remained for a longer time* before the crowd. Pilots and their passengers were hanging out of the planes, waving and blowing kisses to the crowd, and the crowd, delighted and laughing, cheering and shouting, responded in kind. It was amazing to see this cloud of rags and metal churning the air like a rowboat going upstream and how that audience reacted. It was *terrific!* It was personal, a one-on-one exchange that became an instant love affair.

So let's return to the question we still haven't really answered. What kinds of planes are we talking about? We started off with the Taylorcraft L-2, a sort of kid-from-down-the-block ragwing that donned khaki and went off to war. But there were also the ubiquitous Airknockers, the Aeroncas with their deep bellies and sway-backs and 65 hp. Do you see the pattern? Almost every one of these ragwing warbirds, and most of their metal brethren, were civilian jobbies drafted for military service.

The Interstate Cadet had become the L-6. With its three seats and 90 hp, the Stinson Voyager became the L-9. But the one air-craft that always commanded the greatest interest was *the* bird, the Piper J-3 Cub with yellow paint and tandem seating and 65 horses banging away up front. Why the J-3/L-4 to command the greatest attention? Aside from the fact that it's a great airplane (despite certain characteristics not always endearing to new pi-lots), the Cub was rarely separated from other airplanes. Or, to state it from the public's point of view, *all* small airplanes were Cubs. It was really that simple. The public was not educated then and it's really not that different now. If it's smaller than a 747 then most likely it's a Cub. It became the branding iron, the catchall name. That tendency, plus the fact that the Cub as the L-4 per-formed incredibly well throughout the world, made the name stick.

Look at the record. The Cub flew as a trainer of civilian pilots and aspiring military aviators. It showed up almost everywhere as a winged jeep — running errands, shuttling people and small cargo, carrying photographers and medicine and ammunition and USO entertainers and dogs and beer and whiskey and cigars and cigarettes; if it could be stuffed into the venerable Cub, it was car-ried, and so it was a liaison, transport, utility, observation, shuttle, photographic, and general handyman airplane. We come full circle to the old saw: it was military, all right, but was it a *warbird?*

All you purists can leave the room now. If the L-4 and its stable-mates didn't make it as warbirds in the purest sense of the word, then neither did the Gooney Bird, or the Focke-Wulf FW-200 Kurier (because it's a modified airliner) four-engined bomber, or the Ju-52/3m (another bomber-from-transport), or the T-6 or — ah, *they're all warbirds.*

Keep in mind that the lowly Cubs flew combat missions from aircraft carriers, they dropped grenades and bombs on enemy troops, and the rocket tube–equipped Cubs opened the mighty Ti-ger tanks like overripe tomato cans.

Case closed.

A giant step above the lowliest chug-chugs like the Cubs and Airknockers were the more powerful civilian jobs, some with one

From really heavy iron to the ragwing ... Martin Caidin offers final flying words to his wife, Dee Dee, in a gleaming rebuilt Piper L-4 Cub. Happy Miles in the back seat is already falling asleep. *Photo by Becky Ritter*

and others with two engines. Most representative of the latter breed was the Beech Model 18, more commonly regarded simply as *the* Twin Beech. This was a husky brute of an airplane, a tail-dragger with two snarling Pratts out front, and hauling people and cargo behind 900 hp. The Twin Beech quickly separated the men from the boys. It demanded an experienced touch, or it would groundloop faster than a hound dog with one rear leg afire. The aluminum-shiny Model 18 became the C-45 Expeditor, a twin-engined machine that should have been called, simply, The Everything Airplane. It was modified into the AT-7 advanced multi-engine trainer, and it became the AT-11 bombardier trainer along with Plexiglas nose and Norden bombsight *and* a bomb bay filled with hundred-pounders. It flew for everybody in the world, *including* the Germans and the Japanese, who commandeered for their own uses every one of these machines they found or captured.

Cessna's wooden multi, the T-50, became the AT-8 and the AT-17 and became renowned, cursed, and loved as the UC-78 Bamboo Bomber. (For those new to the game, the prefix U represented Utility, one of the most sensible designations ever assigned.) Lockheed's twin-engine Model 10, sleek but with a touch of aging, and famous as the Model 10 and 12 that set world records (including those of Amelia Earhart) was pressed into service as the UC-36A and the C-40. The venerable Beech D-17 Staggerwing, one of the most beautiful biplanes with retractable gear and a husky 450-hp engine, became the C-43 series.

Getting the idea? Just about *everything* was drafted and served throughout the world. The classic Fairchild 24 became the UC-61 and the UC-86 transports. Howard's tough and famed DGA-15P (DGA, by the by, stands for Damn Good Airplane) put on khaki to become the C-70, Spartan's CM-7W sported its colors as the C-71, Waco's SRE emerged as the UC-72. Cessna's bewhiskered DC-6A of 1929 vintage was now the UC-77, and the Harlow PJC-2 became the UC-80.

The successor, or more properly, the stablemate to the old Piper J-3 Cub, was the J-5A, and *that* became the UC-83. Those familiar with the gleaming Luscombe 8A-2 blinked as the airplane changed into the UC-90. If you saw an Akron-Funk B-75, you had to learn its new designation of UC-92. Cessna's C-165 was transformed into the UC-94, the Taylorcraft BL-65 became the UC-95, and even the old Rearwin 9000KR went to war as the "new" UC-102.

This just scratches the surface, for there were also hundreds of primary trainers, fabric birds and metal-skinned tremblers and Vibrators from Ryan, Stearman, Vultee, and other manufacturers. On second thought, change hundreds to *thousands.*

Now, that represents the enormous arena from which to draw a new (spell that rebuilt) warbird for today's flying. And it *is* within reach of the "little guy" in aviation, who really makes up far and away the greatest number of people who take to the skies. Where buying and paying for the operation of a T-6 (let alone a Corsair or a Mustang) was hopelessly beyond the reach of the little guy (and gal), the only real difference between flying a civilian Cub or Airknocker and flying an L-4 or an L-3 is a *coat of paint.* That, and your attitude, because the attitude of the audiences at airshows is that they want more of the littlest warbirds.

And 65 horses tugging your ragwing through the air won't burn fifteen bucks of gasoline *for an entire airshow.* Makes it interesting, doesn't it?

There's more than one way to skin a cat, so goes the old saying, and there's more than one way to get into the warbird game where your horizons are brought to you courtesy of a ragwing flivver. Once you make the decision and get your warbird, you can add the spats or boots, leather helmet and gloves and scarf and swagger stick or anything else that makes *you* feel good. If you already own an airplane like the drafted civilian machines we've described, all you need is the paint and joining a group, local or regional or national, where flying is more important than posturing. It's said and done.

If you don't have your machine and you want "in," there are still other ways, many of them in direct proportion to the thickness and well-being of your checking account. Obviously, you can scan the pages of Trade-A-Plane, the bible of the used aircraft business in the world, and what's offered will seem like a cornucopia of winged riches. *If* you can hack the dollars, you can flat buy whatever airplane you want (almost all of which in the flivver class will be under ten grand), paint it any way you want, and you're a warbird owner. (Obviously, the color of the paint doesn't prevent you from using your machine for personal and business flying.)

But what if you can't afford, like so many others in this era of economic depression, to rip off a check and bring home your prized possession? What if the checkbook is thin and lean? You want to get into the business and you may even go partners with a friend, but you still want the airplane at minimum cost *and you want to make it a fun project.*

So you're moving swiftly into the rebuilding game, but again there's a difference in your future, and it's a difference with a vengeance in your favor. You can do this rebuild at home, in your garage, your living room (and likely bring on a divorce), or in a hangar at your local strip. The key to this new adventure is that if you're interested in aviation, you have some knowledge of the business, and you're pretty good with things mechanical, as well as with your hands, you can hack it. And it's fun and it's rewarding in many ways. There's no other feeling in the world quite like that experienced when you take to the air in a ship you've reclaimed from that Great Big Basket where old planes go to die.

I don't want to step across official or legal boundaries to offer up advice on how you *should* go about this, but the basic fact is that it's perfectly legal for you to rebuild your own machine, with or without a partner, even if you are *not* a licensed FAA mechanic.

The trick is to have available one of those A&P (Airframe and Powerplant) mechanics with the FAA ticket that makes it legal for him to supervise your work, to inspect what you do, and sign his name to the results. Always be sure those inspections of your work are done in stages that permit a clear study of everything you do. And get your advice from him *before* you plunge. The people with experience know the pitfalls as well as the right way to go.

There's another enormous advantage for someone who wants to create with his own hands the jobbie that will commit him to thousands of feet in the sky. All across America there are groups and chapters of the Experimental Aircraft Association and the Antique Airplane Association. Almost every one of those people has scads of experience in rebuilding old ships or starting new projects from the ground up. The telephone books or local airport crowd can lead you to founts of tremendously helpful advice about how to proceed. *Ask questions, take notes, compare the advice you receive, and when you feel your patience has worn to a thin nub — have at it.*

Two people went through all or part of the above with the avowed goal of rebuilding a very wrecked Aeronca 7AC, a 65-hp machine of ancient vintage, wonderful service, and a disastrous conclusion to her life through power lines. Two pilots could hardly have been more unlike one another than Vern Renaud and Chick Autry.

Vern Renaud is a captain with Eastern Airlines. He is that sort of airlines captain whose pleasant countenance, wavy silver hair, and broad smile they plaster on billboards all over America, and whose face and calm words have been known to reduce little old ladies to panting and hopes they will be marooned somewhere with that "marvelous young man in the wonderful dark suit and all that simply charming gold braid." Renaud has umpteen ratings for all kinds of flying machines. I have flown with Renaud for lo these many years and can attest to a shameless guilt and vice on his part: he absolutely loves to fly. When he is not flying those enormous monsters like the Lockheed L-1011 TriStar, of which he is a confidence-inspiring captain, he will be found scrunched in the cockpit of a Waco, or driving a Stearman, or manhandling with deft grace the corrugated ancient known as *Iron Annie*. He is tall, witty, and suave.

Not so his partner. Chick Autry is a walking tree trunk. His forearms are like Renaud's thighs. He is one tough mammoo, a detective, ex-marine, ex-army officer, and ragwing pilot of long standing, who has made it a lifetime habit to shamelessly steal flying time in anything that has wings. Grasshopper driver he may be, he has logged much time in everything from the T-6 and T-34 to the B-25 and Ju-52 bombers. But his favorites remain the clattering little ragwings. Long ago, in that dim past when he and Renaud were still regarded as comparative youngsters, Autry had rebuilt not one but several planes from wrecks or simply rotting discard. He had long been itching to have at it once again.

Enter the third character in this scene, a swaybacked Champ with the calling card of N85226 or, as Vern and Chick referred to the ragwing, as "Double Deuce Sex." Vern Renaud had bought the airplane when he still lived in the Far Cold North of the northeastern United States, where the Champ proved herself by flying through miserably hot and humid summers and braving the stinging cold of howling winters. The airplane had spent "the first thirty years of her life," Vern Renaud explained, "training pilots. At one point she was so bone-weary that her owners tore her down and rebuilt her. Sometime after that she came into my hands and I painted the airplane in a beautiful cream and orange. When I moved to Florida I left the Champ behind for a brief stay until a friend of mine, another airline captain, would ferry her down, a trip to which he looked forward with great glee. Who ever expects disaster on a flight like *that?*

"The trip was going peaches and cream when double disaster struck. Not even the greatest flying skill in the world can keep an engine running when your fuel is contaminated. My friend was bringing her in for a landing in Maryland when the engine coughed, spat violently, and died. Directly before the airplane was a power line. The Champ slammed into what is almost always a killer situation. Incredible flying brought her down in a controlled crash that kept the pilot and his wife in the rear seat from getting so much as a scratch, but it sure tore that airplane to pieces. As far as I knew that was the end of the Champ and the end of the story. I got the news by telephone, accepted the inevitable, wondered how I would tell Chick what had happened, and put it all aside because it was time to leave for work."

Work for Renaud meant getting to Miami International Airport for his scheduled run in a DC-9 jetliner. Vern Renaud continues:

"It was really strange how I wound up telling Chick the sorry news about the Aeronca. I was taxiing from the terminal down to the active runway at Melbourne Regional Airport in Florida with a planeload of passengers. The tower told me to hold my position for an aircraft on final. I couldn't believe it. There came the great winged shape of the Ju-52 I'd flown for years with Marty Caidin, but he was rumbling down the pike with — you guessed it — with Chick in the right seat. I announced the arrival of the Junkers to the passengers in the DC-9, and everybody was at the windows for a good look when the top hatch of the Ju-52 cockpit slid back and as Marty flared to land, Chick climbed halfway out of the airplane and waved at us in the DC-9. Not the everyday approach, for sure. While they were rolling out I took the time, because it's never better than *now*, to tell Chick what had happened.

"When I returned home a few days later Chick was waiting for me. My wife had told him I would sell the wreckage for what loose change it might bring, and Chick wasn't having any of it. He told me in no uncertain terms that we were *not* giving up the Champ, and that if I persisted in those feelings he might feel inclined to break both my legs in a few places, and that was just for starters.

"You can't beat enthusiasm and Chick had it. In just a few moments my feelings about the Champ went from despair to buoyancy. We just might do it!"

Chick whipped the details into shape. "I couldn't understand why Vern wanted to just quit. I'd forgotten that long before he became one of the best pilots in the world he'd been a mechanic, and *he knew* the problems better than I did. I'd worked on rebuilding planes before and I'd recovered a bunch, but Vern understood we had a long and hard job ahead of us. Well, my *not* knowing might have been the best thing. Anyway, we had to get the thing down from Maryland to Florida and I was gung-ho to get cracking. We ran into the first problem immediately. It's the most important thing you need to make an airplane fly. *Money*."

Events like this come in threes. Vern had just gone through a financially debilitating shift in his professional plans, Chick discovered his financial situation was a mirror image of his friend's, and they had a busted flying machine on their hands. To the rescue came Vern's wife. With a wistful sigh, Ruby sold jewelry she had cherished for years and threw the cash into the pot to reclaim the shattered Aeronca.

"It helped," Chick said with a grin, "that Vern had been teaching her to fly and she had this thing for the old taildraggers. Talk about being hooked! We put every loose dollar we could raise into the venture. The first order of business was to get a man with some airplane smarts into action. Tom Reilly of Orlando shook his head, laid down the tools with which he was rebuilding *big* warbirds, and went off to Maryland. He was back in a few days with the wreckage of the Aeronca lashed to a flatbed trailer, moved the parts and pieces to a hangar, and went back to his heavy iron.

"The only way to start this job was from the beginning," Chick explained. "That meant gathering every piece of data on the airplane we could find. We drove the FAA records division crazy, we chased down old Aeronca company records, but it paid off. We tracked the little bird back to her military days. You see, Aeronca had been involved with their little planes and the military since the L-3 rumbled into World War II skies. This was what you call a skinny early version of the Champ. This was the L-3. There were also glider versions, the overnight mods, so to speak, when they took out the engine and prop, skinned a new nose to the bird, hung some metal on to keep the CG in place, and used the thing as a training glider. Then the war ended, but not the military role for the Champ. Aeronca turned out the 7AC, the military took a hard look at it, and she was drafted again as the L-16, with an 85-horse engine. Our Champ was somewhere in between. There's always an oddball. We were it, an ex-military Champ with 65 horses."

"The only way to do this right was to keep meticulous records," Vern added to the details. "Chick had dug up more logs and paperwork than I believed existed. In the hangar we spread out everything. We numbered every part. We took pictures of everything we did, we put screws and nuts and bolts into separate tie bags. It's cataloguing, but it's vital. We had our work inspected on a steady basis, but we also recognized that when everything was done, *we* were going to fly this thing. The moral is to do the work for your own safety, not just to please some inspector."

The Champ had a broken longeron. The landing gear was bent and twisted out of shape. There were broken spars and ribs. The engine air intakes were a crumpled mess. The prop had taken a beating. Instruments were busted. The windshield was useless. Wires were cut, lines severed, hoses chewed up, and the fabric fluttered from rips, gashes, and tears. It meant a total recovering. But the engine had survived without apparent damage except to cylinder cooling fins and a lot of rash.

"Listen, I could go on for days about the *details* of what we had to do, but the list of *unexpected* work would be even longer," Chick said with a shake of his head. "I guess that's what had Vern so spooked from the beginning. You never really know what you're going to find once you're into the thing. Who expects bent screws? Think that's a detail? You got to get them out of metal and you can't screw them out. You can't hammer and smash like you might with a wrecked car; this thing is going to carry your butt and your soul back into the air. Do you drill? Better be sure you don't mess up things because replacement screws go back in and they cannot be wrong sizes. Before you even go to work you've spent hours figuring out the details."

Vern agonized over the instruments. "For me and Chick, a string tied outside was enough to fly the airplane," he sighed, "but other people would be flying the Champ. Ruby was already working out a new military paint design and she'd be flying, and so would Carol, Chick's younger daughter, so it meant having everything *right*. We didn't want to put back instruments that might be damaged and finally we made the only sensible compromise. We sent *all* the gauges off to an instrument shop. Those that passed their tests, with new placards certifying them, went back into the panel. Those that didn't, we traded in as junk on new gauges. But the cost — !"

"We also found more of the unexpected," Chick said sourly, "when we ran into rust and corrosion that had never been picked up before in any annual inspection. That stuff scares me, especially since we were going to base at Merritt Island, and there's the highest salt-air concentration in the world. Oh, my, the sanding and scraping and filing we did. Call it knuckle-banging and skin-scraping. We took *all* the paint off *all* the areas, and I mean we put this thing back to bare bones. Sure enough, we found some more rust, and by the time we got through that metal was better than the day it left the factory."

Vern grinned. "And we smelled like a combination of a perfume shop, paint factory, and nail polish tub. We took off not only the old paint and fabric, but decided to Ceconite the bird. Do it the right way. There was so much thinner and glue and other chemicals you could smell us downwind a country mile. I suppose we overdid things now and then, but we sure wanted the *right* bird."

"If you want to talk about drugs," Chick added, "then you've got to be careful about the most dangerous of all drugs in a job like this. The moment you finish one thing, you want to do more. You're always trying to make everything perfect. Hell, the Ceconite looked so good we decided we needed new overheads and side

154

panels in the cabin, and then we thought the panel looked ratty, so *that* had to go, and Ruby commented about the ceiling looking great, but why sit on ratty seats, so *those* went into a corner of the shop for complete recovering and . . ." His voice trailed off as he studied his scarred and scraped knuckles and hands. The familiar sound of a weary sigh followed.

Ruby laughed at Chick. "I'll tell you what really drove them crazy," she said, pointing a finger at herself. "*Me.* I wanted a very special paint job for the fabric lady. After all, if we were going to resurrect her in her old military colors, I didn't want some grubby old flat paint. No way! It had to be something so special that anyone who saw the Champ would remember her from the first look. At the same time the fabric lady had to be within reason. And guess what decided us?"

They looked at one another and all three grinned at once. "The corrugated cloud, that's what," Ruby continued. "That iron monster had been a part of our lives for years. We'd all flown in her and had flown the Ju-52, and we got the idea that it would be nice if our baby could look like an offspring of the giant bird. To refine our scheme, and to add some zing to the little lady, we added slick wheel pants, a propeller spinner, and some interior refinements."

"Everything but gingham curtains," Chick grumbled. "But that's how it happened. A beautiful military green, a dark forest green, really. And it had to *shine*."

Things don't always work out the way the first script is written. They'd started work on the Champ at the Merritt Island Airport, decided that after doing much of the detailed work the only smart way to continue was to bring the rebuilt parts to a professional to hang the wings to get the exact angle of incidence, control cable security, and the hundred odd items which the pro can do faster and almost always better than the best-meaning amateurs. That way they could also have the airplane inspected and signed off in the proper manner.

"Finally, after nine months of work on the airplane," Vern went on, "the big day came to bring her home. Ruby and I went to Sanford Airport and we were really excited at the thought of flying her home. Just *seeing* the airplane gave us our first disappointment. Where was the gleaming, shining military Champ? This couldn't be *our* airplane with the ghastly flat and dull olive drab. The nose was a horrid mustard yellow. How could anyone mess up a basic order for a paint job? Well, we weren't going to *drive* back to Merritt Island. We checked the papers and everything was signed off and then we checked out the airplane. First glances are almost always questionable, but generally we seemed to have survived the rebuilding as planned. I don't like that word *generally*, so I took my time examining connections, moving everything that wasn't bolted down, and trying to get the feel of the little machine.

"Ruby reminded me the day was flying from us and the sun was dropping to the horizon. There was still time for a test hop, and I told Ruby to wait while I took the Champ around. That wasn't an order she welcomed, but I want crew only whenever I test anything, whether it's a Champ or a DC-9. She fired up, taxied smoothly, and leaped off the runway. I was just getting my first feeling of exaltation when the throttle stuck. I just couldn't move it, so I declared an emergency, about as mild as I could make one, brought her around the pattern and shut her down. She deadsticked like Champs usually do — beautifully. We spent another twenty minutes of hard work to loosen up the throttle linkage. By that time I'd spotted a few other things that disturbed me, but we needed only 25 minutes in the flight from Sanford to Merritt Island. I decided we'd just get out of there and attend to the few squawks the next day. We fired up and right after takeoff I gave the controls to Ruby, who sat up front. I sat back to enjoy the ride, the sun low to the horizon but behind us, casting that marvelous late afternoon glow across the countryside.

"Then that 'old feeling' began to chew at me. It wasn't anything definite, but when that 'old feeling' works on me I come straight up in my seat and I *know* something's wrong or about to go wrong. I looked down. *Gasoline was running along the floorboards between my feet*. Terrific! The first thing I did was scan the world below for a place to land. Free-running gasoline means the chance of fire very suddenly and being up this high, and suddenly a thousand feet was *very* high, was no place to be. The surface didn't invite a landing. We were over the area of the St. John's River and a vast swamp awaited us.

"I leaned forward and spotted the problem: the small primer line on the bottom of the fuel tank had broken. The tank was behind the instrument panel above Ruby's knees. I leaned farther, bending over my wife's shoulder and squeezing my fingers as hard as I could over the break at the primer fitting. To my surprise the flow of fuel stopped.

"What *now*? Since the leak was under control the best thing to do was press on, get home as quickly as possible. The short flight of twenty-five minutes I'd anticipated was still twenty-five minutes but began to feel like twenty-five hours. To say the least I was uncomfortable and I had practically crawled into the front seat with Ruby, who was now twisted like a contortionist to fly the airplane. We flew over Ti-Co Airport and if the tower operator had trained binoculars on us I know he would have had a hard time figuring out what was going on up there!

"Contorted or not, Ruby swung into the pattern at Merritt Island and brought the Champ down smoothly. As soon as we could we shut down and I clamped the leak. We went home, Ruby, me, and my thoroughly cramped fingers.

"Early the next morning we fixed the fitting, and Chick and I went upstairs to cavort. And cavort we did, giving the little bird the freedom she'd been denied so long. We came down and took up the kids and friends who'd come out for rides. But before the day was over that sense of unease returned to me. We couldn't figure it out until I pinned it down to a subtle vibration that simply shouldn't have been there. We had some new visitors; Marty Caidin and Terry Ritter showed up. They're like two old hound dogs sniffing around fresh bear tracks when they get near a rebuilt plane. They went slowly around the bird and we found them poking at the curved metal around the air intakes of the engine. The air slowly began to turn blue and then it blistered as our friends poked and pried. They showed us new cracks in metal and Terry rapped his knuckles on the prop and stepped back. Chick and I took a long, hard look. We couldn't believe it. *There was a bend in the metal prop,* and it was vibrating the plane just enough to cause that uneasy feeling. That also started metal cracking. It had escaped detection during the entire nine months of rebuild. Well, off came the prop and the Champ was grounded — again.

"Never one to waste a moment, Chick decided to use the time to paint the airplane the way we'd intended. We got rid of the horrid mustard nose and painted the entire ship a gleaming bright green. Chick painted on invasion stripes that marked Allied planes in the invasion of France in 1944. We added the wheel pants, military lettering, and codes, and Chick went quietly berserk inside the bird, replacing the metal side panels with thick foam and brown vinyl, tucking a beautiful carpet along the floor and adding all sorts of what he calls doodads and finishing touches.

"We now had a beautiful bird and made a series of flights where

157

flying was spelled fun and pleasure. But the unease stayed with me, and when I landed on Merritt Island after an hour's flight one day, the engine sound became louder instead of becoming quieter. There's that *Oh, Oh* sensation that sort of wobbles your knees as the engine roar turned into a howl and then a tortured screeching as the main bearings failed. One good thing was in our favor. It *could* have happened in the air . . ."

Chick rolled a cigar stub in his teeth. "Three more months on the ground," he grumbled. "No way to fix the engine. We traded her in and saved pennies and quarters and dollars and we went for a zero-timed engine. Vern will tell you it was all peaches and cream from that point on. But it wasn't. You see, on a flight just before the engine tore apart, the rudder cable running through the plane came loose from its connections. It had never been properly assembled in the first place. To most pilots this could have been a final disaster. Vern calmly wrapped the cable around his hand and then hand-flew — literally! — the Champ home. The way he landed no one could tell anything was wrong. Well, while *he* took care of the engine I went through the Champ from stem to stern. There were a couple more things I didn't like, but now I had time near home to fix them."

The saga of rebuilding headaches ended there. For the past few years the Champ has been worthy of its name: a champ. And we had a celebration flight after the first checkout of the new engine. They were having an old-fashioned warbird airshow at Patrick Air Force Base on the ocean and, naturally, *Little Annie* (as the Champ had become known) and *Iron Annie* were invited to join in the fun. I simply had to turn the tables on all the gleaming heavy iron on the ground.

The announcer told the crowd one of the unusual warbirds, an L-3, would be coming down the runway at a hundred feet with an escort off her right wing. Vern and Chick rumbled down the centerline of the main runway at a blistering 75 miles an hour, and we were their escort — 23,000 pounds of Ju-52 with flaps and ailerons down to 25 and 15 degrees, props in flat pitch and howling, and hanging in tight on the *real* Champ.

Well, Friend, It's Flying!

Take three categories of flivver, from a ghostlike butterfly to a high-legged dragonfly that does impossible things in the sky, and what have you got? The Taylorcraft L-2 with 65 horses, the Stinson L-5 with 190 ponies up front, and the Fieseler Storch with 240 German horses prancing through an inverted, air-cooled V-8 engine (if it sounds familiar you're thinking of Messerschmitt bf-108B airplanes . . .). When we speak of warbirds, pilots who are struck with the Walter Mitty syndrome want to know, right *now*, how they fly, what it feels like, and as you describe the machines their blood runs hot and mist curls through their eyes.

Slow down! If you want differences in handling techniques and aircraft variations on a theme, you can find all you want with the ragwings. Herewith, then, a brief report on flying the three aforementioned flivvers, running from the bottom of the line to the top, for if ever there was an airplane that defies common sense, good looks, and gravity, it's that Storch.

Starting out with the L-2, you wonder what all the hullaballoo about the ultralights comes to, especially if you're flying one of the rigid-wing jobs with solid tail boom and secure goodies of that nature, including three-axis control. The Taylorcraft L-2 I flew took off with a weight of under 1000 pounds, and it was a skinnied fuselage job with tandem seats and the feeling of a greenhouse. It's hardly different in essential respects from the J-3 Cub with those 65 horses up front, the same (virtually) gear and tailwheel. And this rebuilt L-2 with its military colors was hardly different from the J-3 I used to fly uncounted decades past, a faded yellow machine that lumbered into the sky without radios, without an electrical system, with a plywood seat and an old raggedy cushion, and the absolute minimum of gauges. It's the old flying by feel and you do everything slow motion, *except* for your feet doing a brisk tap dance on the rudder pedals to keep it going straight.

You could always feel the ground in these things. It may sound strange, but it's not. Every thud and bang and slam against a rough field transmits through the airplane, but without the tin-canning the metal Spam Cans throw back at you. It's a nice feel even if it does rattle your teeth a bit. You bring in the power smoothly and your engine challenges all sewing machines around, and you're not sure if it clatters or tries to roar but doesn't quite make it, but the airplane moves ahead and the tail comes up with ridiculous ease, and if you'll then hold that stick steady and keep tap-dancing with very short quick jabs on the pedals for heading, why, before you know it the L-2 sort of lazily floats upward when it's ready. You discover the old and long-forgotten joy of taking off without bothering to look at the airspeed. It doesn't seem to matter. This thing will fly when its wings get good and ready and it happens fast enough and you continue the upward float.

You can do everything lazily, and that's wonderful. The wind is your friend, the wings are comfortably poking holes in some invisible foam to carry you around, and when you get to 700 feet or so, level off, set up cruise power, and *relax*. If you want to do big things with maneuverability, you're in the wrong airplane. Oh, you can throw it around and of course you can push it straight down, but *why*? Is that what you came up here to do? Say hello to the birds flying around with you, enjoy the lazy bumps of thermals, and putt-putt along at 75 or 80 mph. Enjoy, enjoy! Go sightseeing, be with the world, smell the grass from below, slide the windows back and let the air blow in your face and muss up your hair (if you still have any, right?). I've always found it fun in the Taylors, Pipers, and Aeroncas of this ilk to bring back the power to where you can see that prop turning and bring up the nose a bit and fly at not much above stall speed. I like the feeling.

Coming downstairs to end the armchair sojourn gives you all the latitude you want. You can laze down with some power or bring in the carb heat and the right trim and come back on power and make like a glider. As you come in on final and get close to the ground you'll rediscover the old rule that each of these little buggers has its very own individual characteristics about landing. The T-Craft, for example, fights with the ground. When it gets into ground effect it becomes a reluctant elevator. It doesn't want to go up and it rumbles about coming down as if it's stuck just a few feet in the air and wants to keep floating forever. Be patient. Let her keep settling, be ready for the burble over the wing you can't see because suddenly the ground comes up at you very quickly. If everything has played it out right, you'll put her down gently in three-point or the tailwheel will touch a tad before the mains and it's cause for a grin, or if you let it all fall away a few feet up, why, she'll fall like a mattress and there you are. A few stabs at the tap dance again and before you know it, she'll surprise you by mushing to a halt and you certainly will need some power to get back to the coffee pot. As I said, relax, enjoy; it's worth the trip back to the old values.

The Stinson L-5 is a step upward in the ragwing category, but it's a whole quantum jump in the way it feels and the way it flies, and it demands much more from the pilot. You're out of the 65-hp marshmallow class and don't forget it. Up front there's a great wooden club of a propeller being spun around by 190 hp, and I flew this bird solo at just more than twice the weight of the L-2, or slightly more than 2000 pounds. There's no question you're in a heavier, huskier airplane. You've got the power and the weight *and* flaps and ailerons that droop up to 15 degrees when you crank in flaps and the ship is just plain solid.

I hadn't flown the L-5 for a long time, so after going through the drill before taking the runway, I let her run. I knew that if I wanted to haul back on the stick she'd leave the ground at 60 mph, but in an airplane new to me I like extra speed (the old money-in-the-bank syndrome). After all, the indicator might be off, the engine might cough, the controls could be sloppier than expected, and a little extra speed goes a very long way. She lifted the tail easily enough and I brought in right rudder, and more and more right rudder. At 70 she flew herself off and I was pushing in even *more* right rudder. Climbout at about 85 mph and upstairs at just under 600 feet per minute, the RPM showing 2275. Nice. Solid. No nonsense. *Reliable.* That was the feeling.

At 1500 feet I leveled off, eased the power back to 2300 rpm and watched the airspeed build to just about 113 mph indicated. So what's different? The L-5 is sturdy and she's comfortable, if noisier than a boiler factory during a hailstorm, but if you ever look inside the bird, beneath her fabric covering, you'll see torque tubes that connect to the ailerons and elevators, and when they built these ships they didn't stint on ball and roller bearings, and all that adds up to a solid, immediately responsive flying machine. I like that phrase: *flying machine.* Because the L-5 is that. It's no aerobatic ace, but then I like lazy curves in the sky better than I do crisp aerobatics, and you get the feel of driving ahead solidly with the L-5 and no nonsense about it.

If you're up to snuff, then landing the L-5 is almost sinfully fun. You crank in the flaps and everything out there on the wings droops, and with all the burbling she wants to come down in a hurry. She'll deadstick like an old pro, but this was somebody else's airplane and I hadn't had time to get all her *feel*, so I kept in some power and let her rumble and chug and kept the needle on 65 as we got near the fence. It's an easy deceleration from 90 to 80 on base, and as you roll out onto final you're a tad over 70 because it feels good, and then you play the throttle and gravity to 60 or 65, flare her steadily, just touch the power, and she'll kiss the tailwheel an instant before the fat tires touch and the big mushy gear ab-

Heavy metal takes the headlines, but the ragwings often steal the show. An ancient Tiger Moth rests quietly at Ti-Co after low-level bombing strikes by the ragwings set the airport ablaze. *Photo by Paul Brown*

sorbs whatever you're doing. *Keep that stick back.* Those six cylinders and that wooden club of a prop can bring the L-5 to stand on her nose if you're heavy on the brakes. But why bother? Galumph, wheeze, and bounce gently. What could be nicer?

Well, whatever the L-2 and the L-5 can do, the Fieseler Storch, despite its 240 hp, can do better. There are all kinds of airplanes. Some of them are successful. Some of them are grandly successful. Others are also ugly, and some are so ugly you know they were designed during a terrible hangover. The Storch is grandly successful and incredibly ugly. It looks as if it is always starving. It's a dragonfly and a great mosquito and a bad cousin to a praying mantis, and its legs are long and spindly like those of a stork, and the name *Storch* sure fits it well.

The United States built the Jeep and the Germans built the Storch. During the Big War there was simply nothing like it for discomfort, performance, ruggedness, and incredible reliability. It did things most pilots wouldn't want to try in a helicopter, and it

162

had the equipment to do it. They hung a wing of 46 feet on this thing, installed full-span leading-edge slats, added Fowler flaps, and jiggled the system so that when you lowered the flaps past 20 degrees the ailerons also sagged. You increased wing area by almost 20 percent and you did incredible things with the camber. (Many times with the Storch I wondered what might have been added to the performance with a constant speed propeller. But even with the thick club out front it's still amazing. And this is a *1935* design . . .)

The first time I wrapped my hand about the stick I had a flashback that I was seated again in the replica of the *Spirit of St. Louis*. This was the same kind of deliberate Ryan monstrosity. It's a *club*, the working end of a baseball bat! Everything worked well for starting up, except that in the cockpit, with all its glass, you feel you've been trapped in a nightmare of struts and wires and chains. The old pros who have been flying the Storch in France (a whole bunch of them were manufactured there) grinned and told me to use 45 mph as the figure for taking off. "You point her down the runway and you wait until you have the forty-five and you take off. But I warn you, the tail does not like to lift. Push *hard* on the stick during your roll."

This was sort of crazy. Just about everything I'd flown, except some taildraggers with sick engines, *liked* to get the tail up and would do so without any effort from the pilot. But they sure meant what they said about *push* with this thing! The wind was at about 15 mph straight down the runway (I thank Thee for small favors) so I didn't have to wrestle with sideloads. I figured getting the tail up had to be easier at slow speed with the Storch than it was with a 23,000-pound Ju-52, but I was wrong. At very slow speeds, with 25-degree flaps and full bore in the Ju-52, I can get the tail up in about 50 feet of roll, but it takes a lot of muscle to do so. It took about the same effort with this ungainly, stick-legged caricature of an airplane! The tail came up, complaining and resisting all the way, and I wondered if it would fly off tail low; while I was thinking about it the tail came up sluggishly and at about the same moment we were flying. Got to watch it here; with all that forward pressure there was a danger of nosing down, so I relaxed all the muscle work and — again amazingly like the Ju-52 — the airplane sort of lofted upward, but without any nonsense to it. Again there was a similarity to the Ju-52 when I thought about it; cranking trim changes the angle of incidence of the horizontal stabilizer so

163

that it acts like a stabilator, and the trim changes are really powerful.

I took it upstairs for some slow flight and simulated short-field approaches. This thing with flaps and ailerons drooping had incredible drag, but when you put the nose down it tried to run away with itself. You don't need 60 mph in the Storch to land; it's sort of a blistering pace. But that's what I had. So I played around upstairs and got the feel at *very* slow flight to see how the control pressures would change. I came down ham-handed, but then I approach all new planes like they were nitro until I feel them through their full regime. The airplane doesn't land. It just quits flying. Finally I was coming around on steep final at just under 40 mph and she flew just fine with all the appropriate pressures, and I had my point picked out and dropped her in as slowly as I dared. With that wind it was ridiculous. She touched, I had the stick back hard and was on those brakes *at once.* I had to measure it later. *We didn't roll 60 feet.*

With that wind and increasing confidence, I held her steady for the next takeoff, flaps at 20 degrees, brakes hard, and full power, and kept the stick full back as I released the brakes. Guess what? She moved soggily into the air in what I estimated was about 70 feet and even then I think I overestimated the run before the wheels lifted.

The trick for the really tight landing is much the same as in other planes. Bring her in with everything hanging out, let her come down like a stone, and as you flare, short and sweet, pop just a touch of power to keep the elevator working, and drop her in. She'll stop right there and then.

In other words, the Storch needs only a heliport for its operations!

And there ain't none of the big iron can do *that*, friend.

Holy Moses!

Thou shalt maintain thy airspeed lest the
ground reach up and smite thee.

THE ELEVENTH COMMANDMENT

Some years back I received a letter from a young sailor who, when not wearing his U.S. Navy uniform and doing whatever sailors do these days, appeared grimly determined to challenge the heavens. He had several things going for him. An unquenchable enthusiasm, for starters. A bevy of angels working frantic overtime to take care of him. And what appears to be a battered old ragwing that had once seen military service and then had been written off the roster as a collection of rag, wood, and metal long overdue for decent burial. That letter was, and remains, in every sense a classic. George Moses, and I am certain he never was aware of his inimitable contribution to aviation lore, stumbled and staggered his way into a classic chapter of flight. I offer you his letter as it was written, and I could not bear to change a word. He had scrawled and scratched this letter longhand and, except for a few personal details of interest only to George Moses and me, *this is really the way it happened* —

——————— ☆ ———————

Thanks so much for your long letter and what I guess are your detailed orders. I thought you might just be giving me some advice or instructions, but the second and third time I read what you wrote I really began to get the message. So I thought about how I was going where I was going and I guess I wasn't so much confused but I hadn't really thought about it too much at all. Anyway, it appears that your suggested routes for the Green Bomb and I to take is a little tardy but not really. Know what I mean?

Since January I have flapped my way through the cumulus to Asbury Park, New Jersey, then back to Portsmouth, Virginia, later to Beckley, West by God Virginia. The weather kept me from going on to Lexington, Kentucky, so I hopped aboard the great grey dog. *Blech.* Only way I know to describe a Greyhound. Soon as I could I was back in the air, I can tell you *that.*

On most of these routes I followed pipelines, railroads, and highways, and sometimes even my compass. In all this flying I have learned a wealth of experience and lessons. My bird what only goes sixty knots indicated has seen some breakneck speeds of ninety knots plus coming up from Macon, Georgia, and I scared the hell outta me. I shudder as I recall this and I swear to the great sky boss I'll never do it again.

My first takeoff from Macon I had loss of power on getting off. I was at four hundred feet and climbing out when it happened. The engine still sounded smooth. But still, I thought, it's got to be carburetor ice. My full power in the sixty-five horse Continental is 2300 RPM. She dropped to 2000. I yanked on carb heat and Great Shades of Orville and Wilbur. That jewel dropped right down to fifteen hundred. If I'd have had a radio I would have called for a laundry truck to be standing by, I was so scared. Still at full throttle, I began settling. Damn thing just wouldn't fly. The field was to my right as there was a right-hand pattern in effect. I was still thinking I had carburetor icing so I was afraid to shut off the carb heat. I sweated complete engine failure for a minute that seemed like an hour as I roared over a clump of woods. Finally a long runway reached out my way, and I wasted no time diving for it. Knowing it wasn't the same one I had leaped off from, I waggled my wings on the way down so the tower would know I was really in trouble. Man, that carb ice can be costly.

Well, I made it down okay, and then I found all that jiggling with carb heat hadn't done a bit of good, because it wasn't carb ice at all. It took a whole day for all them fancy mechanics to find out it was a bum right magneto. Finding out cost me thirty-five bucks and to me that's a fortune. It was also thirty-five bucks of gasoline, the way I look at it. I phoned the Navy at Norfolk the next day and they gave me two days' extension on my leave, or I'd have been AWOL in addition to being broke.

Believe it or not, *now* comes the big sin. Because of time, present weather, and future weather, like the whole world was crowding me, I pressed on. The weather was maybe eighty percent IFR conditions all the way to Portsmouth. I never got more than a thousand feet over the ground at any time, and the real truth is that I stayed at three hundred feet most of the way, and that was hugging those railroad tracks. Half the time I was in rain heavy enough to drown a long-legged dog. I swear at one time I seen the devil himself, because I was completely socked in, only two hundred feet up, and I was *lost*. I splashed onward after fifteen minutes of circling some farm roads, wanting desperately to land, but knowing I'd never make it with narrow roads and rain and trees and power lines and God knows what else. I finally found a river ten miles west of where I'd been circling, and by God at least I now knew where I was.

Hooray — an airport I could reach safely! I went there like a homing pigeon with the Mexican sidestep, crazy to get on the ground, and I landed and taxied up to an old hangar and shut down, glad I could get some fuel. Turned out I was the only airplane and the only living human being on the whole field. It was like Antarctica when it was melting. So I removed the rear seat and shoved it up front, curling up in the back seat to let the winds rock me and the Green Bomb to sleep. Well, I fell asleep all right but not for long, because waterproof is something this airplane was not. The rain leaked in heavier and heavier, and I woke up wet, cold, cramped, and pretty miserable. Boy, this was fun. I dragged myself up over the front seat, with my feet touching the back of the baggage compartment, and my head touching the panel, and I loosened up my sore muscles with a half-healthy stretch.

My knee bones popped with a noise so loud it scared hell out of me. So again I repositioned my aching carcass, half in the baggage compartment, and the top half of me laying across the foundation frame of the rear seat. After an hour of squirming I dropped off again to sleep, only to come wildly awake from a too-realistic nightmare of some punk hoods dragging me outta the airplane to beat the hell out of me. After a time I dozed off again, changing position a dozen times. I kept coming awake from the cold and cramps and water dripping all over me. I figure I got maybe a total of three hours sleep. Finally at four in the morning I said to hell with this, climbed out of the airplane, and walked through the rain to a gas station I spotted down the road alongside the field. At least they had a radio there.

I felt I should have stayed wet and cold, because the weather reports I heard on the radio were real scary. Yet I was even more scared to remain at this wreck of an airport and spend another night like this twisted into the airplane. I carried a can of five gallons of automobile gasoline down to the airplane and poured it into the tanks. She runs real good on auto gas, I should mention. I waited for the first sign of daylight and it came cold and grey, but at least the rain was now down to a drizzle. I fired up and took off as fast as I could, water spraying from the tires before I got into the air. I made it all the way to Orangeburg, filled the airplane with real aviation gas, and left immediately for Huggins, North Carolina.

God bless the police. The Huggins airport was run by a flying patrol cop. He was terrific to me. He bedded me down in the airport lounge on a big soft couch, and he kept the gas stove going full blast all night to keep me warm. I slept like a dead man for twelve hours, and the cop said I didn't so much as twitch, and he began to wonder if maybe I wasn't really dead.

Next morning he piled me into his jeep with six huge dogs and we all roared off into town for a terrific breakfast. When we got back to the field the weather was better than it had been; I said my goodbye to that wonderful cop and all his dogs. With a sky of broken clouds and high winds I flapped my way north slowly to Wilson, North Carolina. It was a real record-breaker for me; I'd gone a whole hundred and fifty miles nonstop and without an emergency of some kind. I skirted two big airports on the way so I could stay well clear of the FAA boys, what with not having radios and flying now on fumes. But the navigation was wonderful, because I had a double set of train tracks all the way into Wilson.

But I couldn't get any gas there. I begged a guy in an Apache for help, and he was kind about it, too. He drained five gallons of gas from his airplane and I loaded up my ship again. I took off and scooted on to Portsmouth, sort of whistled to myself while I skidded into the pattern at eight hundred feet, and squeaked onto the runway. By God, I'd made it!

Maybe the worst happened after I was shut down. Talk about a tongue lashing! I got scraped up one side of my butt and down the other. The paint had peeled back from all the leading edges of the wings and it looked like the fabric was just about to follow. I was a bit ticked off at first with getting reamed out like that, but the more they hollered and the more I listened I think they should have taken their feet and pounded my butt up between my shoulders. The truth of the matter is I should never have even tried to fly through some of the weather in which I'd bumbled around. I'd let time push me, and they made sure I understood that the fastest way to lose all your time on this world is to do what I did by being impatient.

Oh, well. Time to go again. My next trip over the mountains of West Virginia was surprising because the navigation was so much easier than I'd expected. I had a little trouble going south by Spartanburg, North Carolina. Then, on my way from Athens to Macon I wandered into a pretty good crosswind because for a while I got lost. I was supposed to pass between two lakes but because of the wind I mistook a cloud shadow for a lake on my left. I sure thank the guy who drew those lakes on that chart. He did a great job of putting in every detail exactly the way it looked from the air, and having those details saved my butt. You know yourself how that run goes from Macon to Portsmouth, but this time I had the gods with me and they gave me a tailwind all the way.

When I got near Macon I knew I had to land at Smart so I could telephone Macon Tower for permission to get into their field without radio. Unfortunately, on my way from Portsmouth to Beckley I got lost again. I think I was near Hilltop, and then I didn't know where the hell I was. There's two airports just ten miles apart. The lower one, well, I couldn't see it, so I headed north for a river, and then I spotted the other airport. I believe it was called Plainview, but I never was sure.

I didn't have any charts with me, so that made it a bit more difficult, I guess. Well, anyway, when I got things sorted out on the ground, I took off like I was on a crazy roller coaster. That runway was ridiculous. Bad as that was I got the surprise of my life at White Sulphur Springs. The pattern wrapped itself right around the mountain! The field nestled in the valley and the only way to get in was to hold a continuous turning glide all the way to the ground. It was scary as hell not being able to see what might be coming at you from around the other side, and I saw right away that I'd better remember that when I took off, the climbout was going to be through a valley the floor of which climbed just about as fast as I could climb in my plane.

Anyway, it went pretty good and then I was on my way from

169

White Sulphur to Beckley. Just when things are going nice for you it starts to rain and now wasn't any different. This was a light drizzle where there wasn't much water, but it beat the visibility down to almost nothing. I had my neck turning constantly on a swivel watching out for them Big Boppers of Piedmont Airlines. Well, I made it.

So on this one trip I logged nineteen hours and forty minutes and I flew a distance of twelve hundred nautical miles, which includes all that wandering around and following the curves and turns in all the railroad tracks when the weather was hugging the trees. The truth was I *had* to stay with all those turns, because the visibility was so bad I couldn't even make a short cut from one rail curve to the next. Radio and television towers don't grow in the middle of train tracks, do they? I sure hope not. My mileage I logged has got to include the circles I flew, around and around, when I got lost so many times.

Now, in March, before this trip, I had went to Lakewood, New Jersey. I followed the parkway from Atlantic City to Lakewood, and my first real big blooper was to fly along dumb and happy while watching a fog bank dropping steadily from 3500 feet right on down to just 500 feet. This was my first real low flying, by the way. I suppose I could have climbed above that fog, but it seemed to go on forever. I found out later it topped at 8000 feet, but I didn't have any radios and I really wasn't too hot with being able to use a compass, and I didn't also know, or not know, which way the winds were blowing, so I stayed low and kept going lower. I broke that Golden Rule of When in Doubt — *Get Out*. I should have done a run home, you know, do the old one-eighty and run for it while the running was good. Not me. I flew for a while at 500 feet and then it got worse and I went scooting over a toll booth at maybe 200 feet up, tops, and I hugged that road on the way to Lakewood, and the saints were with me because the fog lifted about ten miles from Lakewood and I even climbed to 1000 feet to get into the pattern.

I spent the night with a buddy, and the next morning I called the Navy at Lakehurst and the weather people told me I was crazy if I planned on flying, what with winds gusting from all over the place at nearly thirty miles an hour, to say nothing of intermittent rain and a broken ceiling. To the south, Norfolk was the same: lousy. But Lakewood airport didn't have anyone running the field at the time and I didn't want to leave the airplane unattended, so

I sort of ignored all those terrible reports and I took off, headed for Asbury Park. I managed to find the parkway, but the winds turned really bad. I mean, they were gusting with real hard blows better than forty or fifty miles an hour and my little airplane was taking the beating of her life. It felt like I was driving over a rutted road and people were throwing rocks at me.

Then I took the wrong turn off the road and I was lost again, so I headed for Monmouth County Airport. I didn't really know how lost I was, or what kind of mistake I'd made, until at the same time I saw a sky filled with U.S. Army airplanes and a control tower sticking up from the ground like a giant sore thumb. By now I was sort of very desperate to get out of this sky, which was beating me up so badly, so I skidded, bucked, and sunfished around the pattern with a lot of help from those gusting winds wagging my wings like we had palsy. Later I found out how really upset those tower people were. They said they flashed every light they had at me and were even thinking of firing flares, but I swear to God I never saw even a single light. Anyway, I missed the runway because the winds were throwing me all over the place, and I came around the pattern a second time. All the army planes had just disappeared and I had the pattern all to myself, and on my second approach to the runway I chopped power and pulled on carb heat and found myself going down the runway at about a hundred miles an hour! Holy Smoke, I was landing *downwind!* I poured the coal to the ship and climbed around again and I found my mouth as dry as cotton and my hands as wet as if I'd stuck them under a faucet. I popped a wad of gum in my mouth and chewed like mad, and really fought the winds.

This time I made the right approach but the winds were getting even worse and I had full throttle and I was diving for the runway and my speed over the ground was about twenty miles an hour at the most. Up ahead of me, on the field, I saw a crash truck with all its lights flashing like mad, rolling fast to get to the runway. I tightened my shoulder harness just as tight as it would go and bounced my way down. I was amazed at what I did. Everything was right. I touched down in a level attitude, a wheels landing under full power, and it was like settling in like a helicopter. Except that it wouldn't drop the last few feet and I used up half the runway trying to get those wheels on the ground.

It was really crazy. If I eased off on the power the airplane went up like an elevator, so I needed the power to *force* it down. I finally stopped, just five feet short of a real big ditch at the end of the runway. The winds were so wild by now that I was standing still, full power, wheels on the ground and the tail up in the air! I sat there for a while, forcing myself to breathe slowly and trying to stuff my heart back into my chest. A bunch of men stuck their heads up slowly from the ditch; the last thing they'd seen before they hauled ass was me coming straight at them with the engine screaming. After sitting on the end of the runway, getting the tail down very slowly and praying for help, the crash truck showed up. Four men ran up to the plane and grabbed the wing struts and the tail and hung on to help me taxi back to the dirt-sand tiedown ramp. Without their weight the airplane would just have been blown back into the air.

That poor airplane got tied down every way I could, but it sat on that field and for the rest of that day and long into the night it got a terrific sandblasting job. I never expected it, but the army people and the civilians who worked there were all nice to me and I stood there with my mouth open when the army pilots congratulated me on my good landing. I didn't tell them that wheel landings are all anyone can do in my bird with any degree of safety and that if I'd tried to three-point it I'd have killed myself.

Well, the next day the winds were strong but not buffeting like they had been, so I took off and circled and with a nice stiff tailwind to help me along I headed south for a nonstop flight to Salisbury, Maryland. I made it okay, and at the ramp I gassed up and set out again. I had to taxi out onto a frightening spiderweb maze of taxiways and runways and I was more lost on the ground there than I'd ever been in the air. By the time I'd taxied out to way over to the other side of the field I couldn't even see which way the wind Tee was pointing.

Blast my hide if I didn't pick the wrong runway. I was going like a raped ape down the field and not flying when the truth dawned on me that I had a real strong crosswind from *behind* me. The ground was racing by, I mean, I was really scooting along, but the airspeed indicator read a big fat zilch. Then the wind started shoving me toward the side of the runway and toward all those trees lining the runway about twenty yards away. With my tail finally in the air the rest of that takeoff roll was on the grass and I was heading right for those trees and I couldn't do a thing about it! I had just enough speed to jerk her into the air, and when I got the wheels off the grass I made the damndest ninety degree turn you

172

ever saw. Or anyone else who was watching, for that matter. It sure felt uncomfortable, and when I broke out into the open near the middle of the field I could feel all the eyes of the FAA watching this idiot George Moses. I managed to wind my way around the field so that at its boundaries I crossed the threshold of the runway I was supposed to have used, and just climbed away whistling through dry lips. But now I ran into a wind shift and I began to settle earthward again despite my banging on the throttle and both praying and yelling curses. I got very closely acquainted with the trees before I started climbing again.

On my next cross-country trip, or whatever it should be called, things were pretty uneventful, and I made sure to stay as far away as I could from Salisbury Airport. I'd had enough of that. Have you ever landed at Rehoboth across the water from Cape May? It's a nice enough field, and the people are friendly, and they give great service even to little guys like me, but sometimes I think they're apologizing for their runway. It's a roller coaster. I think they had an all-night earthquake when they poured the macadam and that's how it finally dried. For a while I thought I had just forgotten how to fly. I bounced twenty times trying to land and felt like an idiot. Then I watched other planes bouncing like crazy and I figured we couldn't *all* be idiots, right? That would have made one hell of a convention right then and there, for sure.

I'm really learning the ins and outs of this flying business by now. I should also say the ups and downs. I never realized how far and how long a wingtip vortex could be from a real big jet or how strong they could stay after the jet passes. I was watching a real big bird descending above me and many miles off, and I knew I was ten miles or more from this dude. Obviously his wingtip vortices continued to settle in air that was absolutely calm. I'm glad I was flying in the same direction because finally I moved into one of those vortices, and my little airplane, just as pretty as you please, rolled over on her back, stayed there for a while, and then rolled right side up. For a few seconds, I was dumbfounded as the world turned upside down, and I did everything but throw those controls out the window; it had absolutely no effect. Maybe these things seek me out.

We had a snowstorm, but where I keep the airplane the winds kept the snow from piling up and the plows opened the field, so I fired up for a short trip to visit a friend of mine. At his field I saw they had scraped the snow right down to the very runway surface.

173

There wasn't a mark on it, so I came around into the wind and I landed in snow that was four feet high. Boy, was I ever surprised. It was soft and pure white and I touched beautifully and I must have rolled twelve feet or something, but the snow was everywhere and spraying in through the glass and the prop just stopped, like *that*, and I was in snow up to my keister and I couldn't even climb out of the thing because the snow had jammed the side of the airplane shut. It was like being shifted by magic to some steppe out in Siberia. Some people finally came out in a snowplow and dug me out. It was different, all right. You should have seen that take-off. They did a fast plow job for me and I went down that field like a hound dog jumping in and out of drifts. When I got home the little plane was full of snow just everywhere.

I've had only one real bad moment, a near-miss with a low-wing Piper or Beech. It was so close and went by so fast that the airplane was just a blur. Have you ever figured out why they call it a near-miss? That sounds pretty stupid to me. If it's a miss that's terrific, but a near-*hit*, now that grabs you where they really got your attention. I was coming up from Kitty Hawk and had the afternoon sun in my eyes, when this really swift bird filled up my windshield in a right diving turn. I turned to ice but I snapped out of my shock and whipped it over into a tight right turn. It was more like clawing my way around. Maybe we were 200 feet apart when we went by, maybe it was a lot closer. He came from my one o'clock position and we seemed to be at the same altitude. The last I seen of that guy he was still diving like mad for the water.

I'd been wearing some real badly scratched plastic-lens sunglasses, and let me tell you I opened the side window and threw those suckers away from me as fast as I could. The truth is that they were also prescription glasses and I really couldn't see very good without them, but that was better than trying to see with them where the scratches just dimmed the world and about hid it from sight.

Well, when it gets to be August I'm off on some more real good trips. I plan to do some flying to Macon, and then travel north up to Boston, work my way through upstate New York. The mountain flying should be fun. I might do some flying through Pennsylvania as I work my way back down south. I guess I ought to prepare a little better from now on. I mean, I'll have charts with me, and for sure, the right glasses. I'll take along a first-aid kit, and even some survival gear. I can get a portable emergency transmitter from my navy squadron. Since I'm planning some long overwater hops I suppose I should use a life vest. Next summer I've got my flights planned from Virginia to Oregon and California, and I'm already plotting my trip down into Mexico, and hit the American southwest. I think I'll like the desert.

One day maybe I can fly some of the heavier warbirds. That would really be neat. Keep an eye out for me.

———————— ☆ ————————

You can count on it, George.

Coming Up Sixes

A midair collision can ruin
your whole day.

There just ain't nobody in Warbird Country who isn't familiar with the Six, otherwise known as the North American T-6 Texan. Long ago it was called the BC-1, then BC-2, and then they changed its designation to AT-6 and they also labeled it the SNJ. They called it other names in special models and foreign variants, but no matter what you ever did to it the airplane was still just the Six. All the fancy trimmings and doodads people added to them didn't change a thing. This wasn't a debutante and no matter what fancy slippers you put on she still snarled and coughed like a rough-hewn stevedore of an airplane.

There are more of these T-6 warbirds than anything else in the world, since between the American, Canadian, and Australian governments more than 16,000 of these things rolled off the production lines (16,376, to be exact). They were in every form burly airplanes, built for punishment to teach advanced students on land and on aircraft carriers how to survive an angry airplane, which the Six most truly is. Square winged, with a snarling six hundred horses and a big prop, with cursedly narrow gear, and violent tendencies when you don't coddle and caress her, they have been both the love and the hate of the whole warbird movement. Not as hot as a Mustang or a Corsair, they are still devilishly tough to handle the right way, and if you can fly a Six with quality you can fly

176

anything. Among the warbird fraternity there's a saying that you start out in the Hellcat, graduate to a Corsair, climb into a Mustang, and *then* you're ready to fly the Six.

It's a good idea to get the numbers out of the way, because if you're going to be involved with warbirds, there simply is no escaping the presence of gangs of T-6 airplanes all around you. Thus this brief history of production and types. There are so many legends about the background of the Six that even the nonsense has become legendary. Keep this book with you when you get into arguments about the Six. Talk with authority and use these numbers to win beer bets with your friends.

Long before the outbreak of the Second World War, North American Aviation moved handily into the military trainer business. They produced their NA-16 design (NA-16 refers to the sixteenth design of North American and is a *company* designation) and offered it to the Army Air Corps, the long-deceased ancestor of today's United States Air Force. NAA (North American Aviation) won a production order for their airplane as the BT-9 (Basic Trainer, 9th Major Model in the BT line). Since some changes were made between the test model and the production model, NAA changed their company designation of the BT-9 production airplane from NA-16 to NA-19. (Stay with us.)

In 1937, NAA produced a new and improved trainer design that got the company tag of NA-26 in its test model. The Air Corps ordered the airplane in quantity as the BC-1 (Basic Combat, 1st Major Model in the BC line). The moment it went into production, NAA labeled it the NA-36. To confuse matters somewhat, a few models were built as the BC-II, and the Roman numerals are very specific, but no one seems ever to have understood *why.* They're just *there.*

The BC-1 was the direct ancestor of the AT-6 and, in fact, *was* the AT-6 before it got the latter name (they changed from BC to AT, which stands for Advanced Trainer). Where the BT-9 had some 450 hp and fixed gear and was a bear of an airplane, the BC-1 had 600 horsepower, retractable gear, a constant speed propeller, and other refinements and aeronautical instruments of torture.

Once the BC-1 was on the scene, the U.S. Navy liked it so much they ordered sixteen of the airplanes, *but* under their own designation of SNJ, which, under the navy system, used SN to represent this category of trainer and J to identify the manufacturer as NAA. Still with us? Because if you are, you have just become aware that,

177

despite anything you may have heard, the SNJ did not spring to life as a new navy design, but was simply the air corps's BC/AT-6 series modified for naval use by strengthening the fuselage to take a carrier arrestor hook, to mount different radios, and be made resistant to salt-water corrosion.

Soon after, the BC designation would be dropped in favor of AT-6, but SNJ would remain unchanged. Just keep that as a side-bar note for reference.

Anyway, North American had its eyes on the foreign market. They had on their hands their NA-16A model. This had already been rebuilt into BC configuration with all its advancements, and when that was done, NAA redesignated the airplane the NA-32 and shipped it to Australia for tests by that government. Soon after-ward, they finished work on their NA-16-3, which was the second prototype in the line, and now identified as the NA-33.

Let's stop for a moment. Australia liked the airplane so much they made a deal to rush it into production in Australia as the Wirraway, to be built under license by Commonwealth Aircraft. The early models were built in Australia, but used imported en-gines from Pratt & Whitney. As soon as it geared up for production, Commonwealth manufactured its own licensed copies of these en-gines, designated R-1340-S1H1-G engines of 600 hp and swinging a three-bladed propeller, as well as being fitted out with bomb racks and machine guns. Through August 31, 1945, Australia turned out 717 of these airplanes.

Turn back the clock to 1938. The NA-16-3 had also attracted the attention of the British government, and it ordered this airplane, to be built as the Harvard. The moment NAA had the contract, they called the production model of the Harvard the NA-49. The British liked the plane so much they ordered a second batch, and *these* Harvards because of minor redesign became known as the NA-61. A total of 430 Harvards were built for the British and Ca-nadian air forces.

(Deep breath.) In the meantime, NAA had improved its early de-signs of the BC-1. It had a new dash 45 engine and a three-bladed prop, and they called it the NA-54 and sold it to the air corps as the BC-2.

Okay so far. NAA still tinkered with the design, and got an order for some test articles that were bought by the air corps as the BC-1A. Working backwards, NAA promptly dubbed *this* model the NA-59.

The navy also liked it and put in an order for the SNJ-2 trainer (which NAA immediately designated the NA-65).

Changes continued. The demand for the airplane was so great it was built at a new Texas plant. It now had a dash 49 engine, was designated by the company as the NA-66, and was sold to the air corps as the AT-6A.

So far, so good. The British and Canadians also liked what they saw and ordered the airplane, but they called the AT-6A the Harvard II. Then everybody came up with the idea of increasing production. Why not have the Noorduyn company in Canada build the airplane? Why not, indeed? To distinguish it from other models, Noorduyn called it the Harvard IIA and churned out 1500 of these models.

Our air force liked the Noorduyn model so much it took a bunch of them and designated the Harvard IIA as the Noorduyn AT-16.

Everybody continued cranking out various Texan and Harvard models until finally they went as high as the SNJ-6 and the AT-6J. Production ended generally when World War II cranked down because no one needed that many hot trainers. But a war was coming again in Korea, and when it arrived the demand for what was now known as the T-6 became overwhelming. Surplused models were dragged back into service and modified and improved. The airplane was so much in demand that in 1952 Canadian Car and Foundry went back into production with the model, now known as the Harvard IV, and cranked out a couple of hundred of these new variants. To top off the numbers game, the Harvard IV was also manufactured (50 of them) as the T-6J-CC for other foreign buyers.

There's a sidebar development somewhere in here. North American was still hot for the foreign market, so they beefed up the basic AT-6 design by installing a 785-hp Wright 1820-75 engine with a three-bladed prop, and hanging a bunch of machine guns on the airplane. It also did 250 mph, which was pretty neat for a T-6 frame. This model became the NA-44, but the air force (ours) took over the production order as the A-27 attack bomber.

Meanwhile, back at the NAA ranch, the company got a request for a bunch of low-cost fighters for Siam. They beefed up and fattened the airplane (now called the NA-50A), stuck on an R-1820-77 engine of 875 hp that delivered a speed of 270 mph, and prepared to ship the birds overseas. The war changed all that, and the U.S. Air Force stepped in to claim the airplanes, drafting them into wartime service as the P-64 fighter. They never saw combat, and,

Hot rod of the warbird world, the chunky and rugged T-6 is the In-be-tween Machine for pilots who want more in life than the Spam Cans have to offer. Jim Garemore of Ocala climbs out in his SNJ-5. *Asgard Flite Photo*

miraculously, at least two out of the batch of six survived and are still flying today.

So if you add it all together, we built a total of 15,649 Texans and Harvards, 717 Wirraways, 10 A-27 bombers, and 6 P-64 fighters for a grand total of 16,382 airplanes.

☆

Which brings us back to *now,* and the fact that there remain un-counted hundreds, many hundreds, of these airplanes still flying. The problem is that many of the T-6 birds are being flown by peo-ple who have no business in the machines without prior benefit of some really sensible and directed training. This has been a sore point not only with pilots who have seen friends and neighbors die unnecessarily, but also with the FAA, which on one hand doesn't want to come down as an Iron Grandfather on people having a good time, and on the other hand is responsible for keeping people alive. Things got so bad the FAA published a special warning and safety paper on the matter, and some excerpts right now may save *your* life if you're about to step up from the civilian Spam Can into the huskier birds.

There is nothing wrong with coveting a time-honored military airplane, provided that you can find one in airworthy condition that is within your economic grasp. And there is nothing wrong with making a "pet" out of an AT-6. The danger is the fatal taint of a challenge to the airman's pride: "If you can fly one bird, you can fly them all."

This is not necessarily true. Different planes have different flying characteristics and varying performances, which can become very important in an emergency. Light modern civilian aircraft are specifically designed to be forgiving of pilot error, a feature which increases the safety factor and the sales appeal but offers little as preparation toward moving into an unforgiving airplane. The difference between flying a 600-hp warplane and a 145-hp civilian job is considerable.

Having 500 hours or even 5000 hours in a 170 or similar aircraft certainly means that you are an experienced pilot. But it also means you have built up a specific set of habits with regard to flying which, although they keep you accident free in one type of aircraft, could contribute to a mishap or worse in another. Flying experience is, in part, specific; in fact, the problem of *unlearning* certain habits associated with hundreds of hours in a given plane can be the most difficult part about changing airplanes.

No formal checkout and no minimum number of hours of dual instruction are required for transitioning from one aircraft to another in the same general category . . . The readiness of a pilot to fly a different airplane safely depends not on any minimum legal requirement but on his ability to handle the aircraft in question.

Warplanes are something like wild animals: beautiful but savage — and very expensive to own. If you have your heart set on taming one, get some professional help.

☆

Down in Lakeland, Florida, there lives a close friend of mine, a brother in our fraternity, really, who deals in the sales of heavy construction and engineering equipment as his profession. Jack Kehoe flies Cessna 310s and Comanches and other Spam Cans both for his livelihood and because he enjoys the flying. But he also owns and flies a pale-blue-and-gray camouflaged T-6. The Big Six itself.

Kehoe's story is that like so many of us, he was (and is) a hell of a good Spam Can driver. He has loads of pilot ratings, and we all used to trundle on down to Texas every year to do our thing with the Confederates. Then was born the Florida Wing of the CAF and Kehoe felt the fire boiling up through his belly and with his friend, Bone Crusher Kerwin (he of the Ultimate 108), they bought themselves a Big Six. They got into the stuff hot and heavy. No one, *but no one*, can give you a better road map to your own future in warbirds than Jack Kehoe, who might title his words to this chapter *How I Found an Old T-6, Scared Myself to Death Learning to Fly It, and Skinned All My Knuckles Rebuilding the Mother — and Went Broke.*

One and all, I give you Jack Kehoe —

—————————— ☆ ——————————

Would I do it all over again? You've got to be crazy or spaced out to ask a question like that. My first reaction to that query is nonstop profanity. *Then* I might be able to speak coherently. I know, I know. You told me that if I put all this down on paper, and I answered your thousand questions, I could save lives of people who wander into the same mess I found. I can prevent trauma both physical and mental. I could do all these things simply by relating what happened to me over the years since tumbling down that bottomless pit called warbirds.

In the beginning, or once upon a time, or whatever we might recall that magic moment to be, I was in Okinawa. You know, that big island well south of Japan, and I was a member of the occupation team. Among other things, those people who could do so flew every chance they could get. I wasn't a greenhorn to flying or some G.I. in rumpled khakis. Hell, I had my private ticket. I'd even picked up outlaw time in everything from small military ships to eight hours in a B-25 bomber, which is as close as you can get to this side of heaven with only a new private license in your pocket.

Then a pilot offered me a flight in a T-6, the old North American trainer with 600 horses and squared-off wings and oodles of sex appeal. To a Spam Can pilot the T-6 was *it*, and I was in hog heaven as the airplane shook and rattled during the runup, and thunder sang sweetly as we galumphed down the runway and started a long climb through towering white pillars lifting high over the ocean. I was still wandering through my own reverie when the pilot's voice crackled over the intercom. "Hey, Kehoe, you buckled in tight?" I cinched the straps tighter and gave him some fast and impressive patter. "Yessir! Sure am, captain! Go for it, I'm ready!" *Real* impressive, right? Wrong. It was my luck to be invited upstairs by a pilot who'd had his stomach surgically removed. And who didn't know or care what was up or down. He got me sicker than the time I was thirteen years old and smoked my first dago cigar. That vile stuff came rumbling and boiling up from my guts into my stomach and I swallowed it. I wasn't going to let that sucker know what he was doing to me. Of course I was sick for a week after getting back on the ground, and my stomach and throat tried to reject me from their presence, but I kept cool. I think.

That's when it began. This business of Coming Up Sixes, which was like a haunting refrain in the back of my head. I didn't really hear the music for twenty-four years, and then, it was 1974 and I was in Lakeland, Florida, and the trumpets sounded and I could hear the wind and smell the cold air, and the whole thing was touched with tragedy but there was no way to stop. I had a friend, Wayne Thomas, proud owner of a rebuilt T-6 and, wonder of all wonders, a gleaming blue F4U Corsair, the famed cranked-wing fighter from great air battles of the past. Wayne, along with Bud Clark and Marion Robles and a small gang of enthusiastic gophers, had rebuilt that bentwing machine into a jewel. He finished a flight in the F4U and shut it down and climbed into the T-6 for some air work. Wayne was a jewel of a pilot and he rolled the T-6 down real low, as smooth as silk, and when he was inverted the engine quit and he had nowhere to go, and nothing he did helped. She split-essed straight into the ground and he was gone in a blur of torn metal and boiling dust.

What did I do *now?* No stopping, that's for sure. Wayne Thomas had taken me upstairs in that same T-6 and we'd cut high blue and flashed through white clouds, and his engine sang with that extra special note of honey, and we'd talked about warbirds and the Confederate Air Force, and the gatherings of the clan, and I could not and never would forget that he rolled and looped that T-6 with me in the back seat and I not only did *not* get sick, but I never knew the first signs of discomfort. My God, what a difference in the sensations of flight when the pilot is a part of the airplane and he loves flying as did Wayne. The die was cast and my emotions had been stamped into the metal. I was on my way into a new world, to meet and love new friends, to experience new joys and new sorrows, and there would be so many scars! The kind that furrow the skin and the others between your ears that only you or your closest friends ever know are there.

That cloud of dust had to and did become a memory, and everything Wayne had said was coming true with heady speed. A couple of the warbird pilots and owners started the Florida Wing of the Confederate Air Force. Hot damn, right in my own back yard! Jack Kehoe dashed off to the first meeting to become one of *the* select group, a charter member, no less. Boy oh boy — fighter pilots in beautiful P-51 Mustangs; flamboyant author Martin Caidin sitting at my table; honest-to-God heroes of the Second World War; and one very wildassed, fast-talking, convincing doctor, Leo Kerwin, drilling words into both my ears. I had been bit, the fangs were deep, and when the blush of pain and pleasure wore off I awoke to discover I'd consented to be a sponsor for a T-6.

That's one way it happens. You slide down the chute of pleasurable moments and buddies gathered about a table with fist-pounding and hard drinking, and it's all *real*, and you're up to your socks in responsibilities before you can turn around. According to that fork-tongued doctor I would find it real easy to be a T-6 sponsor. "First of all," ran the words of his siren song, "it won't cost you any money. Really, all you're doing is helping to show faith in this glorious establishment." Remember some other famous statements, like "The check is in the mail"? Same song. Funny I never realized at the time how much his siren song sounded like Oral Roberts before the pulpit. According to Leo Kerwin, I couldn't miss, I couldn't lose, I was terrific, and away we go.

Looking back on the orchestrated verbal onslaught brings me to wonder, as every potential new warbird owner should wonder before getting in over his head, would I do it all over again? Sure, I would. What the hell, I've already been through four marriages and you can't get screwed much better than *that*. Besides, if Leo Kerwin hadn't woven his net around me, even though his flashing hands were something like the hairy legs of a tarantula, N7988C wouldn't be nestled, *right now*, in front of my T-hangar, ready, willing, and very able to fly.

But, in the "old days" there we were, four fledgling sponsors, all the paperwork signed. Johnny Bolton, who ran around the skies in a P-38 or a P-51 as the mood suited him, has sold us a T-6 for a fair price. Terrific! You can't do better than buy a T-6 in top shape, right? *Wrong!* Jump in and fly, baby, right? *Wrong!* No maintenance problems, right? *Wrong!* In fact, it was a triple-damned *Wrong! Wrong! Wrong!*

Before the paperwork even cleared the hungry lawyers and the government offices, two of the four loyal true-blue sponsors flaked out of the deal. Number Three managed to wheedle his way into the airplane to fly the hell out of it without paying anyone a dime. Who paid? You guessed it. Good Old Fork-Tongued Kerwin and Fat, Dumb, and Happy Kehoe made all the payments, that's who.

Bless Leo, though, he did have a heart. He saw *my* heart bleeding to fly that airplane, and decided to bring the T-6 from Ti-Co on the east coast to Lakeland so I could at least start checking out. However, as he taxied in with verve and dash he spun her around sharply, and I watched with wide eyes as he peeled the tailwheel clear off the airplane, and when the screaming and shouting was done, we all piled into my Twin Comanche (I paid for the fuel, naturally) and rushed over to Sanford. God smiles sometimes; we found a hangar with the tube and other parts we needed to make that T-6 flyable again. I was getting a solid pain where I sit, and it sure as hell wasn't from too much T-6 time. But it was part of the learning process. *Always* check the tailwheel tire pressure to 50 pounds minimum and 52 pounds maximum. When do you check it? *Now*, and it is always *now*, not when it looks to be low. Another lesson: always check the mains while you have the gauge in your hand. What the hell, your knees are already scraped and you have holes in your nice new slacks.

The tailwheel was fixed, my frustration wasn't quite yet boiling over, and we hustled into the airplane, fired up, enjoyed the soothing rumble of the big round engine, and Leo rolled out to the active, flying the airplane and dominating the conversation. He was doing a damned good job with the basic fundamentals and I found his talking didn't bother me a bit. Finally he said what I had been wanting to hear: "You got it." My turn to fly, right? *Wrong.* So he screamed at me: "You got it, dammit!" *Now* I could fly, right? *Wrong.* That unmentionable radio had no intercom capability and I never heard a word! You know what that means? One, that it would cost a hell of a lot more dollars in the very near future, and two, that I knew instinctively the solution for just about everything was more money from yours truly.

I was kicking the side of the airplane and Leo was looking back at me to see if I was dead, and by hand signals we worked it out that I couldn't hear a thing, and the stick banged between my knees and he held up his hands and I took it and I *was* flying my own airplane. Finally! I flew straight and level, climbed, turned, let her horse around, got to know the touch and the feel, searched for the messages a good airplane gives its pilot, then into clean stalls, and into dirty stalls with gear and flaps down, setting up landing patterns and flareouts at altitude, Leo's hands and fingers doing the talking for him, breaks 360 degrees to the right and then 360 to the left, feel her fly, feel her tremble, do it all, get into all the regimes, feel the response with sudden throttle movement, slip, skid, wallow, and by golly, I know my airplane now! Right? *Wrong.*

Down we go into the pattern, real slick, and come about on final, rolling out with the nose down, speed up, remembering all the warnings never to let this sucker come even close to a tremble of a stall at low altitude. She'll kill you. But it was all right in the groove, and by God, I'm excited, grinning, thrilled, all-powerful, too dumb and happy to be scared of the Big Six. I brought her in for a three-point landing, eased over the fence, held the airspeed smack on, and I set her up to plant the mains and the tailwheel at the same time, a perfect landing, I've got the stick coming all the way back to the edge of the seat, man, I am hot snot and plunk we're down and — *wrong!* All of a sudden that Six careens off the runway, one wing grabbing for sky, the other trying to dig a furrow in concrete, and its brakes, throttle, aileron, rudder, everything moving like mad and Jeez, we've had it, we're going to pile up this thing! *Wrong.* We got her straightened out. But we came close to bending metal. First lesson above all lessons: don't mess with this mother. And never forget the old adage: your landing, your entire flight, never ends until the airplane stops, and is tied and chained to earth. Believe me, my friends and nonfriends and those who hanker to love the Six, this airplane will eat your lunch while you're still stirring your breakfast coffee.

As soon as I could spare the time after this momentous introduction to the Six I hauled tail to Ti-Co Airport where Leo would give me my final checkout in our airplane. The fun I looked to with such anticipation drowned in cockpit sweat. Mine, of course, because Leo Kerwin demanded not three or five landings, but no less than 15 bumps and grinds about the circuit. I was real pissed over the whole thing. What the hell was I supposed to be? Some greenhorn student? However, Leo did me a favor. Man, did I learn! That kind of practice makes perfect, right? *Wrong!* I thought I'd learned, but in truth it was probably a year later and maybe a couple of hundred landings down the line, some good, some blah, that I became competent in putting the Six back to earth.

Only the pilot knows if coming home is done with a really good landing. Nobody else. *Just because it looks good doesn't make it good*. Hell, I've made wheel landings some folks called brilliant, but some of those times was when I was set up for a three-pointer and just forgot to pull back on the stick and luckily recovered in time.

While we're at it, let's get to the big question. Which is right for the Six, the three-pointer or the wheel landing on the mains only? After all the years now behind me and all the landings, both good and bad, it's really a dead heat between planting and wheeling on the bird. My navy pilot friends who went through the SNJ (salt-covered AT-6) training program swear by the three-pointer. That makes sense. When executed properly the Six quits flying at 52 knots with full flaps and gear down and, if you're close to the ground at quitting time, you assume the bird will stay down. If your brakes work you can stop where you want to stop. Think of carrier training in the SNJ that required use of the tailhook and the *need* to plant it on in a three-pointer so the hook will grab a cable and snap you to a stop. You start out planting it on and it becomes the *only* right way to do it. The marines and the coast guard offer vehement agreement.

Now we cross the runway to where the blue-suiters regard all this with disdain. My old air force buddies such as Bob Casey, Roy Nelson, General Spaulding, Colonel McWhorter, and others, all of incredible talent, insist wheel landings are the best. When you line up to wheel it on you have a better view of the runway, you have less chance of stalling the Six too high above concrete, it's easier and safer to go around for a missed or balked approach since the airplane is in flying configuration until the tailwheel smacks the ground. The strange thing is that both groups have valid points and both groups of pilots fly the Six like they were poured into the airplane.

Well, I'm flying my own Six, and what's best for me? You could call it variations on a theme to meet unusual wind or field conditions. One in particular is a wing-low, one-wheel landing in a high crosswind condition when the runway length permits. I fly the Six 10 to 15 knots above normal approach speed right down to the threshold, which vastly improves response and maneuverability. You don't do that on a carrier deck, however, unless you like swimming with your airplane. And *don't* try it on a short or a soft runway. It's a good way to roll your airplane up into a ball.

To get into a short or a soft field I'm convinced that the full-stall, full-flap landing is the safest way to go. When it's executed properly you use only half the runway distance normally consumed in a wheel landing, perhaps even less than that.

Now, let me go back to those moments soon after I was cast loose into an unsuspecting world with my still "new" Big Six. Several airshows and *seven wingtips* later, along with one major right wing spar repair (God!), it became a major task simply to get the T-6 off the ground. My partner, he of the very capable lofting amidst the clouds, was obviously snakebit with landings, and the down time (which means you can't fly, pardner) was becoming a nightmare. It got damned right tedious every Friday afternoon to rush across the state in the twin, joined by Dick Fields (thank God for *his* help as a pilot, master mechanic, and troubleshooter) in repairing the dings, bends, scrapes, breaks, and curlecued pieces of T-6. But something good always comes from something bad. They give you horsepoop, grow roses. They give you lemons, sell lemonade. They give you dinged wingtips, get Dick Fields, and from those early days we formed a marvelous bond. He has an uncanny touch of wizardry with sheet metal and rivets, and most of all a love of aircraft and the thrill of keeping warbirds alive. Dick and I somehow always made the airshows exhausted, bleeding from working with sheet metal, and always fighting the clock, often right around the clock. You want to survive your life with a warbird? Get your own Dick Fields, brother.

Back to showtime, not only on the flight line, but with the lawyers again in the midst of things. We went back to the negotiating table. There were some hard feelings, snarls, and a few kicks under the table, and when it was over 7988C was *mine*, for better or for worse, for poorer and much more poorer.

Before I drag you into the trauma of sole ownership, let me get to a terribly critical area for anyone who wants to fly with other aerial machines — formation flying. Leo Kerwin had worked long, hard, and with true concern to have Hall Bond, a master checkpilot with the Confederate Air Force, come to Florida to qualify a bunch of our pilots for *safe* formation flying for our first big airshow. This Hall Bond was something else. Before we could even attempt to qualify in formation work, he made us prove we could fly in a safe and sane manner, that we could control our aircraft in any situation, and that we fully understood the responsibilities of being a formation pilot. Bond was an incredible man at the controls, he was a gentleman, and he imbued us all with his profound respect for safety. Every one of us is forever indebted to his opening the skies to a whole new world of flight, one I'd never suspected to exist. Even with a couple of thousand hours under my seat in many kinds of aircraft, with a commercial and instrument and multi-engine ticket, I was absolutely unprepared for formation work the way Hall Bond insisted it be flown. The only thing I can describe to you that's close to the Bond System would be a night instrument approach with a 200-foot overcast, quarter-mile viz, monsoon rains, low fuel, diarrhea — you get the idea.

Soon after I was the proud sole owner of the Big Six, Dick Fields and I worked up a progressive maintenance schedule. Let me tell you, flat out, that anything else is crazy. One of the Eleventh Commandments should read: *Always Stay On Top of Thy Bird's Needs.* The military had great guidelines to get maximum use of their iron machines and keep their pilots alive. All we needed to do was start someplace. But where? Our tires were worn, the brakes a hollow laugh, the radios erratic, the lights only sometimes, I had mag drops of 150 to 200 RPM (terrible), the paint was ratty, and *then* we discovered that the fabric was *legally* intolerable. It had dry-rotted and wanted to tear itself free of its framework of ailerons, elevators, and rudder.

We looked at one another, nodded, and made the *only* sensible decision. Start from Square One. We were going to take the Six apart piece by piece, we were going to do everything the right way, and make her like new. We projected a down time of four to six weeks, and I should have known the evil chuckles from Martin Caidin were an ominous warning. Because when the four weeks went by we were still disassembling and I had grave doubts about my decision. At such times you wonder if the best move wasn't to sell the airplane "as is" and look for one in better shape. It was too late. The bridges were burned and the drawbridge was up; the airplane was in too many parts and pieces to sell.

And so, in the finest tradition of true pioneers, we began. Before we knew what was happening hundreds of parts were strewn across my hangar floor. The skeleton of 7988C loomed naked and cold and shivering under harsh lights. If an airplane could whimper, this one whined. If she could have bit me I think it would have happened. Sure, shake your head about these feelings, but I've had the winged machines communicate with me, perform beyond anything in the manuals, be good to me, save my life when I was stupid with them. I listen, I feel, and now I heard metal bones rattling in the shadows.

189

The next lesson was one to pipe up the blood pressure. Heed these words well, my known and unknown friends out there. *Before* you start this kind of job, your buddies in the Confederate Air Force will swear they're going to help. So will the mechanics you know, and the hang-arounds, and the talkers, and the enthusiasts, and the hangar fliers, most of whom are blowhard drunks and big-mouths. Offer a ride and they'll trample you on the way to the airplane. Wait for them to show up to work and with very rare exception you'll be singing the blues to yourself in a land devoid of all other human souls. When the real nut-cutting begins they vanish into the woodwork. *You have very few friends who'll bust their chops to help.* I hope you never forget this warning, and always remember the few true-blues who are always there.

Days, nights, holidays, in my sleep, and during every spare moment, my world was the Six. Every Friday night Dick Fields left his job in the Piper Aircraft factory and drove to belabor the Six, and on Sunday night he was on his way home to snatch some sleep before starting work Monday morning. He put in nearly 300 miles every single weekend *for ten months!* He also brought friends with him every time he could sweet-talk someone into working. Some of the work we got was great and some not so good, but the willingness of these people to resurrect an iron bird was marvelous. Without all these people it simply couldn't have been done.

And there were the special people. We had some friends and some other unfriendly types who ignored cross words and glaring expressions of the past, because like *me* or not, they believed in what we were doing and they came to strip paint, scrape away old metal, feed and water the troops, and all of them put forth a great effort. And some of them didn't like flying, but *did* respect the past. Mike Araldi was a genius with his hands and inspired us through thorny moments. He glass-beaded the airplane and taught us how to do it, but along with the teaching he did most of the work himself. Along with priming and stripping and using special chemicals; wow. Ron Bumgardner and his girl friend could break away only rarely, so they showed up one day *and spent 72 hours nonstop* doing all the precision lettering, and the insignias and other work just so we could make our first airshow with the restored machine *looking* like the masterpiece we all struggled to create. My son, Mark, at that time was going to college, working part time, chasing girls, and hobbling about on a badly injured foot, and still managed (along with moaning and groaning and genuine pain) to work his butt off on the bird with us. At one point we were ready for really stripping down the Six. I mean every shred of paint, oil, grease, dirt, and whatever else had to be removed from the airplane. We needed all the help we could get because as fast as we finished we would be into priming and painting, and it was racing the clock.

There was a huge roll of thunder over the airport, and only a radial engine, or a bunch of radials, sounds like *that*. We looked into the sky and the big shadow was that tri-motored monster with Martin Caidin at the controls. He wheeled the Ju-52 up to the ramp and shut it down and unloaded parts and pieces we needed. He also left his wife with us! Dee Dee, who's been family from Day One with the Kehoes, stayed on for days, and worked days and nights, scraping, sanding, suffering from paint stripper burns, getting bit by everything that flew; and there was never a complaint about the crazy backbreaking schedules we ran. She, too, was entranced by this very special airplane. She was also a pilot and she'd been through some rebuilding campaigns of her own, and she could feel that what was happening here was so different as to be unique. The airplane seemed to be taking on the hopes and intensity of effort of all the people working on her.

I'm missing some names, but those I do miss here don't *need* recognition. Every time they see that Six in her new glory they're part of her. Of course, there were people we didn't even know who left their imprint on the bird. One day as we're tearing out hair and breaking fingernails on the engine a Cadillac Eldorado pulls up, ass end and tailpipes about an inch off the ground. Out steps this tall drink of water, beer in one hand, girl friend in the other, and a beautiful little eight-year-old girl. His voice boomed out at us.

"Hey, there, folks! Joe Araldi said you needed someone to adjust your valves and here I am." I'd asked Joe Araldi, or begged him, to find someone who could help us with that big Pratt & Whitney engine, and I guess Joe waved his magic wand, and here's Jerry Van Winkle, himself.

There's always *the* question: "How much?" I had to know what this dude would charge to adjust the valves, check the timing, and perhaps replace push rods, O rings, and valve cover gaskets. He sort of grunted, "Not much. Let's get it done. We'll talk the green over a cold one when we're through."

It sure was easy to grin and say, "Okay." I'd heard about this character and his, uh, unusual expertise. No shop, no books, and no conversation unless he started it. But did he ever have tools in the trunk of that Eldorado! He could get *any* radial engine running under any conditions day or night. Do you believe in rainmakers showing up when the world is parched? I do. We destroyed cases of cold beer, worked, drank more beer, and worked harder. That night he joined us at my home and started some serious drinking between heaps of steak. He roared through the whiskey to two in the morning, turned to look at me, and said, "I'm going. See you at the plane at seven sharp." My God, he meant it and he was hard at work when we arrived at 7:05 A.M. That afternoon we cranked the engine for the first time in six months, and it fired as the second blade came around. We were stunned. He was a miracle and he was gone as quickly as he appeared, beer in one hand and a twenty-dollar bill in the other. "Figger I drank twenty-five bucks of beer, and me and my lady and our little girl ate some thirty-five bucks of steak, and at least twenty in sippin' whiskey, so you owe me twenty, and it's been nice working with you folks."

Anyone else would have charged me $500 for what he did and *maybe* the work would have been good, but with all the screwing you get in this business the odds were against it.

Never forget for a moment (especially all you folks who want to do the whole thing) that in appearance alone our effort was monumental. We took off all the old paint and started from the tubing with all new chromate and paint, new hydraulics, new electrical system, new control surfaces, ailerons with a high rate of roll, all new lights, tires, brakes, glass, decals, and even instruments. We used gallons of paint stripper, the hottest stuff available, that cost about $35 a gallon. We felt crushed when we found intergranular corrosion (the most insidious kind) in a wing, even some snake skeletons in the tail, and more intergranular corrosion in a wheel well. That meant forming new metal to replace anything with a hint of corrosion. Dick Fields's hands looked like mad raccoons had chewed on them. We searched every AD note (Airworthiness Directive) that demanded changes and had only one of those to deal with. Money was going out the ying-yang and there wasn't any way to stop when you get in this deep. Sort of like eating peanuts and drinking beer.

Before we were finished — *ten months later!* — we had more than 3000 man-hours and an investment of $35,000 in the Six. Oh, you fork-tongued doctor, you!

Then came the day when all the hardware work was done. We could hardly believe it. We were down to the new paint job; a gleaming, beautiful SNJ would emerge from the homestretch. We gathered bright floodlights and everyone went to work to do the final job in one entire night so that at daybreak we could see the new miracle shining in the sun. My God, how we all worked that night, being eaten alive by every bug that ever migrated to Florida. In the morning, exhausted but proud, we looked at an SNJ that had the mumps. There were little knots and bumps and dimples and lumps all over the airplane! Remember the floodlights and the bugs? You ever count a few hundred bugs stuck to your brand-new paint job?

So we stripped it down again and took her inside the hangar and filled every crack and opening with rags and newspapers and sprayed bug killer everywhere until we were gasping and we worked all night *again*. This time, well, she sure did gleam brightly in the sun. Most beautiful damned airplane I've *ever* seen, and by God, now it was time to *fly!*

Four of us who flew the Big Six, USAF or USN colors didn't matter, got together to form the Jay Birds. Morris, Deems, Borchin, and Kehoe; that was us. We busted buttons with pride when the four Sixes formated together amidst high cloud mountains. The four of us — George, Chip, Jerry, and Jack — hit some real turbulence, but not the kind you find in the clouds. It was about this time the CAF (Confederate Air Force) started turning the screws on our wing commander, Dr. Leo Kerwin, and things were getting very dicey. Rumbles were heard about leaving the CAF and starting our own group. We ignored the politics and concentrated on the flying. From the first flight we made together the romance began. We were a *team*. George Morris was an ex-navy commander who had flown about everything with wings in the navy, starting as an SNJ instructor and running the gamut to the newest bent-wing jet fighters. Chip Deems and Jerry Borchin were both ex-military pilots and already knew all the fundamentals. I had more time than the others flying instruments, and I continued to fly just about every day in my job. Chip was flying huge C-130 turboprops in the active reserves and doing crop-dusting when he was home. Jerry was flying with Braniff, and when he came home he was flying balloons and his Stearman PT-17 or his T-6 or a Cub or anything else that snarled and had wings.

Airshows were sprouting all over the East Coast and we were in the thick of them. We flew our long cross-country junkets in formation to practice every moment we were upstairs. We were at Oceana Naval Air Station, Patuxent, Cherry Point, Beaufort, Langley — you name it and we were there. We began to fly so tight only inches separated our wings. Safety, precision, discipline, and a profound trust in one another. The crowds cheered and yelled and waved when we flew and we were proud. Hell, we used to grin and bang each other on the shoulders and backs and hug and dance on the flight line, we were so jazzed with that kind of flying.

The performances were not always good. There were some stinking blunders, some pilot error, and sometimes the conditions that brought these on were beyond our control. But when we goofed, no matter *what* the reason, George "The Skipper" Morris was all over us, not just with critiques, but with ways to prevent the mistakes from happening again. Of course, Gentle George *has* been known to lose his cool, hurl his hat to the ground and stomp on it, and remind us he hasn't forgotten a single verb from those salty phrases of his old navy days.

This is perhaps the best part of the gathering of the warbirds, anywhere in the country. We sang together, ate and drank together, flew together, and shared it all. Yet Skipper demanded professionalism. We briefed before every flight and critiqued when the engines were still hot. We couldn't sign an autograph or have a beer or rush off to the john for relief until the critique was over. It didn't matter whether we flew a short hop or a full show; we critiqued. Everything we did was well calculated for our safety *as well as for that of the crowd.* To those of you who will one day perform before thousands of people, *they* are your absolute and ultimate responsibility.

Even the wonders of life wind down or go their separate ways. Jerry Borchin and Chip Deems finally had to sell their Sixes and go on to more pressing matters in their lives. Once they left, the plans George and I shared to start a new Jay Birds team just never came to pass. Something was missing forever, and maybe that's the way it should be. Of all the Six pilots we knew, we seriously considered only one new prospect, a sawed-off, brute-shouldered wop by name of Jim Garemore. He hammered at every flight and every maneuver as if this day, *any* day, was his last shot to get into the air. In fact, we thought so highly of Garemore that even before the team broke up, we invited him to become an alternate because of his flying skills *and* to show how deeply we all respected him.

Today, well . . . the shows don't happen as often as they once did. Fuel costs have stopped the famous dawn patrols over cities and towns with the first light of day. The really great team flying we did has yielded to more cautious, basic-maneuver demonstrations. It's great for the crowd, but it lacks the snap of the old Jay Birds. Even coming down in our landing breaks, four Sixes going *SNAP!* — *SNAP!* — *SNAP!* — *SNAP!* three seconds apart and sharp break left, gear down, flaps down, prop flat pitch, okay, everybody come around and land in formation. I miss that and I miss my friends.

That's hardly to say there's not talent around. There are brilliant performers all about us, but let me make it clear there are also some real bungholes who don't belong in professional warbird flying. They know so little and think they can do everything. These are the people who never take time to *understand* what's going on about them; they miss the meaning, they have no conception of the blood, the sweat, the lump in the throat, and the tears. How do you measure those countless hours of working shoulder to shoulder to recreate a long-dead and near-extinct iron bird? Discipline, trust, dedication, pride, and honor. They have *not* left us. In the T-6 gang there's Rick Thompson, Ken Cooksey, Hank Ratliff, all with that little something special. George Baker and Tom Crevasse, and others, of course, still make the Six sing and dance lightly in the bright sun.

Well, I look back often. Somewhere back then, when we finished the restoration (resurrection is more like it), 7988C got her final touches. A brand new avionics package with *all* the goodies, the main and the backup radios, transponder, ADF. A complete Collins Microline with digital readouts and all the "nifty sex electronics" any pilot dreams of. The Collins people, bless 'em, came to our aid nights or weekends to meet some of the very special problems of operating their equipment in the harsh environment of severe maneuvers and g-loads in an airplane never intended to carry their wares. Hey, the woods are still full of great guys and they were some of them.

Once the Six was resplendent in her new shining blue armor I moved with her into a new world of aerobatics. I pleaded and begged with George Morris to teach me the *real* basics. And I gave that eternally patient man all kinds of fits. I was damn good on the gauges and I mastered formation work, but I simply couldn't get the feel of the barrel rolls and loops, the two basic maneuvers Skipper wanted us to do with absolute smoothness and precision.

More than once we had to quit in the midst of a training session because I screwed up so badly I needed time to *think* rather than fly. George waited patiently while I screwed my head back in place and we went upstairs again, and even then sometimes I floundered and came back down admitting defeat for the day. It was not easy, and it was too often not good. I had a wall before me I couldn't climb. Then, one day I was airborne with my son, Mark. He had just made his first solo in an old ragwing and was panting to try the Six. We did an hour of basic maneuvers at which Mark did very well, and suddenly I had the urge to go for a loop. I took the controls, cleared the area, heard every word George had ever spoken to me being repeated in my ears, and down we went, airspeed coming up to 180 mph, now, pull back steady and keep the nose moving at a constant rate through the maneuver — my God, it's working! — over the top, beautiful, WHOOPS! What the hell is wrong? She's not coming over, I'm flat on my back and the airspeed is almost nothing. Oh, Jesus . . . I've heard enough about these flat inverted spins. They're killers. And why should Mark buy the farm because of *my* stupidity? I reacted, shouting to myself, *Snap that aileron, get her over, recover.* I did, in a sort of half-assed Cuban Eight. I never did tell Mark, and if he reads this, he'll know how badly his old man screwed up that day.

I wanted to quit the aerobatics. I was crushed, but I just couldn't quit. I went back up, alone this time, and at 5000 feet I put the nose down, got her to 160 mph, pulled up in a 30-degree climb and put in the aileron. I was going for a roll, but halfway through the nose fell through the horizon and I was split-essing out of the sky at better than 200 mph and down to 3000 feet before I could recover. I was disgusted. I climbed back to 5000 feet trying to figure where I had screwed up again. *Then there was the light.* I had forgotten a critical move — forward pressure halfway through the maneuver. My next roll was fair to middling, and the roll after that I lost only 200 feet, and the roll after *that* was cause for idiot shouting and singing and rejoicing because I had it! Never again did I lose altitude in the rolls, but more important was that in winning this private battle *everything* fell into place, and I had become an aerobatic pilot and I was *comfortable.*

Then came 1979 and Homestead and *all* the pieces came together in the great air races and airshows of South Florida. They were all there, the Bearcats and Mustangs, the Lightnings and Sea Furies, Airacobras and Kingcobras, Hellcats and Corsairs, Spitfires and the greatest racing planes in the world. *All* the top names in air racing, brought into this single great event by the Whittington brothers in their attempt to return classic air racing to Florida. Those who came for the races were just as eager for the special demonstrations of aircraft and pilots, and a lot of people looked forward to *Iron Annie* and her redeemer, Marty Caidin. In those days Marty and I were inseparable, and where one went so did the other. Marty was extremely selective about who flew close formation with him and, in fact, when one SNJ pilot at an airshow flew in tight without permission, and didn't back off immediately, Marty threatened to ram him and we were afraid he would damned well do it with that iron bridge of an airplane.

Rarely did we fly more than ten feet apart on the longer cross-country flights, taking every chance to practice and perfect our routines. When I called him to hold her steady for some really tight inside work, the huge Ju-52 rode a rail and I would work my way in, literally within inches of the German bomber and with wings overlapping. That took enormous confidence on the parts of both pilots, let me tell you. Marty in his wisdom knew I loved that corrugated monster he flew as I loved my Six and we were long before this brothers in flight and in friendship, blooded by many things as soulmates.

Marty also had some juice with the Feds who were monitoring the races and airshow demos, so he called on his friend Red Gargaly to let me try for my aerobatic waiver, which was, next to my letter of authorization as Pilot in Command of the Ju-52, my dearest wish. Now, Gargaly did me a favor only in agreeing to officially critique my flying. That man never yielded an inch in performance demands from anybody. Marty and I had a 15-minute slot between the race heats to entertain that crowd of 100,000 spectators. We'd been doing a routine for a while so it wasn't any big deal for Marty to set up the scenario. There'd be head-on passes, he shoots me, I shoot him, we do a comic battle routine and even one wildassed on-the-deck run around the pylons to bring the crowd whooping and hollering to their feet.

But this was *my* big chance, the biggest ever, my first time to perform any aerobatics before a crowd. Just before takeoff I cornered Paul Poberezny, chief honcho of the Experimental Airplane Association, and who is, according to many pilots, the best all-around T-6 aerobatic performer in the business. "Paul," I told him straight out, "please help. I've got a shot for my FAA waiver and I

197

don't want to blow this one." In five minutes he outlined for me a perfect and safe aerobatic plan and the speeds at which I should do those maneuvers with a 500-foot belly cushion if I screwed up.

We took off in a pair and beat up the runway and then Marty lofted the Ju-52 slowly out of the way and gave me the stage. "You got it, Kehoe. She's all yours," he called. Sweet words! And into the test I went, knot in my throat, my mind racing, and diving for that 190-mph Paul recommended to me, and down to the 500 feet he told me to nail precisely, and back on the stick into the loop, and over the top we went and she was perfect, plenty of room to recover as I came down the back side, and the airspeed was good and I went up again into my first vertical roll *ever. It worked!* It was all happening! Around I came looking for *Annie* and there she was, right where I expected, exactly where Marty had briefed our positions. He had it all lined up for the landing in 60 seconds to give me time for my last maneuver, which, if I pulled it all off on our schedule, would bring me into position for us to land simultaneously before the crowd and that FAA watchdog studying my every move.

Oh, please, Lord, let me do it right — help me! All those great pilots down there were watching everything I did with hawk eyes and I pulled her up into an inverted climb, watched *Annie* slide by beneath me in perfect position, and while upside down I banged the gear free, split-essed over the top, and there was *Annie* directly in front of me and we touched tires simultaneously and it was all over and we taxied in and shut down. Red Gargaly grinned when I sort of stumbled up to him with pleading eyes. I never said a word. Red ended my agonizing with a firm handshake and words I'll never forget. "Well done, Jack." *I made it!* He approved my waiver for 500-foot aerobatics and the next day, all my anxiety gone, we did it again and I finished the act with a whistling low-level knife-edged pass, my first one ever, and into a snappy four-point roll and when it was all over I had my waiver down to a hundred feet!

Let me tell you, people, everything I ever wanted in flying in my entire life was now mine, and best of all was sharing it with my friends. Dick Fields was in his glory; he had done more with his mind and hands and sweat than anyone else to bring that Six into life. Marty and Dee Dee grinned with me; they knew how I felt, and they kept the thrill alive all that week and stepped into the background so I could be the man of the hour amidst that mob of racers. Hey, you can't shake the reality that the racing pilots were

198

really the heroes, for they're the ones who rub wingtips with death screaming around those pylons.

When the roar of the crowd and scream of Merlins dies down and you go home, there's the more prosaic element of life. Keeping the bird in shape, or you take a chance of a sudden violent end to everything you've built. We do our own annual inspections. Sound strange? Well, not really. First, it keeps down the cost, which can eat you out of house, home, and hangar. Second, if you really put your muscle to it and remain absolutely honest, and don't screw around with shortcuts, there isn't anyone who can do them as well as the people who risk their lives in the airplane. Dick Fields checks me and I check him. It's the old game of "Gotcha!" and it works. Always trying to catch the other in messing up somehow, finding those little mistakes that in an unsuspecting moment can kill you. We play this game for keeps, for life, and intimidating one another during inspection time is marvelous life insurance. Dick Fields is a skinny sort of guy but with a persistence that would nose out an alligator. "You want to be a good airshow pilot, then you got to understand each and every function of this airplane and its engine and all its parts, and if you don't want to do that with me, get yourself another boy." That's as final as you can get. Dick built airplanes and rebuilt them and tested them and he's seen death too many times, so when he gave me all the dirty bird jobs it was (I learned after a while) for my own benefit. I learned and I'm still learning.

Since that "once ultimate" day of putting the resurrected Six back into the air we've put a lot of hours and miles behind us. We now have a newly majored engine, almost every component new or rebuilt, with a total cost of some fifty grand and about 4000 man-hours. There's no doubt in my mind of cables failing, bolts coming loose, or any other sudden surprises. She's honey-smooth and I'll fly her anywhere, anytime. There aren't any shortcuts — that kind of magic is really a fairy tale. There's money and there's work, and if you're not ready for that, *stay out of this game*.

The years pile up and so do the major occasions. After the Great Restoration we took awards in every major show in which we participated. Our work was recognized by those who *know*. We covet our craftsmanship awards, and the plaques we've received at the EAA's Sun & Fun gathering at Lakeland, Florida, are the ones I prize the most. They're given to the restoration job by the aircraft owner that the judges decide is the best of all the aircraft attending. Those of you who've seen the marvelous work done on warbirds, anywhere in the country, know the competition and how proud we must feel.

Of course, there *are* events where the damned sun don't shine too good at all. Tom Shaw is a pilot friend from Atlanta, an avid warbird enthusiast, and member of the Valiant Air Command, who flies with us and at every airshow event works his butt to a fare-thee-well with the dirty ground jobs. He and his son Steve park cars, set up bleachers, put up chow control lines, clean up the grounds — anything that's needed. Our friend up Nashville way by name of John Baugh called one day. "Hey, we're opening a new museum in Tullahoma, and we've got the finest Staggerwings in the world, and we need you." John Baugh with the gold-plated tobacco juice cups in Mustangs and Messerschmitts, who can say no to you? So I called Tom Shaw, told him of the event, and did he want the back seat? Does a fat bear poop in the woods?

We pushed our way north in a driving rainstorm. At Fulton County Airport outside Atlanta we were in an angry front. We were down to 500-foot ceilings and a half-mile visibility and it was cold and it was raining cats and lizards. What the hell, I'd told Baugh we'd make it, so we pressed on, soaking wet from just getting into the airplane. It was raining like a tall cow dumping on a flat rock and the whole world was wet. We should have stayed on the ground where the weather was terrible, because we launched the Six into a black, undulating, snarling sleet storm.

Good things come in unexpected packages. Bad things come at any time, like right now as I watched that gleaming, shining, sweat-created new blue paint peeling off the wings in the driving sleet. I did everything but sing and beg Atlanta Approach Control for some help in getting out of the worst of the sleet and turbulence, but it doesn't help much if you're not in a fat winged egg with lots of stews you can introduce to those cruds when they're off duty. I heard the old familiar refrain of "Continue your heading, maintain your altitude, and we'll get back to you." One day I'll get them in *my* home town, but in the meantime the damage was done.

By the time we pushed through to Tullahoma the sky had closed in. No longer the 1500 feet and five miles I'd been given in the forecast. As has been so common, reality had nothing to do with the FAA weather briefing. But I hadn't come this far to let this cock-amamie system make me break my promise to John Baugh. I scanned the charts; A VOR approach was in order, but I could

Pale-blue aggressor colors mark many a T-6 today to keep their military authenticity in flying mock combat for airshows. One of the first to sport the fancy new paint threads was Jack Kehoe's Texan. *Asgard Flite Photo*

never make it with the ceiling and visibility I faced. *Unless*, that is, I cancelled my IFR flight plan when I was directly over the field. I did just that. Free of the shackles of officialdom, we came down on instruments we trusted, broke out directly over the field at 200 feet, dumped the gear and flaps, and circle-landed with a field wide open to us.

They had some madman waving his hands and jumping with wild joy. Who the hell expected to see a Six punching through *this* crap? There was more joy than common sense to our friendly greeter, because I followed his signals closely and ended up with my airplane buried to the axles in grassy mud. All this time to start sinking the airplane!

I forgot all that when I climbed down and looked at my airplane. I was sick. More than half the paint was gone. My pride and joy looked like it had been through a threshing machine. There wouldn't be any awards for 7988C this trip. However, the local gods sort of grinned, and the Six won a most exclusive award as being the *only* warbird to get into the field that day.

Shortly after the sleet scrubbing, I selected the new paint scheme for the Big Six. She had always been a leader in being different and there was no need to change that philosophy. When we were through with the next monumental effort, she appeared to the world in Air Force Aggressor colors, a sort of pale-blue-and-gray-ghost scheme that gives her a very special look, indeed.

The world is quieter now. The runways await us, the bleachers wait to fill. We're ready, and she awaits the next call.

Please call.

———————— ☆ ————————

Terrible George

If a pilot, deep within himself, doesn't
consider himself to be the best damned
pilot there is, he belongs on the ground.

KEN STALLINGS

That the T-6 is sexy and alluring, that it is a powerful and heady perfume, is a grim reality of life. Grim because too many friends who leaped off into the wild blue did so without really knowing what they were doing. We've been beating this issue with a big stick ever since we got into the business of flying these machines, and just as long as we're talking warbirds and pilots just coming into the game we're not going to ease off one bit. We'd rather have you with us instead of drinking toasts after your permanent departure.

Pick a dandied banker, spiffy and absolutely correct in his three-piece suit and shined shoes and neat-o attaché case, and throw in a beautiful wife by name of Joan and some kids who can wring your heart inside out with a shy smile; you peel off the label and there's one of the old masters of pilot instruction known among the warbird trade as Terrible George. Or, if you're inclined to formal introductions, George Morris will do quite well, thank you.

This, ah, banker earned his name of Terrible George as a U.S. Navy instructor in the SNJ, and he also crushed, stomped, cussed out, and taught to fly uncounted students in the T-28 and a wide variety of other aircraft, many of which suffer a reputation for terrible manners. But in the SNJ/T-6, George went far beyond instructing or simply flying. He became an artist in the airplane.

No one, but no one, puts on smoother or more beautiful aerobatics in the Six than does Terrible George. He transforms a bulky, powerful, snarling machine into a graceful swallow, a bird that defies gravity and the laws of aerodynamics.

In this chapter, George shares with *you* the touches of flying this airplane that can come only from the long-experienced master. Join us for an insider's private affair —

———————— ☆ ————————

Thanks, but I can only stay a minute. Understand you're a T-6 fan. Great airplane. Sure, I'd love to talk about flying the Texan. Where can we start?

What's that? I'd love one. Make it a Scotch, and, ah, light on the water. Fine; thank you. Now — what a comfortable room — about flying the Six . . .

You already know the history of the bird, but let me say that it's legendary in its own time, and that's saying a lot. It's been flown by more military pilots for more hours than any other airplane ever built. It's been described as the "best scout trainer in the world" and "the most widely used airplane in history." Maybe legendary isn't wide enough, because this airplane is an institution unto itself.

My own experience with the SNJ, which is the designation under which I came to know this beast, spans more than three decades and what I'm proudest of is that I've never had an accident in this thing. From this vantage point of my own experience I can make some remarks that are terribly important to people who are about to fly this machine. You start off with the unbreakable rule: the Six demands your respect *and it's going to get it one way or the other*. It requires a humility and a sensitivity to let you be good in the airplane. There's only one way to fly the Six and that's as a professional. Okay, now for the second rule: accept the Six for what it really is — a trainer.

Before we get into the flying, let's examine what seem to be those contradictions I just gave you. The first is a caveat about treating the airplane with anything less than veneration, and a serious personal commitment to putting forth your best effort to become proficient in the Six. The second point admonishes the Six pilot to avoid judging this aircraft as an instrument of ego enhancement.

Anything that goes beyond the quiet feeling of accomplishment derived from gaining true flying skills, and the sheer joy of flight itself, is both suspect and dangerous.

Sure, I know the Six in many cases was flown solo by kids who had scarcely more than twenty or thirty hours' total time in *any* aircraft. It also killed quite a few *high*-time veterans who ignored my point number one. So, respect this bird if you want to keep on drinking good Scotch like this. Let's get on with the flying.

There's an old saw that familiarity breeds contempt. Be careful of that. It's a sucker hole into which you fall permanently. Your own attitude as a pilot, being familiar with the machine, all its systems, operating limitations, normal and emergency procedures, is what you *must* follow to attain flight proficiency. And everything I just said is magnified tenfold if you don't have the enormous benefits of military training.

Before you ever turn on the switches in the Six, do your work on the ground. *Get the flight handbook.* It's your bible, your teacher, your survival kit. You can get pilot manuals and operational handbooks for the SNJ and T-6 series from many publishers. I'd suggest getting your hands on any other flight training handbooks and programs the navy or the army used with the airplane. There's always some extra word of advice in one that the other doesn't have. Then, read everything you can on the machine. Just about all the aviation magazines have carried articles on the Six, and when you go back ten years or so to read these stories, you gain all the advantages of seeing just how other pilots view the machine, and their own experience with it.

What are you learning? The general background, first. You become familiar with the territory. Every time you read or hear something about the airplane *it has meaning for you.* You never waste another word once you do that. Know the characteristics of the bird. Know the airspeeds, power settings, engine and systems operating ranges, all the procedures, and get them down cold. Write down all the trouble spots. List all the warnings. Know the danger areas. You'll come to recognize them *before* you get into them.

Don't ever take that airplane up yourself without knowing your emergency procedures. When you think you have them down pat, I'll tell you right now that you *won't.* Because if you concentrate on doing things by reflex, the odds are you'll mess up. That means you need practice, practice, and more of the same; and you get that by reading the manuals, sitting in the bird on the ground, and doing all the emergencies until you can, literally, do them with your eyes shut. You reach out and touch every control, switch, and handle in that thing until you identify them blindfolded and you can move any which way and always come up with the right answer.

Sounds too much, right? Well, remember what I said about military training. *My* students could do that or I wouldn't let them go. There might be a fire, a hydraulic problem, a runway disaster facing them, or an electrical failure or a hung gear or a runaway prop or anything. Being upstairs as a lone neophyte is not the time or place to learn to survive emergencies in any airplane, most especially the Six. I'll add another point. When we were instructing, our cadets were given at least two simulated emergencies on *every* dual hop. I'll repeat it in different words: in an aircraft like the Six, your response to the unexpected needs to be automatic, expeditious, and *appropriate.*

At this point, like right now, you can even test your mental attitude. If, regardless of your experience level, it is characterized by a disdainful sigh and the old rolling of the eyeballs along with the impatient comment that "I know all *that* stuff," just be very aware of that reaction, and carefully evaluate its validity and whether it's appropriate.

Okay, the glass is almost empty, and so much for tests and attitude adjustment. Let's move on to some rudimentary counsel, the basic stuff. *Learn the procedures of your aircraft and you have eliminated ninety percent of all the trouble into which you may ever get.* Let me give you some basic rules of my own.

ONE: Follow the preflight procedure outlined in the handbook. Check *every* item *every* time. (Just remember Kehoe and his tailwheel.)

TWO: Go through your takeoff checklist prior to rolling onto (taking) the runway. Check *every* item *every* time.

THREE: Go through your landing checklist prior to beginning your approach. Check *every* item *every* time.

FOUR: Go through your shutdown procedures and secure the aircraft carefully. Check *every* item *every* time.

FIVE: Learn your cockpit layout so that you can locate every instrument, switch, lever, knob, control, *whatever,* and you can *operate all systems blindfolded.*

SIX: Be safe.

SEVEN: Don't stall. Repeat this rule before and after each meal and every other time you think of it. *Don't stall.*

The student aviators who soloed the Six after a few dozen hours of dual instruction, without any previous flight time, had something very special going for them. We called it ground school. It was intensive. These kids had a course of programmed learning that prepared them to handle the mental and physical challenge of controlling the aircraft at the conscious level, while supported by a formidable body of knowledge at the subliminal levels.

This learning discipline was *forced* upon them. It was *not* fun for the cadet. It may be less fun for you, but you've got to discipline yourself. Think of it this way. The cadets had *only* the flying to worry about, from ground school on up. They didn't worry about earning a living, the wife and kids, the neighbors, political meetings, taxes, or anything else except hard work on the ground and in the air. They had tunnel vision. They *had* to hit the books and the classrooms before taking off. If you want to make up for this lack on your part, then it's going to take a lot of self-discipline to compensate for what you'll never get in your own life.

But your family is going to be awfully lonely if you *don't* do these things. Now, that's no guarantee, of course. But I'll tell you what, as I sit here and enjoy this fine Scotch of yours. You give me any hundred pilots like yourself, with all your years of experience, *but lacking this military training,* and turn you all loose in the T-6. And you know what? Somewhere between ten and thirty of those people will be dead within a year.

One last thing before we crawl into the cockpit and strap 5000 pounds-plus, and 600 snarling horses of very tough machinery to our butts. It's in addition to everything I've told you, plus so much that's been left unsaid. You want to stay alive? You want to become a good T-6 pilot? You want to become proficient in the airplane?

Get yourself a good instructor with military T-6 experience. Whatever you spend, it's got to be cheap. The cheapest insurance you can buy. Besides, he'll let you become *good* at what you're doing. Then you're flying safely and capably instead of showing off. The military instructor with T-6 experience is your link with the past and your bridge to safe and enjoyable flying in the Texan. It's a magnificent airplane. Why should you be any less than a magnificent pilot?

Let me say a few words about the preflight inspection. I'm not going to go through the drill here and now, because you'll never remember all those many details. But I can lead you down the right path. Completely aside from the preflight as it's outlined in the handbook, which you must carry with you at all times and use as your only reference to survival, you should take the time to become acquainted with the airplane.

And I mean slow, easy, and comfortable. Walk around it. Study it. Do you really understand all its parts and sections? Find out what control moves what system to the trim, for example. *Look inside the airplane.* When you go to a doctor he doesn't restrict his examination to your exterior skin and a glance down your throat. Why do less with the machine in which you're going to bet your life? Sit in the front seat. Then the back seat. Open everything and look inside. Find out what works, why it works, how it works. Another example. Look for the control sheaves. What's that? You never heard of a *sheave?* Then you're not ready to fly the Six! Find out what it is and what it does, and after you've done that, drop a few rags here and there in the airplane, and you'll be stunned to discover how easily and quickly a forgotten rag can *foul your controls.*

There is no way to overemphasize the need for meticulous *detail* in your walkaround and inside-the-airplane preflight. Never forget that your airplane doesn't receive the full-complement maintenance and "hang the cost" program of the military. Something doesn't work in the navy or army training program? They change it. They have warehouses full of parts and limitless manpower. Do you do everything with a blank check? If you don't, then *you* have to make up for the difference.

More than you ever did before, look for tears or breaks or bulges, and always keep an eye out for the wrinkles that denote possibly severe structural damage you can't see otherwise. The *only* SNJ/T-6 you can fly has been around for a long time, it's been flown long and hard, and I can just about guarantee it never has had the proper maintenance through the years *your life deserves.* All of a sudden snapped rivets or dried-out rubber or neoprene fittings or gaskets are life-attention matters, and don't you forget it.

I'm presupposing, of course, that your airplane *has* had a really meticulous, spyglass inspection before you'll fly it. Let me tell you something about buying a T-6. If the records don't show that it's been done, you'd be wise to consider a wing pull. They take the wings off the airplane and they check everything. I flew a Six that on the books was in great shape, but a friend of mine beat me around the head and shoulders until I did a wing pull. Guess what. The wings of this airplane had come from a different model than the fuselage. For argument's sake, we'll say we had T-6G wings on a T-6D fuselage. Whatever the models, there were old fuel cell bladders in the wing that hadn't been connected for years, and they were crazy for collecting rust, and that wing was structurally deficient.

If they can fool an old hoss like me, friend, you can be pretty vulnerable yourself.

One more jarring note, aside from all the many details you'll learn yourself. The longer you're around propellers, the more easy you feel about them. *Don't*. Especially with that big Pratt & Whitney. Propellers bite, cut, mutilate, and kill. And I've seen foolish people move a T-6 prop and have that prop swing on them without warning, *with the switches off*, and separate limbs from the body. Let me tell you, you'll see it only once to *never* forget it. Humility and respect begin long before you climb into the cockpit.

Most pilots today sneer at the idea of a fire guard standing by when they start their airplanes. But sooner or later, a T-6 during startup is going to catch on fire, and if you're right there with a fire bottle when it happens you can handle it immediately. Let me dig back into the bag of memories to explain. We were flying an airshow at Patrick Air Force Base in Florida. The whole VAC gang was there. The air force had firemen and engines and equipment up and down the line. One T-6 pilot, a 40-year veteran in the front seat, started his airplane. Fuel ran down beneath the bird and it backfired and it caught on fire. *No one was standing by the airplane —* no one from the fire guard crews, that is. The pilot had no idea why the engine wouldn't start. He kept cranking and pumping fuel and the flames raced down the belly. Other warbird pilots saw what was happening and grabbed extinguishers from their own planes and ran like mad to the burning T-6, *whose two pilots still didn't know was ablaze!*

When they saw the frantic signaling they left that Six like raped apes. Smart. The air force crew ran up with big extinguishers, and one brave soul rushed right up against the flames and blew his extinguisher into the engine exhaust. *He had been fire guard only on jets and really didn't know what to do*, and his bravery was wasted because it didn't do a thing to stop the flames. The other pilots poured their stuff into the engine intakes and got the fire out. A few seconds more, however, and that T-6 would have been a giant fireball. So have the fire guard ready and *be certain he knows what to do.*

This isn't the time or place to go through every detail, as I've mentioned before. Your handbook, your own studies, and that instructor I hope you'll get will attend to that. But do follow an old system. When you're in the cockpit and going through checklists for prestart and start or anything else, *touch every item as it's called off.* I really mean that. Physically touch it. It becomes habit, it's good procedure, and good procedures are like parachutes. They can save your life.

That's one more item. It's macho to fly without a parachute these days. On many flights you really don't need one. But if you're learning or you're flying in bad weather or at night, or doing aerobatics, you're crazy, friend, *not* to have the chute. In fact, you should have that chute in your airplane *any* time you fly, and that means a chute in both seats. The Six is designed to use a seatpack chute as a seat cushion. Anything less simply takes away from you an event, a procedure, and the equipment that can save your life when everything else fails you.

Let's talk some about basic flying. What? Sure, I'd like a refill! That really is great Scotch. You're also being a gracious host to this somewhat overweight and graying mentor, and I hope you keep listening.

So let's get back to the first basic maneuver. It's like the First Commandment. You can't do anything else without going through Number One. What's that? Taxiing. I'm talking about taxiing. Oh, you don't think the conversation is really getting more exciting. Well, how do you think you get to the runway? And if you can't maneuver between planes and obstacles, my friend, you *won't* get to the runway. You'll scrunch up against another plane, or a fuel truck, or a sign post, or get friendly with a drainage ditch.

Seriously, if you'll observe T-6 drivers, you'll admit quickly that their movements along the ground are somewhat like an albatross with a busted leg. Many a guy who flies trikes and has thousands of hours finds taxiing the Six a humbling and frustrating experience. People new to the airplane use excessive RPM, excessive forward speed, and excessive braking. They do almost everything to excess. It's a terrible waste and it isn't safe. Your competent T-6 instructor can demonstrate proper techniques for minimal use of power, and use of rudder, supplemented by brakes to S-turn the aircraft and taxi smoothly, safely, and effectively. Learn to do it

North American's ubiquitous T-6 is the Ultimate Training Machine. You either fly it the way it's supposed to be flown, or you get bitten — and fast. But when you're right, it's the Fun Machine! *Photo by Bob Reid*

right. Many folks never have, but it's never too late. Want to be humbled? Put a safety driver in the front seat and then taxi the Six from the *back* seat. I promise you an interesting time.

When you're all through phumphering down the taxiway and you go through all the proper procedures of your pre-takeoff checklist, you roll out to the runway and set up every last detail, and then you discover something that is just delightful. It's a secret you should share.

The T-6 wants to fly. It is eager to take wing, and that's a wonderful feeling. Let her go! With proper technique, that cast-iron monster will lift off like a feather. Don't force the airplane and don't restrain her. *Let her fly when she's ready,* and she'll never disappoint you.

Proper training on your part means you know the basics, so at this moment we needn't burden ourselves with directional control on the takeoff roll, or the need for smooth application of power, or holding the stick full back during the initial run, or dropping your heels to the deck to get your leaden feet off the brakes. You know all about that, right? Let's focus attention on transitioning to flight.

As speed increases during the roll, relax the back pressure on the stick. As the speed continues to build, ease in a little forward pressure until the tailwheel comes unglued and the nose lowers smoothly to the takeoff attitude. This is a nose position *between* level flight and climbing attitude, and you'll come to recognize it with experience. Maintain this attitude throughout the takeoff run. As the airplane approaches liftoff speed, apply a gentle back pressure to the stick and the Six will fly smoothly from the runway. With a little practice you can do it every time.

Soon, you will disdain the takeoff technique of the less proficient T-6 driver. You'll be critical of the nose-low position during the takeoff roll, and the obvious ham-fisted over-rotation as he yanks his steed abruptly into the air. You might even be tempted to share your skill and knowledge with those less fortunate. *Do so with humility.*

Watch Your Attitude

One point becomes abundantly clear to the neophyte T-6 driver: *this is a trim-tab airplane.* Normal flight, climb, turns, level flight, glides, and landing approaches are best accomplished when control pressures are trimmed constantly out of rudder and elevator. Thus everything is accomplished with a smoothness that marks the old pro. Besides, you don't have to work so hard.

Later, as you get into formation flying, you'll appreciate beyond your wildest dreams the value of trim in flying a smooth lead or maintaining a solid wing position.

Strange to say, there's no hard-and-fast agreement on the power settings to fly the Six. That's because the different services had different ideas on this subject. They all worked, and I suppose the planned missions affected the handbooks that went to the aviators. So I'll use more recent experience with a used airplane, which means *all* T-6 airplanes. To me, the optimal operating ranges of the dependable P&W R-1340-AN-1 have dictated the settings, and airspeeds have been established accordingly for various aircraft powered by this fine round engine. (I hate to bring in Martin Caidin at this point, but he studied R-1340 operations and wrote a definitive work on the *used* engine that almost all of us also use as our bible.)

In the navy's flight training manual, power settings and airspeeds (in knots, of course) were as follows:

CLIMB: Clean: 30 in. MP and 1950 RPM = 95 knots
      Wheels down: Same power = 90 knots
      Wheels down and half-flaps: Same power = 80 knots
      Wheels down and full-flaps: Same power = 75 knots
NORMAL CRUISE: 23 to 28 in. MP and 1850 RPM = 120 knots
ACROBATIC CRUISE: 26 to 28 in. MP and 1950 RPM = 130 knots
POWER-OFF GLIDE: Wheels and flaps up, idle throttle,
      and you get 95 knots.
      Power-off glide with wheels down
      and flaps up = 95 knots.
      Power-off glide with wheels up *or* down
      and half to full flaps and the throttle full
      back and you get 80 knots.

☆

Want the best (most efficient) climbing situation? The Flight Handbook always has the answer. METO, or maximum continuous power, is 32.5 in. MP and the RPM at 2200, and 95 knots airspeed, all of it calculated on a standard day at sea level (29.92 and 59° F).

You will see quickly the great range of power through throttle and propeller. If you want maximum range, then you pull back to 1600 RPM and go to 25 to 26 inches MP, and keep leaning until she smoothes out. Now remember this: unless you have a favorable wind at altitude, you won't really save any fuel climbing for efficient cruise because you'll waste that fuel in the climb. If your airplane is neat and clean, you'll true out at 120 knots. A quick calculation with these figures tells you you're doing almost as well as your wife's 1970 station wagon (you've got the Vette, right?) by giving you about six miles to the gallon.

Okay, I'll admit that this stuff is so boring that we're both ready for another drink. I'm really not trying to interpret the manuals so much as emphasizing to you that there is *always* a source of reliable information. So let's go back to flying, and probably the one area that needs attention even more than landing. What would that be? No, *no*. Not aerobatics. You're too eager. *Slow flight*, that's what.

The unique thing about naval aviation is landing an airplane on a boat. Any fighter jock wearing the blue suit of the U.S. Air Force will tell you this is an act so unnatural it's almost a perversion of returning to earth. Although they won't admit it publicly, many naval aviators agree. Be that as it may, one thing necessary for a successful carrier landing (often called a controlled crash) is flying slowly. *This means on the ragged edge of the stall.*

As an SNJ helmsman with low time, you may encounter some apprehension of an approaching stall as the airspeed hovers at about 70 knots. Consider that fledgling carrier pilots with less than 200 hours' total time brought the SNJ aboard undersized flattops at airspeeds in the realm of 58 knots. I say all this to stress the point that the aircraft is capable of operating at very high angles of attack, low speeds, and reduced power settings. No sweat, right?

"Slow flight" is that flight attitude in which the airplane is flown in the "dirty" condition, wheels and flaps down, and at an airspeed near the minimum at which controlled flight can be maintained.

Slow flight is a *must* for examining the low end of the SNJ flight envelope. As you fly the airplane along the bottom edge of the envelope, you'll gain confidence in your ability to control it in the landing configuration. Making the transition from normal cruise in the clean condition to slow flight, with everything hanging out and back again, while holding heading and altitude, and keeping the ball dead center, may not be your idea of fun. But you may be assured that it's a worthwhile exercise. And if you're *my* student, you do *not* get turned loose solo in this airplane until you can do all of the above, and it is to be done well.

Maneuvering the aircraft — turning, climbing, descending — at minimum airspeed will reinforce the importance of proper use of trim tabs *and* a light touch on the controls. It will also remind you that in the landing configuration — slow flight — when maintaining a constant attitude, *the throttle controls your altitude.* Also, with constant power, *the fore-and-aft pressure of the stick controls your airspeed.* Sure, you've heard that before, but we all need reminders now and then. You see, some folks have forgotten those basic rules, as is evidenced by the inconsistent and sometimes hysterical approaches and landings often made by private pilots.

There are few times when "feel" is more important than anything else in controllability than during slow flight. An instructor can (and will) run you through a series of what I call degraduated speed runs. Under different aircraft configurations he will have you steadily reduce your airspeed, both in clean and filthy configurations, until you're shaking and buffeting on the edge of the stall, *but still flying your airplane.* There is only one way to learn this system and it is in the airplane in the air and flying. Again and again I cannot overstress the importance of learning all these little tricks of competent flight while holding heading and altitude con-

214

stant. You really hone your flying skills with this sort of training.

There is a natural fear about flying so slowly your airplane rumbles and bucks and feels sloppy and you have to fight the controls. But if you use trim properly you won't need to fight. The stick pressures will be light and sensitive and you can truly *feel* the airplane trying to tell you what's happening. *Listen to it!*

Now, slow flight obviously means flying on or near the edge of a stall. There are different kinds of stalls. Deliberate, clean, dirty, hard, soft, rolling, whip, and worst of all, unexpected.

The navy cadet went through a strict routine of stalls. They simulated conditions of flight that might sneak up on him and knock him out of the sky.

Each stall was presented by the flight instructor in the format we called What, Why, and How. We described the stall and the conditions that could lead to its occurrence, as well as an explanation and demonstration of execution and recovery. If this sounds a bit formal, it's because instinctively we all knew how important it was. We demanded that our students know the power settings, entry airspeeds, and sequential procedures and be able to execute each stall and recovery *with precision*. This experience at the lower edge of the flight envelope was ingrained to the degree that recovery from dangerous attitudes was automatic. And many a cadet's *conditioned reflexes* saved him from pranging his machine as a result of an insidious stall.

Again, this isn't a review of the Flight Handbook. It's a reminder as part of this friendly conversation that until you master *all* the envelope of stalls, *you are not safe to fly a T-6 by your lonesome.* Learn your airplane, read the book, then *study* the book, check the dates of your parachute packing, and get your instructor into the air with you.

That same instructor won't quit with slow flight and stalls, because getting into a stalled condition can lead, deliberately or through panic or loss of control, to a spin. And let me tell you, my friend, the T-6 *spins*. It's in her heart and soul. What's a spin? You've never done one? My gosh; I forget. *They don't require spin training in civilian life.*

Maybe that's why so many pilots get killed when they should be coming home to their families. They never truly learned that you can stall an airplane, you can get into an aggravated stall, and your airplane autorotates. What's that? What's an autorotation? It's just another name for spin, or more literally as the old-timers called it, a tailspin. The specific explanation is that, in a spin, the airplane is completely stalled and is falling toward the ground nose-low, following a corkscrew path through the air.

If you're lucky, you can get out of that one easily enough, but there are other spins caused by severe off-loading of CG, or when an airplane spins flat, or oscillates, or goes inverted and spins, or any crazy combinations of these. In some of them, unless you have a parachute and use it quickly enough, it's your last flight.

Once again, you've got to do it to learn it, and above all, nothing replaces experience in learning how to recover from a spin. Your family will love you for it, which is better than for them to cherish your memory because you didn't know how. I'll stay with this subject just long enough to give you a few pointers about the SNJ in spins. Like any other airplane, it will never spin unless it is first stalled (deliberately or accidentally). When you train for spins, you'll learn how to bring up the nose and reduce power and RPM and all the hundred and one things necessary to practice everything properly, so I won't state now what you *must* learn by studying the manual before you test your instructor's patience.

You'll get into a deliberate spin with power off, stick full back, and one of your feet stomped hard against the rudder stop. There are some personal points I feel I *must* make to you. During the spin, keep the stick fully back, and hold down full rudder pressure. *Don't* look at the ground directly over the nose, but look out toward the horizon at an angle. That's critical. Keep track of your reference line so that you'll know how many spins (turns) you've made. This gives you the practice that will let you graduate later to precision spins.

Spin recovery follows specific steps. Make sure you haven't moved that throttle; it's to be in idle (power off). First, apply full rudder opposite to the direction you're rotating. Follow this immediately with positive (and I mean sharp, definite, *positive*) forward stick. Rap that sucker forward, man. Hold the controls in this position until you stop whirling around. *Instantly* neutralize the rudder, making certain you're in a straight dive, without skidding.

The trick now is not to overdo things. To start recovery, gradually apply smooth back pressure with the stick. *Don't jerk it back.* As the nose approaches the horizon, set the RPM (propeller control) approximately two-thirds the way forward on the quadrant, apply throttle smoothly, and then readjust RPM to what you need for continued flight.

There are those common sense rules always to observe. You may be diving with great speed and that's when recovery must be gradual. How do you judge this? Well, there are g-meters which tell you the gravity loads you're pulling, and there's also the seat of your pants, which is best of all, because you can feel the body pressure against the seat, as well as increased pressure on the controls. If you pull out too sharply you can black out personally (by draining the blood from your brain), and even if you hang in there without gray fog in your head, you can also cause the airplane to stall again. At that point it will probably enter a *progressive spin*, which can be considerably more violent than the first one. So you need a good instructor, a good airplane, a parachute, and lots of practice. Strange to say, after you gain proficiency, spins can be fun and executed with great precision.

I have a personal prescription here. Practice this at home, again and again and again, until every move is instinctive, pure reflex. This is one way you'll observe a cautionary note with the SNJ/T-6, which is NEVER TO USE AILERONS TO GET INTO THE SPIN OR DURING RECOVERY FROM THE SPIN. Keep the ailerons neutral. And remember that when you're spinning, your control movements are ALWAYS brisk and positive. I know, I know, you've been taught that in almost all flying, slow and cautious control movements don't overstress the airplane, but in coming out of a spin in the SNJ, those same slow and cautious control movements not only cause excessive loss of altitude before recovery, *they may have no effect on the spin.*

After all the flying, there's always the game to be played called coming home. Let's face it; no flight is ever a good one unless your landing, stopping, shutting down, and tieing down are also carried out just as well. And the Six has an undeserved reputation for ground looping. You should see your face! Like most people, you've heard the Six is a grizzly bear when it comes to operating on the ground. Well, there's always as much gray as black and white in these statements. Because the Six *does* have a record for chewing up pilots and wingtips and ailerons or even buckling the gear. Just keep in mind the low-time students involved in these accidents and incidents, and the difficult challenge that the Six represented for these people, and you'll be more understanding.

Actually, the SNJ/T-6 is relatively stable, as taildraggers go, with wide gear legs and behavioral characteristics that make the "wing down" approach an effective technique for handling a crosswind.

As with all taildraggers, the landing isn't over until the aircraft is at a dead halt. "Trike" pilots have a tendency to relax after touchdown. This propensity is inappropriate (and silly) to landing airplanes with tailwheels. With the Six, the fun is just beginning when you touch down. Tricycle gear types miss all the excitement.

You can always spot a competent Six pilot by his approach and landing. The old pro brings it around on rails. Airspeed is locked on 80 knots (for full flaps), and a constant rate of descent is held through the approach. Transition to a three-point attitude is silken-smooth, and the touchdown solid, without any swerve afterward.

The approach determines in large measure the success of the landing. To make a normal landing, you plan your approach carefully and you visualize a point a foot or two above the ground for the three-point attitude. The airplane is kept in this attitude until it fully stalls, and settles gently so that all three wheels make contact with the ground simultaneously. It sure sounds simple enough, right?

I'll grant you that although the approach and landing should be one smooth and continuous evolution, it can be analyzed as having four successive stages:

1. *A normal glide path from pattern altitude at a constant rate of descent.* The path of the aircraft over the ground will correspond with the appropriate landing pattern. As you reach the point in the pattern where the next stage begins, you squeeze off the last of the power you carried in the approach.

2. *Transition to the landing attitude.* You begin to break the glide about 30 feet above the ground by starting to raise the nose of the aircraft slowly and smoothly. This shallows the glide and slows the rate of descent. Do this too quickly, and you'll stop your rate of descent, or even balloon and gain altitude. Fail to do it quickly enough and the main gear will thunk hard against the runway, bouncing the airplane back into the air. "Porpoising" can result from this action. Ideally, the landing attitude is reached as the airplane enters a stall only inches off the ground.

3. *A full stall with the airplane in a three-point landing attitude.* Your aim is to maintain that attitude no more than a foot or so from the ground until the Six settles to a landing. It helps to think of this process as trying to hold the airplane aloft as long as possible. If you've done everything right, all three wheels will contact the ground simultaneously, you'll have the stick all the way back

in your lap, and the aircraft will no longer be flying. But — *wait!* This is no time to relax.

4. *A landing run or rollout under positive control.* Although the aircraft is on the ground, the landing is *not* completed. Not by a long shot. Hold the stick fully back to keep the tailwheel firmly on the surface. This helps you maintain directional control. If the steed begins to swerve, *be quick* to notice the swerve and correct the motion with rudder and, if necessary, brake. The landing is *never* completed until you've rolled to a stop. *Always* keep your hand on the throttle and the stick in your lap during this phase.

Now, when you're parked, the engine is shut down, all switches are off, everything is secured, the wheels are chocked, the airplane tied down — *then* your landing is completed!

☆

All this is preview to getting into the "cutting up a big chunk of the sky" — aerobatics. Once again I can give you only a few pointers and warnings, because the *only* way you learn aerobatics is by getting involved in the process, after learning your airplane and the systems, studying the mancuvers, and going out with an instructor.

First, however, let me tell you the odds are you're about 20 pounds overweight and a little out of shape. That means you're *not* ready for aerobatics. It also means that before you and your lean and mean instructor get into the business of slicing curves and angles in the sky, be honest about your own physical condition. *Get a checkout with your doctor, who knows what you plan to do, because it means strange positions, possible vertigo, and positive and negative g-forces. If he says no, don't go.* Get into shape first.

You need an experienced hand to help you along if you want to do this stuff safely. Sure, you can do it by trial and error. Many pilots do, but it takes more time that way, you make many more common and serious mistakes, and at acrobatic cruise settings you sure burn up a lot of expensive fuel.

I'd add that having the maneuvers demonstrated properly will hasten your mastery of the basic flip-flops and didos. I'll also tell you without any fear of contradiction that learning these things incorrectly is the height of folly and makes you a candidate for a white pine box.

This isn't a lesson on how to fly, not unto itself, but how to fly better than you are now by learning the danger areas in your expanding envelope of flight. And simply moving up into the T-6 from a Bonanza or Comanche or Bellanca is an enormous expansion. Another quantum leap is from normal, everyday flying into aerobatics, but you know what? Most pilots can't even define the term simply, and that's where all this really begins: *knowing* your subject.

Aerobatics (or acrobatics) include all maneuvers not necessary to normal flight. Our cadets in basic training were introduced to aerobatics in the form of the inside loop, slow roll, barrel roll, wingover roll, Immelman turn, inverted stall, split-S, and the progressive spin. There are those who consider these maneuvers to be *advanced* aerobatics; they're not. We considered the above to be what you label "Stage C" aerobatics. There are many additions such as outside loops and snap rolls and a long list of maneuvers designed to test your stomach to its ultimate.

Go by the book, friend. I will *not* abuse this subject here and now by any so-called short-course in aerobatics except to repeat what I just said and provide you with a general introduction and running commentary on what happens with you and your warbird *after* you learn aerobatics, become competent, and then decide you're going to do your thing in — *THE AIRSHOW!*

Now, I'll have that last drink . . .

Let's sit back and take this subject as it deserves; with comfort and pleasure. We're talking about Mr. Excitement itself: warbirds and the airshow circuit. There are dashing and exciting machines out there. The Mustangs and Bearcats, the Corsairs or an occasional Lightning or Sea Fury. No one ever forgets the dazzling image of the sleek cruciform of a P-51 catching the sun's fire as it rolls majestically against a bright blue sky. Or if you're really blessed to experience the moment, there is something truly awesome and ethereal in the graceful vision of the elliptical wings and slender fuselage of a Spitfire. All those names fit so well! There's something right about a *Merlin*, magical in its power, that sails like a winged steed in a breathtaking arc along the contour of a booming cumulus. And in contrast there's the brutish hulk of a B-17, or the stolid form of a B-25 as it rumbles with subdued power along the flight line. Echoes and whispers and memories and a thunder truly sweet is what this is all about.

Yet, for all the reverence and awe these sights inspire, the impressions are often ephemeral. After the images fade, and the experience is filed in our memory banks, those same craft assume the misty aspect of a half-remembered dream. Our minds must work to again conjure the impressions, the emotions, the unfocused images of phantom craft.

That's why I love the SNJ; the Six. With the airshow crowds, the popularity of the Six is assured. Compared to the rarer types, the T-6/SNJ/Harvard, in whatever plumage created by its owners, is a bird that breeds prodigiously. It is a mob scene compared to the other types. Often there are as many T-6s at one time at an airshow as all other hefty warbirds combined. Its ungainly form and shattering noise create a reality you can see and hear and feel as gaggles of the species thunder from the earth.

The Six arrests attention in a most impudent manner, then hammers itself into the consciousness of the onlooker. It leaves the ears ringing, the vision filled with its replicated form, and the nostrils filled with oil vapor, dust, and exhaust fumes. The T-6 works hard to be memorable, and the crowd loves it.

The best thing about flying the T-6 in an airshow is that it's *fun*. This happy little airplane is much smoother and more agile than its appearance indicates; anyone who's flown the bird knows that only too well. And you can have a blast at showing it off to an appreciative audience. That's what they came for!

But fun has its price, and that cost is preparedness and skill. Before you get into the airshow business with the T-6, you need to know everything we've talked about, and you *really* need some work on tactical formation flying and in aerobatics within a large box of space in the sky, a box that is defined and to which you must adhere.

The whole concept of being part of a team of aircraft involves far more than holding a relative position on another aircraft. Formation flying is a discipline unto itself, and it is horrifying in its failure. It requires experience, awareness, and a knowledge of the responsibilities of the specific position in the formation that you occupy. In order to perform safely and precisely as a leader or a wingman, you *must* learn the basics of two-plane and four-plane tactics. *There are no short cuts.*

Once again, this isn't the place, nor is it the time, to get into the hard and detailed specifics of formation work. You've got to follow the same rules we discussed with everything else. But I'll leave this subject with a warning. Never thrust yourself into a multiplane position in an airshow assuming that your ability to hold a wing position without excessive bouncing or jockeying will see you through the weird, unexpected, and dangerous complications of an

After training through all the regimes of single-airplane flight, the time comes when "living together" leads the newcomer into tricky and dangerous formation flying. Here, a T-6 hangs in proper low and slightly trailing position for a formation turn to land. *Asgard Flite Photo*

airshow. You *may* make it just fine, but the other guys in the formation may not take kindly to the challenge and the *hazard* you represent. Some of their adjustments to your erratic and/or unpredictable evolutions may present a poor impression to the audience, as well. And most likely the whole group can expect a visit from the FAA to find out just "what in the hell was going on up there?"

Everybody deserves better than that.

Let's fly, at least in our conversation, an aerobatic airshow routine in the Six. We've practiced the basic maneuvers — rolls, loops, hammerhead turns, and others — and we're proficient. We have also demonstrated our low-level competency to our friends in the FAA, and without that demonstration and their waiver approval in writing, it's a no-go situation. However, everything's clear for us to fly. We have our nerve up and a genuine desire to show folks a nice old airplane doing smooth maneuvers. And we've set our *own* limitations, never exceeding the FAA's restrictions and usually falling well within the official limits. Don't push it, baby; any of the old airshow vets will tell you *that*.

Preparation is the key word in the approach to airshow flying. First, devise a routine comprised of maneuvers that you have mastered. They should flow one into the other in a sequence designed to keep you on the show line and directly before (but *never over*) your audience. You can use the Aresti symbols (the guide for aerobatic competition pilots) if you feel this helps you organize and remember the sequence. How you do it isn't as important as having a definite plan to follow.

Second, work out the key airspeeds you need for initiating each maneuver and establish the altitude floor for the entire sequence. Next, rehearse the routine in your mind. Go ahead and use your hands or a model and take a mental journey through the entire act. When you're sure you have it down pat, and it can be flown within the show area, you're ready to practice.

If there's a designated aerobatics practice area close to where you base your plane that's a great plus factor. If not, find a lonesome spot, *off the airways*, and well clear of population. Make certain it has a clearly defined reference line that you can visualize as a runway. Pick out three checkpoints: your midpoint and two ends. Now you can imagine a throng of a hundred thousand people gaping at you as you enter the "box" and roar down the show line.

Start out with a bit of extra altitude. A thousand feet *above* your FAA limitation is a good fudge factor. You can move it downward later when you feel more comfortable, and you're sure about being able to keep your maneuvers *safely* within limits.

Use a power setting that will keep up your airplane energy and alleviate carburetor flooding in the inverted position. Anything between 2000 and 2200 RPM will do fine. You can set your throttle at 30 inches and leave it there. If you don't get too fancy or extreme you won't need to change power except where the maneuver calls for it.

As an example, let's say you've worked out a sequence that calls for you to go into a loop with a roll on top, a Cuban 8, a hammerhead, knife-edge pass, hammerhead, 4-point roll, hammerhead, 8-point roll, a half-Cuban 8, and an inverted pass with wing-waggle. It's simple enough, but it requires concentration and some work to get it right.

Here goes . . . Putting the nose well down, you intercept the show line. There! Speed builds to 180 knots as you flatten out at your initial entry altitude and approach the midpoint.

223

Now, back pressure on the stick and the nose comes up smoothly as you're pressed into your seat. Up, up comes the nose. There's the vertical. Look out the top of the canopy and pick up the opposite horizon. The nose moves at a constant rate of speed as you ease off the back pressure with the stick. Stop the nose about 15 degrees above the horizon and roll the aircraft. It takes a lot of control movement at this slow speed. Full forward stick and top full rudder and you're inverted again. The airplane resisted your efforts to get it onto its back. Now the stick is full forward. Keep in that forward pressure or the nose drops through too fast. Now she's picking up speed going downhill. Pick up the show line! Move the nose right down to it. The pull is coming on and the g-forces are building as you keep that nose moving smoothly at an unvarying rate. How's your altitude? *Never forget that the altimeter lags in these maneuvers.* Nose coming up to the horizon. Level at base altitude. Whew! What an entrance!

Midpoint coming up. Check your speed. There's 155 on the gauge and up comes the nose as the end of the course approaches. Smoothly, now. Constant rate of movement. Here comes the "float" as you acquire that opposite horizon and are over the top at zero-g. Down comes the nose below the horizon. Stop it. Forward stick. Hang in the straps. Hold the 45-degree down-line momentarily, then roll to the upright position. Right down the line. (Good thing there's no wind today to mess things up.) Ease up the nose and flatten out on your altitude minimum at the midpoint. Now, here you go one more time. There's the rest of the 8, but it's no time for congratulations.

End of the runway approaching. There's the smooth pull to the vertical. Hold it; hold it. *Steady.* Speed is dropping through 40 knots. *Now!* Kick that rudder full over. Around she comes like a pinwheel. Neat. Nose straight down. Draw that vertical down-line. Ground's coming up. Move the nose smoothly up to the horizon. Right on the show line, altitude, and airspeed. Nose up smartly — a 90-degree bank — hold it. Feed in top rudder. Feels terrible. She starts to slide down the wing. Hold it. Roll out, wings level, nose down. Check speed.

Another hammerhead, then down the show line once again. There's 150 knots. On altitude. Nose up slightly. Nail the point. Roll to 90 degrees. Now, inverted with lots of forward stick. Wings vertical again with top rudder. Wings level. Get some speed.

Hammerhead turn, again. Everything checks. Make eight points this pass. Nose on the point. There's 45, 90, 135 degrees, inverted at the runway midpoint, 225, 270, 315 degrees, wings level. Speed?

Runway threshold coming up. Check speed again. Kind of slow. More power. There. Nose coming up. Float over the top and cheat a little rolling out. Nail the down-line. Good. Hold it. Gain energy. Controls are firm. Flat-out down the show line. Roll inverted. Roll it right-side up. Snappy. Pull off the course and point the nose up.

Another opening, another show.

Nice job.

Now, all you need to do is practice that routine a dozen times or so, making adjustments as you go along so you can get from one maneuver into the next, and you'll get it down pat.

As you gain proficiency and confidence, you'll want to dress up your act with a few wrinkles.

Try a snap roll on top of that loop.

Put 4 points into your rollout on the 45-degree shot in the Cuban 8.

Work on a reverse Cuban 8 with a roll-and-a-half on the up side of the 45 degrees.

Put in a half-roll up and another half-roll coming down to jazz up the hammerhead.

For the fun of it, do yourself a 16-point hesitation roll and a super slow roll. A continuous sequence of four slow rolls will test your inner ear.

For the real pro, there are slow rolls and snap rolls on takeoff, rolling breaks, multiple-turn spins, rolling gear extensions, and loops into a landing. There are many variations and enhancements. The possibilities are limitless.

A parting word for fellow T-6 lovers. Always fly within your limitations. Remember that proficiency, preparation, and concentration are essential ingredients of safe flying in airshows. Be safe and be happy.

☆

You've been a marvelous host. You made it a pleasure to visit with you and chat about our shared interest in flying the Six. Thanks for your warm hospitality. Sure, I'll have another one. A nightcap. What? Of course I'm staying the night. You don't think I'd drive after all this drinking, do you?

——————— ☆ ———————

12

The Great
Corrugated Cloud

All good airplanes talk to a pilot. The
trick is to know how to listen.

MARTIN CAIDIN

There are always the rumors. Rumors and hangar stories and gossip are the lifeblood of the warbird movement. Tales drift from one continent to another, carried in cockpits and disbursed in bars or at beer-drinking sessions on the flight line after a full day's flying of the airshow.

Pilots wander through obscure and remote towns, places with names no one ever heard before and about which no one really cares. Or if they had names, they've been forgotten. But on the edges of the broken and chipped concrete, dimly through the tall grass and the woods, concealed in the ramshackle buildings, they have seen *the* planes. The ghosts and the derelicts; *something*. And the listeners lift their brows and pause with their beer cans in mid-lift, and they ask, always, the same question.

"What kinda bird is it?"

"Is it any good or is it a piece of crap?"

"Yeah, yeah, you're the forty-second dumbhead that's come through here with that story."

A bunch of us have chased Spitfires hidden away by sheiks with vast land holdings in the uncharted deserts. We have hunted the fabled like-new Focke-Wulf FW-190 fighter still concealed within its concrete bunker in some enchanted oasis the Allies somehow never could find during the Big War. Some of the machines lay beneath forty to fifty feet of packed snow, and *those* stories have almost always been true. But most of the time the stories and the rumors remained phantoms tantalizingly short of reality. A fighter in good shape, when found after heartbreaking effort, emerges as a crumpled mass of corroded metal with broken metal bones jutting awkwardly through the undergrowth, or a bomber has become a mound festooned with thick foliage and decades of animal droppings.

Some ten years ago new rumors drifted through the smoke-laden bars and the thick miasma of pilot hubris along the flight lines. Down in South America there was a great old ugly machine, but one of immense structural strength. Three engines, radials. Corrugated skin. It had been a bomber, a seaplane, an assault transport, an airliner, a secretive Nazi courier in the steaming depths of the South American jungles. In its time it had carried aloft Adolf Hitler, it had flown Pope Pius, Lindbergh had climbed its metal stairs, it rang with history, bulged with secrets, and was a page of reality right out of the wildest fiction. Where was to be found this incredible machine that went back to the early thirties?

Why (as usual), deep in a jungle. But not so deep it couldn't be found. It had been left on an old dirt road, its one hundred feet of wing now crawling with vines and growth and barely visible. But the road could be cleared, the jungle hacked away, years of neglect and growth clawed and scraped away, and it could be made flyable. It would be the only original, German-built, Dessau-manufactured Junkers Ju-52/3m tri-motored bomber-transport in the world that could be returned to flight. You needed only to go to Quito, more than nine thousand feet above sea level at its airport, and go miles into the jungle depths surrounding the remote airfield, and there you would find the rugged giant the Germans had called *Iron Annie*.

Yeah, sure. But it's true! *Right; right.* It's the last one in the world! *Uh huh.* It's the strongest plane ever built! *I know, I know.* You don't understand! I saw it myself!

Now, *that's* different. Okay, our friend had seen something, but *what?* A wreck of a plane standing on its ancient gear can be no more than a shove from becoming a pile of broken metal bones or decayed wood or dusty fabric. It's got to be better than that. You

227

need something to build on. But this story was getting better.

"I suppose it's *the* Ju-52 they've been talking about for years?"

"That's right!"

Still strong reservations, but mounting interest. "Get any identification numbers?"

He had done just that. Everyone was sitting straight up now. The registration; what was the damned registration! Our wanderer removed a folded paper from his wallet. "Here it is. HC-ABS."

Everyone exchanged glances. *My God . . . that's it. That's the plane that left Norway for South America! Her last registration had been LN-KAF, and before that it had been LN-DAH, and before that she carried the Dessau Werke Number of 5489. We'd been tracking down that ship for years, and the phantom in a million-to-one shot turned out to be real!*

But the hard realities were that the airplane had been abandoned for years under the worst conditions, and no one knew what shape the plane had been in when it was shoved aside and forgotten. It was, if not dead, a long-dying creature. It might well take some miracles, large *and* small, even to hope for renewed flight. But we were damned sure going to try.

☆

George Hamilton went to Ecuador to perform the first of the miracles — getting the airplane out from under its monstrous jungle growth and back to an open area where the resurrection could begin. George did some careful studying of the airplane's history; that is, what he could discern through poor records and the memories of many people who were involved. The airplane, if nothing else, seemed to be immortal. It had endured hard and driving service all through South and Central America. Just operating out of Quito at 9300 feet could be called "cruel and unjust punishment." Figure that operating this ancient monster with full loads and old engines and fixed-pitch props at sea level had to be an adventure in itself, and then consider that this particular Ju-52 had been flown, often heavily overloaded, *with takeoffs from an airstrip at 9300 feet!* We discovered that HC-ABS also was operated from terrible airstrips in jungle depths and high atop mountains, and carried such massive overloads the gear seemed to groan under the weight.

They didn't just fly this airplane; they pushed and shoved and drove and pounded and slammed and jerked and hauled and banged her about so severely that any future flight seemed beyond all hope. There were problems other than mauling the thing in the air. Any maintenance performed on the airplane was a cruel joke. If there was a hole, cover it with tape or a tin can. It uses oil? It didn't matter what kind; just pour it into the tanks. Corrosion? The whole airplane had endured a thunderstorm of corrosion inside and out. If corrosion showed then the answer was simple: paint it. *This* airplane had been painted by people stomping its wings and fuselage and *swabbing the paint with long-handled mops!*

The airplane was still flying when the engines started to come unglued. The corrosion chewed at her vitals. Control systems choked and clogged. Valves stuck, lines froze, brakes crumbled. *Then* they gave her up to the elements, which meant rot and mildew, hail, temperature extremes, all of which comes under the heading of brutal neglect. When George Hamilton found her, the tires were rotten, the hydraulic lines crumbling, the electrical system a mishmash of leftover residue of untold creatures that had feasted on the wiring. A condor built a nest in a gaping hole in the tail. Snakes and rodents and insects took up domain in her wings, her deep belly hatches, in the tail, and in all manner of secret compartments.

George shook his head in dismay and disbelief. Then he went to work. That meant hacking away a lot of jungle growth. George wisely used smoke bombs under and inside the old carcass to drive out the thousands of creatures living in the Ju-52. The engines hadn't turned for *eight years*, and there was a superabundance of rust, dust, fungus, mildew, algae, corrosion, and anything else that comes under the headings of vile, foul, rotten, and disgusting. George was assured during the six months of preparatory work, by the local mechanics, that every detail on his checklist was attended to. He should have known better than to trust them with a system even as obvious as fuel lines.

The day arrived finally when it was time to try to ignite the engines. They turned over; radials have a habit of being virtually indestructible. George looked out of the cockpit and stared in disbelief as aviation fuel cascaded back of the wings and *kersplashed!* on the ground as if sprayed from high-pressure hoses. Someone nearby idly flipped away a cigarette butt and a huge ball of fire boomed along the ground and roared upward to encompass the Ju-52. Hamilton hammered the throttles frantically and the Ju-52 lurched forward like a wounded elephant stung with a spear.

The prop blast flattened out the flames and the airplane rocked and swayed forward to safety.

Kapitan Christian Drexel, former Lufthansa and Luftwaffe flying master, checked George out in the airplane. Three days and ten hours later both Drexel and George were satisfied. They stuffed the airplane with every single spare part they could find until everyone knew that the airplane was terribly overgrossed, but not by how much. The Ju-52 has a reputation of flying with anything its crew could stuff into the airplane, and George found no reason to contest history. He went to the end of the runway, thought about his altitude of 9300 feet, muttered a silent prayer, and pushed the throttles all the way forward. Everyone was stunned; the airplane took off in almost the same distance as it had flown when it was nearly empty.

Iron Annie, named by the German troops for the rugged machine she was, headed north.

☆

On November 22, 1970, and after a long ferry flight with no more than four or five emergencies per hour, the Ju-52 ended up in Dixon, Illinois. It didn't move again for more than a year and a half! And it was still coming unglued within its seams, despite frantic patchwork at its new home. What made things worse was that now the airplane had to endure bitter cold along with all its other travails. Meanwhile, the official word from an FAA inspector was that, despite the ferry flight, the airplane legally was unairworthy. They had found severe corrosion in a main carry-through spar in the center section.

Replacement took fifteen months, during which the engines further deteriorated, instruments failed, and everything else began to fall apart. Some more frantic patchwork got the machine flyable so that in May of 1972 it made a few local flights. For the rest of the year it flew a few more times between massive fixit and patchit programs. In all of 1973 it flew but five times. Then came August of 1974, and its owner cried, *"Enough!"* He had the airplane flown to Missouri, where it went on the auction block. An aircraft dealer bought it and had it ferried to Charlotte, North Carolina. For four months it sat on the airport, a battered, beaten-up, rundown flying wreck.

I found it there. What were the words to describe the *sight* of the airplane? Forlorn, scabby, filthy, messy, neglected, beaten, sorrow-

Scabby, filthy, battered, the great bulk of the Ju-52 looms high over airline captain Vern Renaud (left) and Martin Caidin. At the moment the Great Flying is still a dream for the morrow. *Asgard Flite Photo*

ful; you name it and there's a rotten word for it. But if you have 20-20 foresight, you can see through the mists of towering repair bills, of rebuilding problems, of impossible tasks, and in that ethereal realm of imagination you can bring together not just the misery of the moment, but the glory of the past and the wonders that *could* be. So I laid down $52,500 and bought myself a junkyard with wings.

You learn old tricks very fast when you absolutely *must* know them. I'd been flying behind many kinds of engines, but I had *not* flown behind ancient radial engines. My education, or lack of it, caught up with me quickly. First, I didn't have the chance to bring my own airplane down from North Carolina to Ti-Co Airport in Florida. I was, as it happened, in California, and I did not want to leave the Ju-52 in North Carolina any longer than necessary. Ron Skipper and Ted Anderson brought her for me. Skipper had been flying large and heavy taildraggers for a long time, and if anyone could handle the Iron Bucket, he was the man for it. Off they went in bitter cold, endured several days of trying to get the airplane to a semblance of life, and departed Charlotte just as I was returning from California. I was at Ti-Co to hear the lumbering, groaning, thundering sound of what was unmistakably *Iron Annie*. Ron Skip-

231

per brought her around the field at a blistering 92 miles per hour, and eased her tired old bulk to earth. When they parked and shut her down, he climbed from the airplane, patted me on the shoulder, hugged me, and left to go fly somewhere in the world — *anywhere*.

I looked at Anderson and he looked back at me. I kicked one of the huge tires and looked again at Anderson. "Let's fly the son of a bitch," I said happily. "Where's the checklist?"

"Ain't none."

"Then where's the handbook? The flight manual?"

"This is a German airplane," Ted said quietly. "There's a flight manual on the machine, but it's in Spanish and it's for a different airplane."

"That's it?" I asked.

"Yup," he said, nodding, "except for what you know about flying and what I can remember from the trip down here. So, you got it. Let's fly. But first we gotta grease the rocker-arm boxes."

I stared at him. What the hell was this thing? An airplane or a locomotive? Ted must have read my thoughts or suffered the same ones when *he* first encountered the problem. "This way to the train," he muttered.

I learned, quickly, the many idiosyncrasies of the Bavarian Motor Works radial engines (which were manufactured copies of our Pratt & Whitney engines). The BMW 132E engines often took a while to warm up after starting, and while grumbling to acceptable temps inside and out, they did a strange dance of spitting out grease. The engines had *external* rocker-arm boxes that demanded greasing — that meant filling them chock full of grease every ten hours of operation. And they threw grease. A storm of grease. Not tiny globules, but drops and spatters and great big messy globs that smear the windshield. Mix in dust, humidity, and bugs and you can see that the airplane produced as many adventures as it encountered problems along the way.

Well, we refueled, we poured in fifty gallons of oil (a quart at a time), we greased the rocker-arm boxes, we cleaned the windshield, we climbed aboard the airplane, and then we sat. Because I could recognize only a few of the controls that supposedly one finds to be familiar in almost all airplanes. There were little tags and signs everywhere — in German, Norwegian, Spanish, English, and French. They were worthless. So we kept a large note pad at the ready, we drew a diagram of the panels and the cockpit, and then we touched and moved, tweaked and turned, pushed and pulled, trying to figure out just what in the hell was what, and what it did, and kept writing down the details. In the few hours Ted had spent in the airplane, he had already committed to memory many of the things he'd done with Skipper on the way down to Ti-Co. Before the memories could fade we wrote them down furiously.

Starting the Ju-52, in that day and time and in that configuration, was the craziest fire drill you ever saw or ever heard. The cockpit was like a control room of a giant boiler factory, and there were as many wheels and big handles as there were finger-sized things. Imagine also, if you will, we were in the capacious cockpit of a machine with a wing that spanned nearly 100 feet and that weighed 23,000 pounds. The throttles were, to be kind, overly sloppy and their friction knobs weary unto death. We sat two stories above the ground, behind a control yoke of ancient wood that would have fitted well on the *Titanic*. The tires were slick to begin with and had deteriorated to worn smoothness, and the brakes were but a memory. In short, only the left seat had brakes, they were of no meaningful pattern in their operation, when they worked, which was distressingly intermittent; and at their best, they were terrible.

We were supposed to get 600 hp out of the old BMW radials, but no one believed it, of course. They chugged and backfired and smoked and grumbled and we just didn't know how many of those cylinders even had compression. We could count 27 jugs among three engines, but how many worked? Sooner or later we'd have to find out, but for the moment we accepted the fact that the airplane *had* flown here and that was good enough for two eager madmen. Anderson announced that, on the basis of (1) his long association with radial engines, and (2) his brief acquaintance with *these* engines, we must absolutely not, not *ever*, use the overboost or go to the superchargers. The latter were set to operate above 9000 feet only, but even at that height, the engines were so old and crotchety that any real overboost could literally send their internal pieces in many different directions at the same time.

What also confused us thoroughly was the indication that the engine controls marked OIL COOLER and CARBURETOR HEATERS (also referred to as engine preheat) were intended for use only above 9000 feet, only in conjunction with the superchargers, and —

233

"Hold it, HOLD IT!" I shouted in exasperation. "What the hell are we talking about here? Don't use the oil coolers below nine grand? What if the goddamned engines overheat?"

Anderson tugged at his grease-spattered beard. "If they heat up you throttle back and you glide to let the mothers cool off."

"Why?"

"Because no one seems to have used those controls for a hundred years and we're not sure what will happen if we use them. They're probably going to come apart in little pieces on us and really screw up the engines. The same thing goes for the carb heat, because the way they're set now, they're working, and let's not press our luck."

So we made up dozens of those neat little plastic signs saying VERBOTEN! and plastered them everywhere we thought they belonged; we ended up with a cockpit that had more FORBIDDEN! signs in it than a Yugoslavian minefield. It was crazy, because the oil coolers were supposed to be in the OPEN position all the time (unless it was February in Stalingrad, and we planned *not* to go there), to cool the engines. We gambled that because the Germans had flown the airplane in South America they simply jammed the coolers in the OPEN position. The gamble paid off; they were where they belonged and we *didn't* overheat.

To get to the cockpit we had to wend our way through seventeen passenger seats, all lit in a crazyquilt pattern of sunlight streaming through cracked and crazed windows. Weather stripping was a hollow laugh, so when it rained this airplane turned into a shower room under high nozzle pressure. There were 800 pounds of radios and navigation equipment and *all* of it was useless. To me they spelled *fire*, so I cut every cable and line and Ted and I threw them out of the machine. The floorboards were soft and moldy, and every time we walked on them there was danger of plunging into the deep belly hatches — which always plagued us because we often had to go *into* the belly, which became known as the Black Hole of Calcutta, to inspect control rods, flaps springs, fuel lines, cables, and God only knew what else. Ten minutes down there and you sweated off three weeks of beer.

The cockpit windows were mostly broken or jammed. The tailwheel lock didn't work; it had been busted years before. The fire bottles didn't work (and if they did, their chemicals when mixing with flames spewed forth poison gas). We had to empty the tanks and fill them to find out for certain how much fuel they held. We had to load 60 gallons of oil. We loaded 15 gallons of hydraulic fluid for the brake-fluid system, which worked haphazardly and often produced a huge geyser of heated red fluid high above the airplane to drench everything in sight. The batteries, terminals, and cables were horribly corroded; we threw out the lot and put in a new system. We hung new generators and vacuum pumps in the engines and changed all the plugs and tightened everything in sight and taped the exhaust system to hold it together.

And then we were ready to start up the airplane.

☆

Iron Annie had to be approached as if she were a wounded dinosaur with huge teeth, sharp claws, and a flailing spiked tail, to say nothing of flaming bad breath. And you never flew until you had checked off the engine rocker-arm boxes for their last time of grease stuffing, because flying without that grease meant *FIRE!* The preflight check and walkaround consisted of more than 274 separate items, all of which slid by faster with accumulating experience and familiarity. And when you were ready to start, you made certain you had big chocks under the wheels and a fire guard standing by, and a priest with a bunch of extra bibles, and you climbed into the waterlogged pilot seats, and Ted and I looked at one another and agreed to "do it."

Remember, please, that this was the Ju-52 essentially in its Survival Mode. The Grand Rebuilding of the airplane still lay some time in the future. We had patched, fixed, replaced, bent, shaped, twisted, modified, and improved, but only enough to keep us in the air without an uncontrolled return to earth. *Iron Annie* was still in primary form, so to speak. So that despite all that had been performed, the simple truth was that the airplane still featured an unmitigated disaster of a cockpit, with broken knobs and frozen handles and cracked leather and torn fabric and peeling paint and cracked glass and (for the most part) long-dead instruments.

Ted stands up through the opened top cockpit hatch and watches as I move the monstrous yoke through all directions and tromp rudder pedals, and then haul on that terrible, giant wheel to the right of the pilot's seat that moves the flaps *and* ailerons. The wheel is for trim, for lowering the flaps, for lowering the ailerons, and lowering the flaps some more, and it moves huge springs, and it has had many names given to it, the kindest perhaps being Hernia Harry. There is no use checking rudder trim, because the steel cables and bungee cords of that system flailed themselves to death, and we promise ourselves one day to fix the mess, but in the interim we will fly *sans* rudder trim.

Now for the instruments. The clock is frozen. Altimeters set to field elevation (one sags). The directional gyros are all busted bearings; useless. There's one sick radio. Vacuum pump off, and then on to the oddball instruments, gauges, and controls such as cockpit lights (dead), navigation lights (dead), rotating beacon and strobes (ain't got none; check). Tailwheel unlocked, because the locking pin snapped years ago. Fire extinguishers to secure, but they're empty, anyway. Fuel selector checked both sides and back to center; oil coolers OPEN; carb heat COLD; primer to SECURE; primer secondary system — *Snapsebensin* — to SECURE, but it's Norwegian and we don't even know what it does; windows open; prayer books ready . . .

This is just how we did it.

Ted pumps up the hydraulic pressure with a huge handle the size of a baseball bat until we get a reading of 1000 psi, and we pray it doesn't bust open the accumulator bladder. Maybe we'll get *some* brakes with the pressure all the way up. Mixtures in LEAN. Supercharger control to under 9000 feet. Spark advance (my God) to RETARD (like us). Bulkhead master switches up and behind the copilot seat to my right, three more switches on the right bulkhead, all set at ON. Then the quadrant master pulled UP to ON. There are three fuel selectors on the right side of the console; I move number three to the open position for startup. Number three ignition switch to ON, magneto selector for number three centered to BOTH.

Now Ted really goes to work, grasping the fuel wobble pump by the left side of his seat and pounding it up and down in a fast steady motion. The fuel-pressure needle hardly moves. "Faster!" I yell. Ted pumps madly until the fire guard outside stares in disbelief as fuel cascades from the engine to the macadam. Ted yells: "We got fuel yet?"

"You got a great big goddamned leak!" the fire guard screams.

The hell we have; that's how you start this joker. Ted stops pumping for a moment, reaches to the forward part of the console on his side, flips away a protective covering, grabs the T-handle of the Bendix inertial starter, and shoves it down hard as we both count to fifteen. The system winds up from a groan into a whine and then the shriek we want to hear, and Ted hauls up on the T-handle; there's a wheezing, grinding moan, a half growl-and-groan, and all sorts of clanking noises as the prop turns and huge clouds of smoke belch from the stacks. The engine is just catching. I shove the mixture to FULL RICH and do a finger dance with the throttle to number three, and God bless her, she's really trying to light off. I yell for Ted to "Pump! Keep pumping!" and his hand is going up and down like mad on the wobble pump handle because if the engine doesn't start now we've got to do the whole thing all over again. But she's catching, and I jerk the fuel flow from OPEN to RUNNING position, full back, and with a throaty roar, number three is turning. Ted gasps for air, and sweat is all over him.

I'm working the throttle. The generator should come in at 700 RPM but it won't, so I go to 900 RPM and there's the first indication that *Annie* is generating her own current. Back on the throttle to check the generator charge and advance it again to 700 and hold it there and check oil temp and oil pressure and fuel pressure and carb heat and the cylinder-head temp and see what the manifold pressure reads. Everything, to our astonishment, is on the money. There are some more switches to turn on along the side-bulkhead row, and the generator relay has popped out and I push it in and bang on it with my fist and it stays in. The after-bulkhead voltmeter goes to ON.

Okay, that's just the *first* engine. We've got to repeat this entire procedure another two times, if everything works right, to get all three burning and turning. Number two by the grace of good fortune catches, shakes madly, and breaks into a shattering roar. Who cares? It's running. But not number one; she balks and we go through the crazy Chinese fire drill four more times before she lights off. The airplane rumbles and snarls, popping through the exhausts. I'm soaking wet. Ted's arm has cramped and looks like a giant claw, and he's soaked from head to foot. I check the vacuum pressure for the engine-driven pump and the outside venturi and they're both working. We each set the directional gyros and laugh hollowly as they turn willy-nilly, and not even full vacuum will bring the artificial horizons to any more sense than rolling a pencil in zero-g within their instrument mounts.

But what the hell, she's running. We squeak our way to a runway the tower has shut down for us, and we practice moving on the ground. Taxi fast, taxi slow, tail up; try everything short of flying. Feel her swerve, test the sidewinds on her, learn fast that when the tailwheel is on concrete you have hardly any rudder control at all, and unless you have brakes — which we don't — the key to direc-

The nightmare . . . the cockpit of N52JU when we first started flying the corrugated monster. These gauges are in four languages, half of them didn't work, and most were mysteries. But it was fun! *Photo by Julian Leek*

tional control is keeping the tail up and walking hell out of the rudder. We do all these things for about two hours and we're getting the *feel* of it, and it feels right and Ted and I look at one another, and he kicks the radio to make it work, and we tell the tower we want to fly.

On the centerline, forget the brakes, bring in the power steadily, the tail feels light, *walk those rudder pedals!* Keep her going, you've got sixty, seventy, eighty, and the barest nudge back on that huge yoke and this ironmonger wreck of an airplane, this beast, levitates. That's the only word for it. No effort, no straining, just a feathery ride up and away from the concrete and we can't believe it. She's old, she's weary and ancient and tired in her old metal bones, and we know that sooner or later we'll have to rebuild her but, God, was this airplane ever made to fly!

☆

We flew her for several hundred hours, patching and fixing as best we could. We flew her up the East Coast and all over the Florida peninsula and then we flew her to Texas in a hairy trip of rotten weather and storms and a string of mechanical defects and breakdowns that became so ridiculous we learned to live with them as

238

part of our daily routine. She was literally falling apart, but she flew and flew and flew. When we got to Texas at 8000 feet we were going into an airshow, and through the side windows we saw a sky filled with airplanes. I told Ted and our third pilot, Bob Bailey, there was "no way I'm going into that bee's hive until I clean the windshield." Because our windshield was splattered with grease and I had zero forward visibility and I'd already made a few landings like this, with Ted talking me down, but this sky was too crowded. I chopped the nose engine and slowed her down to 80 mph, and Ted pulled on his goggles and leather helmet, jerked open the top hatch, stood on the quadrant, and climbed out of the airplane, rags in hand! He cleaned that windshield, and only then did I realize we had an audience. A bunch of fighters and bombers and trainers, all of them with gear and flaps down, were trying to stay with us at our low speed, their pilots showing their astonishment as Ted stood atop the airplane, 8000 feet high, cleaning the windshield!

We took her down the eight grand to the Harlingen runway and taxied her to the flight line and shut her down, and a great crowd collected. When we shut her down and climbed from the airplane onto the tarmac, Bob Hoover and Art Scholl, the two all-time greats of airshow flying, came up to greet us. Hoover stared with disbelief at *Annie*, engines crackling as they cooled, and he studied the bald tires and the hydraulic fluid already leaking, and the engine oil dripping, and the grease that was everywhere, and he looked at the scabrous paint peeling and tearing, and in a single long glance he understood it all, because this man *flies*.

Hoover looked at me and then at the crowd and back to me and he said, "I always thought he was a crazy son of a bitch." He rapped his knuckles on corrugated iron and grinned. "And now I *know* he's crazier than hell to fly this thing down here!"

Dear Reader, there ain't a better compliment in the world than that from Bob Hoover.

☆

Between that flight from Florida to Texas, and the next nine months, we endured all the heart-stopping moments of an airplane slowly but surely disintegrating under our hands and feet. This brings us back to the heart of all we have shared in these pages. Sooner or later you *must* pay the price to fly with a level of reliability and safety. The cost of rebuilding the Ju-52 to what I wanted was going to resemble the national debt. It would be an enormous undertaking, as much thinking as it was technical and mechanical and electrical. We had flown the old girl down to the nub of her heart. The airplane strained mightily, and we had even stretched the limits of fixing everything as it broke or failed.

It is not the right way to go. It was, in fact, a violation of everything I had ever learned or done in rebuilding airplanes before Iron Annie *came into my life. I was being, in short, more and more stupid about the entire affair.*

There were moments to remember that would have far better been forgotten . . .

We landed at a Louisiana airfield and taxied back on the active runway, the airplane bumping over some junk that someone had left on the runway. What the hell! was our shared reaction, but that was nothing to compare with learning that we had run over parts of our own airplane that had fallen off during our landing!

There was a takeoff at gross weight with a surface temperature of 97° F and a stiff crosswind and the left engine packed it in on takeoff. It didn't quit; it just dropped down to a near-useless 1200 RPM before I had full rudder effect, and still lacked any brakes to speak of. The only way to keep heading was to come back on the other good wing engine until the nose engine gained enough speed to bring power back in and use full rudder to maintain directional control. Not the way to go.

We got some pretty bad weather reports from a station during a flight along the Gulf of Mexico coastline and were directed into a ripping thunderstorm. Without any navigational aids and with the new directional gyros that failed completely (because the vacuum system had failed), we had a very interesting time of it. All we could do was to fly needle-ball-airspeed and let her descend at a steady 500 feet per minute, and the inherent solid stability of that airplane helped to bring us through.

With only one engine running we landed at a coast guard station and when we rolled to a stop, the maintenance chief of the base came out, gaped at the wallowing wreck before him, and was ready to weep openly. The coast guard, bless 'em, patched us up the best they could, wrapped asbestos sheeting and metalwork about our paper-thin exhaust stacks, and sent us on our way with the belief they'd be reading about us in the papers. On the obit page.

Back in Florida in early June of 1976, I decided it was time to quit. Rebuild the airplane or ground her forever; that was the

Keeper of the Dragon. Terry Ritter in a rare moment of pensive relaxation after a day of baby-sitting and coddling The Hulk. "If you love me, rebuild this damn thing!" was his cry. We did. *Photo by Becky (his wife) Ritter*

choice. I opted for the rebuild. But Leo Kerwin and the mob in the Valiant Air Command were having a great big airshow, and NASA had asked us to open the Bicentennial Exposition of the Kennedy Space Center by having *Annie* lead a huge aerial parade, and we were beaten about the head and shoulders to *do it*. Terry Ritter, who by now had been crew chief for several months and knew the machine better than its builders, gathered a crew and worked almost without sleep for three days to get us airworthy for the show. We flew three hard days and the airplane stayed together, but I could *feel* the weariness, the hesitations, the aches, and the pains in that machine. On the final day of the airshow I landed at Merritt Island, told Terry to get her ready for one last flight down to Miami International for her rebuild, and planned what could be a critical juncture in the history of the airplane, to say nothing of our own warm bodies.

Let me emphasize this moment, even if I repeat certain points, because they are almost biblical in their lessons. *An airplane talks to you and tells you things if only you know how to listen, and this airplane was trying to tell us to quit.* We really didn't know if we could make Miami from a few hundred miles away. There were no more patches to make, the internal systems were so far gone they were beyond repair. The engines were coming apart, and the truth of it was we knew we did *not* have 27 jugs pumping out power from all three engines. The electrical system was about belly up and — well, there it was. We loaded up with 300 gallons, a crew of three — Terry Ritter, Bob Bailey, and me — and kept our weight down to 18,000 pounds. Without brakes, despite engines screaming to be buried before their pain became too great, we couldn't stop a take-off. The end of the Merritt Island runway was all water, and I planned to use 800 feet of sod overrun from the west side to gain every inch of space possible.

I fed in the power steadily, she accelerated slowly on the grass, but the tail came up faster than we expected and she began to pick up speed fast, and just as we crossed from the grass to the paved runway a dull explosion shook the airplane. People watching the Great Takeoff Adventure saw a blast of flame from the nose engine exhausts and a huge cloud of black smoke streaming back (we never saw it). *We had blown two jugs in the nose engine and still she was in the air in under a thousand feet.*

We climbed to 7500 feet to take advantage of the cooler air and to keep the engines from predetonating. Just north of Fort Lauderdale, Miami Approach told us to come on down to 2000 feet, and we pulled the plug and let her down at just over 2000 feet per minute rate of descent. The vibration was terrific, the instrument panel jerking so wildly that we could barely read the instruments. We thought the nose engine mounts had broken, but when we brought in some power things settled down a bit, and we lucked out — Miami cleared us in immediately. We landed smoothly and I let her roll off at the second intersection, easing onto a wide runup area beyond the taxiway. Miami Ground cleared us to Aero Facilities but *Annie* had given her last gasp. The brakes were completely gone, things were leaking everywhere, and heat rolled over us from the engines. I nodded to Ritter and Bailey. "Shut her down."

A tug towed us in to Aero Facilities. It was time for the Resurrection.

☆

The first order of business was the philosophy of bringing *Iron Annie* back to life. Not simply as good as new, but *better*. The rules I laid down were not to repair, but to rebuild or to install all new equipment. I had screwed up for so long in getting down to business I was almost a fanatic for doing everything the right way. We looked ahead to five months of total teardown and rebuild. Terry Ritter moved to Miami to live with the airplane, literally, during the Great Transformation.

The BMW engines, we discovered to a mixture of horror and amazement, *had been running on half-power.* Nick Silverio and Dan Freeman, who with Terry Ritter punched this job through, told me that of the 27 cylinders in our three engines, at least 12 were completely dead. How the thing flew was a mystery to us. But now an ancient fact came to our aid. The BMWs were faithful copies of Pratt & Whitney engines, so that meant rebuilt P&W powerplants should fit right to the mounts without any changes. And they did!

We bought three P&W R1340-S1H1 engines that had flown on Grumman Mallards, and modified the system to take the Mallard cowls, far more efficient aerodynamically than the old German cowlings. Paul Gaither of Aviation Propellers showed up with three beautiful, brand-new AG-100 paddle-bladed props (constant speed props; hooray!) that added a lot of useful thrust to the power we developed. At normal takeoff settings we churned out 600 hp from 2250 RPM and 36 inches manifold pressure. But if I wanted to go to overboost I could bring up the manifold pressure to 40 or 42 inches without hurting those fabulous, tough powerplants, and the props would scream with 800 hp each, which gave us DC-3 power but with far more lift.

We removed every piece and scrap of wire, every tube, every hose, every connection. We designed and installed a magnificent new electrical control panel. We now had dual generators and dual vacuums and backup systems for the hydraulics. We installed lights everywhere — landing lights, position lights, anti-collision beacons, taxi lights, strobes: the works.

We converted from the German brakes to a modified system where we split brakes from a B-17, and then we modified the axles and installed C-46 tires. They were heavier and had more drag than the slimmer German tires, but they also had more than twice the footprint and a deep tread and they gave *Annie* great ground control.

Out went the arm-numbing manual fuel pump, to be replaced with a DC-6 fuel pump. Then we thought about it again and reinstalled the old wobble pump as an emergency backup in case we lost all electrical power (we never did). We discarded the inertial starters and went to electrical starters, added quadrant-mounted starter-booster-primer switches (we were able to start this airplane in less than three minutes instead of the usual 30 minutes to an hour we'd lived with for so long). We had never had windshield wipers, and landing the Ju-52 in a heavy rain with a *flat* windshield was near suicide. We installed wipers from an F-4 jet fighter to run off the new hydraulic system. We ripped out the instrument panel and built a designed-to-order panel. Every instrument in the airplane was new. We put in all sorts of avionics: triple-system communications radios, ADF, transponders and encoding altimeters and localizers and all the good stuff. All new antennas, natch. We stripped the fuselage to the bare metal *and removed 800 pounds of paint from the machine!*

Ritter's crew removed all control surfaces. They scoured the interior of the aircraft with high-pressure steam. Every control surface was removed, and every nut, bolt, pin, and connection in the airplane was brand new. We ran lights through the tailcone so we could *see* everything clearly for inspection. I even had the tailcone interior painted a bright, anti-corrosion yellow for better visibility. We had a terrific new intercom system, and we had so many lights in that cockpit that night flying was now a pleasure.

In other words — we were zero-timing the airplane. The FAA at our invitation inspected every move and checked every detail. We went through the whole gamut of X-ray, Magnaflux, dye-typing, and even ultrasonic testing for metal fatigue in any form. *And we found it.*

Ritter called to tell me the gear-axle housings "got some bad cracks in them. They're magnesium; they can't stand the torque we'll be giving them." Ted Votoe and Terry Ritter put their heads together and came up with Tom Reilly, who plays with steel as if it's silly putty, and a few weeks later we had new gear-axle housings of chrome steel. The original magnesium housings from Germany tested out to a safety factor of 38,000 psi. Our new system checked in at *98,000* psi.

New seats in the cockpit; new leather everywhere. The old wooden yokes remained but with marvelous new leather covers. All new glass in the cockpit and the windows. We opened up the old machine-gun turret, installed a fishing seat from a cabin cruiser, and fitted out a mock gun that made loud noises and spit fire. We installed machine guns in the wings and bomb racks under the wings. We put in an all-new thick floor and new carpeting and recovered all the seats. We installed cassette and 8-track tape players and FM radio and put in 10 terrific speakers. Nothing like music all the way. You could hear us on the ground from 2000 feet.

Those amenities mean a lot in the long run. Our crew rebuilt the portable ladder into a true stairway that slid into a belly compartment. We rebuilt the bathroom — à la *Krappenhausen* — with a modern chemical toilet, curtains, and a fan. For extra fun we installed smoke-pumping systems for the wing engines and pyrotechnic holders under the wingtips for smoke grenades.

We did a lot of things during those five months (and for a year later as new ideas hit us), but one of the best ways to relate the changes from the past was that we could load the airplane with 620 gallons of fuel, 60 gallons of oil, 15 gallons of hydraulic fluid, 12 gallons of smoke oil, 10 gallons of cold beer, add twelve people each with 40 pounds of gear, carry 300 pounds of tools and spare parts, and at takeoff we were still a thousand pounds under normal weight. Which meant we could stuff another six people into the cabin.

But the best fun was a lightweight takeoff, a good wind, and overboost. Nothing will communicate the miracle we had all wrought with the Ju-52 better than such an airshow takeoff.

Come along . . .

☆

Your left hand grasps the huge control yoke and your right hand is on a brace of three engine throttles; your feet are pressed hard against the rudder pedals, toes forward to lock the brakes; and slowly but steadily you're advancing the throttle levers. You glance at the overboost switch, which is forward, ready to let the throttles move beyond their normal stop for extra power. Your eyes return to where they belong, scanning the gauges for the green light on for fuel pump, moving to manifold pressure, RPM, carb-air temp, cylinder-head temp, oil pressure and oil temp, and fuel pressure and fuel selector and fuel flow. You continue the scan to the fuel-flow knobs and hydraulic pressure and vacuum pressure and an umpteenth look at the flaps to 25 degrees, the ailerons down 15 degrees, the trim exactly right. The yoke's full back into your chest and you steal another glance at the directional gyro and the flight gauges. Right outside are props to the left and the right and in front of you, the prop controls full forward and cinched down, and their screaming is like a knife through the airplane, and the tail wants UP and it wants to go up NOW, so you keep full back pressure on the yoke, and she shakes and trembles through her body, trembling to be let loose, and you know that when you let those brakes free you'll have the throttles full bore, balls to the wall.

My God, what a feeling! The Ju-52 is screaming and snarling and pounding to be let loose. There's 6000 feet of runway before you and the crowd of a hundred thousand has been told again and again by the show announcer that they're looking at a machine more than fifty years old, that's made of cast iron, that's ponderous and can hardly get out of its own way, and it looks the part, ugly and ungainly and square-sided and slab-faced almost everywhere. This thing is all corrugation and angular bends, right-angled turns and knobs, and God only knows how many protuberances jutting into the airstream. Built-in headwinds, they say. You know what the announcer is bellowing. "They'll be lucky to get that thing off the ground in five thousand feet! They'll be lucky to get off at all!"

We're at 19,000 pounds, a little heavier than we would like for a really short-field takeoff, but a gang of friends are aboard, grinning like kids, and what the hell, there's a good wind right on the nose, straight down the runway at about 12 knots, and that makes up for the extra weight. Of course, in the right seat there isn't too much weight, not with a copilot named Dee Dee and weighing 122 pounds. She grins; she loves this.

"*Annie*, this is Control." The voice crackles through your earphones. "You got the field. Let 'er rip."

One fast glance again at *everything*. Terry Ritter stands between the cockpit seats, and his right hand moves forward to the prop controls, which will stay there until we're well into the climb. You glance at one another and you both nod and Dee Dee's eyes are gleaming and you sweep the panel and all the needles are in their precise rows, and now it's time to have *fun*.

You don't release the brakes as your right hand moves the throttles forward past the usual stop. You've got 36 inches and then 38 and 40 and as you come up on 42 there's no holding her; she's starting to drag forward with the brakes locked, and everything must be timed perfectly. The prop scream is beyond belief as you keep on the brakes and shove that yoke forward, hard. Instantly the corrugated monster is like a ballet dancer and without moving forward the airplane is perfectly level, standing right where it was, and you snatch just a hair back on the yoke and let the brakes go, and for an instant we're standing still, howling and shrieking, tail

REBIRTH! RESURRECTION! NEW LIFE! The brand-new, zero-timed *Iron Annie* shows off her new shape and colors and Martin Caidin tells everyone who said "she'll never fly again" what he thinks of *that* opinion! *Photo by Cecil Stoughton*

up, and then with astonishing speed *Annie* lurches forward.

It's like being in a locomotive that lunges forward from a standing position. The tail has the wind and is grabbing but the brakes are also there if you need them; you don't. With that 12-knot wind down the runway and the props howling their blast backward you have full control before you even know it's happened. You see Terry's thumb stab upward and you know everything is in the green and as you roll faster you *feel* the wings trembling for lift in the air, and you keep one eye ahead of you and the other on the airspeed needle and it's coming around fast, past 40 and still coming. You know she'll fly at 65 but that's pressing it a bit and you've determined to start back on the yoke at 70, because by the time you do that she'll have accelerated to 80 and you'll be in the air and doing 90 before you know it.

You've got 50 and she's really accelerating, *but she's hardly moved from her starting position* as the wings tell you they've got lift. It can't be! It is, it *is!* At that same instant you change your mind, you won't come back on the yoke until she tells you it's time to fly and before you know it the rumble beneath you eases away and the airplane lifts from the ground *in a flat attitude.* You're only doing 58, but before you blink it's 65 and then 75 and now you let the yoke ease back a hair because you want some room for your next maneuver.

The crowd is stunned. They think they're seeing a mirage. The airplane hasn't rolled 400 feet before the big tires have eased upward from the ground. But you forget the crowd, everything except this moment, because now you have enough room, barely enough, and the needle is moving past 90, and in a single fluid motion you shove forward on the yoke and roll the yoke to the left and tromp, and I mean *tromp* the left rudder, and *Annie* rolls into a wicked bank, rolling past 60 degrees, and you keep the nose down because you don't want to bleed away that speed in this turn, and with all your strength you hold down that rudder and keep the yoke rolled left and back in your gut, and that big monster of a locomotive with wings claws about in an astonishing turn, the left wingtip barely a few feet above the grass, but it's all calculated, you have plenty of speed even if you lose an engine or two falter, and it's a hell of a lot safer than it looks, even if you've just taken off in 400 feet and you've made your turn about a thousand feet and maybe twelve hundred from your starting point and you're already going in the opposite direction.

You roll her back level now and center the ball and come back hard on the yoke and the Ju-52 leaps upward like a scalded cat. You're coming back on the throttles, well back to 32 inches and Terry is bringing back the props and synchronizing them so you can pay attention to what you're doing. A gauge flickers, you and Terry and Dee Dee see it, but it steadies down and you're past 1000 feet now and Dee Dee's voice is surprisingly quiet and clear through the intercom. "Fighters at three o'clock, closing for the formation run. They're going wide around us."

You mix into the formation and the crowd doesn't know what to expect because those big flaps are still down and you're into a steep bank and the power comes off, throttles full back and you dump the nose and she comes down like a wounded bird, almost fluttering as you keep slowing and Terry goes to 40-degree flaps and as you fall the fighters come screaming by and Dee Dee hits the smoke switches and *Omigod they're on fire!* and the throttles go forward as the ground comes up and you hold just enough power to rumble down low over the runway at 70 mph as the fighters and trainers beat up the field. Now it's time for Terry to start the flaps back up and you go to full power and start your climb in a wide turn, and this time it's going to be different: a whole gaggle of T-6s are going to chase you down the field and they're always knocking the hell out of you.

Not today. You come around, start the turn in from 1200 feet for the *low* pass down the runway, and the T-6 leader calls for you to start the final turn and descent, and you all grin at one another in the cockpit and it's full throttle *and* the nose down and a hell of a lot of left rudder trim because the speed builds like mad, and this airplane that is never supposed to be able to do better than 140 mph comes out of the sky at 200 indicated and is still picking up speed and you hear the cry of T-6 Lead, "Hey! Slow that thing down, you guys!" but it's too late, that lumbering ancient bomber is now tearing across the field at 230 mph and the tires are only a foot or two above the surface, and you call out on the radio, "All aircraft, the Ju is going to do a sharp pullup and break to the left." T-6 Lead calls that you're in the clear, and directly before the crowd you haul back on the yoke with all your strength and the great old machine bursts upward, nose high, the pullup so sharp that no one even knows the g-loads, but in the cockpit it's tough and in the cabin everyone is pinned to the seats and can't even lift a camera, and you roll her up through 1000 feet and turn off the smoke, and ease away the power and let her slow to 100 mph and everyone is grinning, and it's time to land. Down come the great flaps and the ailerons droop and you set her up very carefully, at 70 mph down the slot and you let her ease earthward, and touch down on the edge of the runway and in just about 420 feet the airplane comes to a dead stop. It's a mixture of yoke back and brakes on as the tires touch, and as she eases to a halt, before the tail can drop, you go forward quickly on the throttles, still holding brakes, and you play the yoke like a violin.

Engines thundering, the Ju-52 stands at the far end of the runway, level, the tail up, and now you work rudder and elevators and

249

The trumpets are silent and the crowd is gone and it's time for the daily after-airshow inspection and checkout. Ted Can-Do-Anything Votoe starts by removing the engine cowlings. *Photo by Ken Rowley*

brakes and the throttles very carefully and you *walk* that thing down the runway at 10 miles an hour, and you know the brakes are heating up but this trick is almost over and you let it all squeeze away and bring the tail down gently, and Terry slides open the top hatch and jams the flagpole into its slot by the left side of the cockpit and you turn on the German marching band music and as you taxi past the crowd, why, that is one hell of a sight to see a hundred thousand people grinning and waving wildly at you and everyone is sharing the thrill.

Hey, don't go away. We have another takeoff in exactly thirty-five minutes . . .

13

The World's Greatest Wingwalk

Skydiving for a pilot is like
practicing drowning for a skindiver.

ANYONE WITH SMARTS

Several years and eighteen hundred flying hours after the rebirth of the great corrugated phoenix, we looked back with immense satisfaction at what we had all performed on the ancient carcass of *Iron Annie*. There had been dire predictions we could never breathe new life into those old metal bones. Pessimists insisted the airplane wouldn't be safe. But no one ever made a stronger machine than the Ju-52, and that knowledge was behind every maneuver we ever flew. We had problems, to be sure, but there isn't an airplane built that lacks that curse. But now we could, and we did, attend to those problems as fast as they arose. We also continued to find ways to improve the airplane. That's a never-ending process, and small details become immense comforts in the long run.

The truth was that we also flew the old girl so hard we often created our need for sudden mechanical work. In 1979 we were guests of the Whittington brothers for the huge air races and airshows held at Homestead, Florida. We flew a couple of airshows every day for a week, mixing in with everything from Sea Furies to Flying Fortresses. In between, we watched the fighters howling their way around the pylons of the race course, until we couldn't stand it any longer. *We* had to do that, and we'd go for a new world speed record for the Ju-52 about a closed course.

The fact that no one had ever bothered to set *any* kind of speed record for a Ju-52 under such circumstances was great. That way, no matter what speed we achieved we'd have a record. It could be rather sluggish. After all, we cruised at 120 mph indicated airspeed when we were on the deck, and we might get 145 to 150 mph wide open. Mustang pilot Johnny Baugh (he flies *Miss Coronado*) climbed into the right seat for the record flight. The chances for any real speed were disappearing as quickly as a mob of mechanics from the fighter pits climbed into the airplane, waving beer cans and shouting encouragement. So we had to make up for the un-expected weight, right?

Instead of approaching the course from three miles out in level flight we climbed an extra thousand feet and then dove for the starting line, coming out flat and level maybe a thousand feet from the entry pylon. We had her pegged to full bore at 36 inches and 2250 RPM and she was singing, and we pounded over the start line at well over 220. Of course, she was also slowing down in a hurry and to overcome the decrepit speed we knew we'd get, spurred on by the rah-rah howls from the cabin, I kicked into overboost to 40 inches and away we went, cutting pylons so low we were clipping bushes with the left wingtip. When it was all over (including oil spraying back from the engines because of the high compression) we had done the course in a world-record time of 168 mph for an official zero-altitude speed run. The FAA observers and the official race judges got together and gave us a huge plaque to commemo-rate the event and our blistering speed.

But for that little affair I had to replace a bunch of valve intakes and exhausts, three cylinders, and a few other engine parts. It was worth it, and so was the lesson implicit in those repairs. First, we *looked for problems;* second, we could now *find* them immediately; third, *we fixed them immediately.* The airplane *never* let us down. That's the bottom line, and you can't ask for more than that. Es-pecially when we flew an airplane far beyond the limits its design-ers had ever intended.

There's always the suspicion, having given you our philosophy about rebuilding and flying these great winged chunks of heavy iron, that we might be overstating the case for ourselves. If you think that's the case, get in line. We also had those same thoughts. Then we had the opportunity to do something about it.

First, Kurt Weil lived in New Jersey, where he was a professor of mathematics and aerodynamics. He was 84 years old, *and the same man who had designed this airplane with Hugo Junkers*. He came to visit us in Florida, and he crawled with me through every inch of the wings and the fuselage and the tail, inspecting with a hard-eyed determination that had us torn between pride at what we had done and fear we hadn't done it as well as we believed. When the old master crawled from the airplane his eyes were bright and shining. He shook his head, but it was in surprise and not dismay.

"It is hard to believe," he said quietly. "After all these years, and the airplane is better now in so many ways than when it was built in 1935 . . ."

The second acid test came in the personal visit from Germany of Kurt Streit. Now here was the most formidable of all the people who would cast a suspicious eye on *Annie*. Kurt Streit had 4500 hours in Ju-52 aircraft! He had been one of the lead test pilots for both Junkers and the Luftwaffe on the airplane. He had flown combat in the Ju-52 at Stalingrad and in North Africa and a few dozen places in between. He had made zero-zero landings in this airplane as a regular course of events to test new equipment *back in 1942*. He was one of the world's outstanding pilots and *the* Ju-52 master.

We flew several weeks with Kurt in the right seat and the left seat. We flew airshows and formations and flathatted across the Florida swamps and had a hell of a time. He taught us tricks with this airplane that only his vast experience could have given him. And *we*, most especially this writer, benefited enormously. In fact, before Kurt returned to Germany, we asked him for the equal of a full Luftwaffe checkout in the airplane. He laughed. "But you've already done everything far beyond what we expected of our pilots!" he said with a huge grin.

No, we hadn't. Because an idea had been growing among a group of us to go after a *real* world's record. And now we were ready.

☆

There's a place by name of Palatka in northeastern Florida where people gather at the local airport beneath signs reading OZONE and ALTITUDE SOUTH, and they come here to fling themselves out of perfectly good airplanes. Skydivers are like that. They disdain the sun-silvered wings to fall like sacks of grain through the sky and risk all on untangling shrouds and blossoming silk, and alight like feathers onto waiting grass and gravel. There came the St. Patrick's Day Boogie and a mob of skydivers met *Iron Annie* and it was love at first sight. They planned a Great Flinging of bodies through the air from the iron bird.

Not that we were new to skydiving. Both Dee Dee and I had jumped. We'd also managed to scrung ourselves up a few times, and after busted knees and twisted ankles and messed-up elbows and a fractured pelvis, that was *enough*. But we continued to jump other people who like that sort of thing. We'd put hundreds of jumpers out at airshows and unexpected gatherings, and the U.S. Army's Golden Knights often jumped with us and we were made members of the army team and it was a great gas, indeed.

One of the army troops, Phil Rogge, asked if I'd ever tried putting people out on the wing of the Ju-52. I stared at him. "Why would I want to do that?" was my retort. He shrugged. "It's fun. On that airplane it would be more fun than with any other airplane I've ever seen."

It was worth considering. Rogge gathered together Andy Keech, Don Yahrling, Norm Ross, and Charlie Burnett, and they ganged up on me. Roger Daigen at that time was flying right seat and was crew chief and *he* thought it was a terrific idea. Now, we'd had them on the wing, but it wasn't the *real* thing. The Ju-52 has rails along the side of the fuselage (no, we didn't add them; the airplane was built that way originally), and some jumpers climbed out and stood against the fuselage before letting loose.

These people meant going out toward the wingtip. That's crazy! Bodies on a wing are the same as enormous spoilers. You might as well hang a barn door flat against the airstream. It would spill off the lift and we'd have the fastest damned stall you ever saw in an airplane. *But* . . . the Ju-52 has enormous lifting power. We could delay the stall if I kept them back from the leading edge . . . Suspicions grew in my mind. I was falling for it.

They showed me a picture of a Lockheed 10E with fourteen maniacs hanging all over the thing. "That's the world-record wingwalk," they chorused.

"The hell it is," I retorted. "They're on the wing *and* the fuselage. You want a record wingwalk they've all got to be on the *wing*."

"Okay, we'll do it," Burnett cried. I hadn't asked him to do it, but it didn't matter.

For our first major test we figured seven on the wing and a cou-

The Great Christmas Cakewalk of 1980. It is aerodynamically impossible, but no one told us that, so we did it. Moments later, the Ju-52 put down her nose and gently rolled over onto her back. What a ride! *Photo by Phil Rogge*

ple of guys atop the fuselage just to see what would happen. *No one knew what to expect.* Especially when they'd be working their way out away from the fuselage.

So we took off the left door and tied nylon ropes and knots around the left engine nacelle and under the wing and along the fuselage and all over the place, and we took off and climbed to 9000 feet. I figured the best thing to do was to cut power so the prop blast wouldn't hurl them away from the airplane when they went outside. We set up the regular routine for a jump run, and I came back on the power to 90 mph indicated (about 115 mph true airspeed) and out they went.

They went sideways from the fuselage, hanging on to that rope, skedaddling their way farther from the airplane, and two more of them climbed up and out through the turret atop the fuselage and there was a whole gang out there now and *what's going to happen next?* Roger Daigen grinned happily at me from the right seat. I should have said he had a broken foot from a skydiving escapade of his own. His smile began to fade swiftly as the Ju-52 started downstairs faster and faster. No power and damned little lift and a hell of a lot of drag, and his smile turned into a glassy, disbelieving stare as the left wing stalled out completely, and we trembled and then shook and then shook madly as the yoke under my hands went crazy and jumped around; with all that unequal lift-drag nonsense out there the left wing dropped sharply, the nose came up and yawed around, and she rolled over on her back just as pretty as you please, shaking like a terrier with the ague.

Just like that, *Annie* was into a rolling vertical dive, shaking wildly, with all sorts of thumping and crashing from the metal flexing, but those lunatics on the wing and atop the fuselage were grinning like crazy and still hanging on. We never got over 140 mph indicated but our rate of descent went like *that* to 4000 feet per minute.

At 5500 feet I shoved forward on the left throttle, the signal to get the hell off, and the people let go and floated away and we came out of it at 4000 feet. Hey — not bad at all!

The idea was planted. We'd go for the world record with nineteen people — *all of them on the left wing only.* That wasn't my first idea. Getting people outside on both wings seemed more sensible. But the forward door of the airplane on the right is directly over the wingroot and that might be a problem. So I took off all the doors and opened the turret to equalize pressure and we went for some practice sessions. Build up slowly for the record. The problem was I never knew of a Ju-52 that had flown with the right door off the airplane. I checked with the German pilots I knew and they told me I was mad. All except Kurt Streit. "*Annie* can do anything!" he said with a laugh in our phone conversation from Germany.

On the first test flight I had a sharp burble at 90 mph during climbout, which left me ready for it when I came in to land. But *why* we had the burble remained a mystery. The airflow about that right wingroot was somehow being messed up. Okay, but we could handle that. We planned a test with six guys on the right wing and six on the left, the latter climbing out the aft cabin door and working their way forward, while the guys on the right wing would ease their way backwards.

We started the test at 7000 feet. Dave Kanamine led six guys out to the left wing, hugging the fuselage, and *Annie* was kicking up a fuss as their bodies sent turbulent air slamming into the tail, and then the six guys started out the right side. We planned for Steve

Weiss to jam his body against the door, plant a foot on the wing and block the wind for the rest of the people. Two jumpers went past him, and Steve *shifted his foot*. That was all she wrote.

A violent blast tore through the airplane. Everything that was loose or mildly connected tore free, and we had a maelstrom of flying parts and pieces in the cockpit and the cabin. The Ju-52 shuddered madly. Even glass covers for the aircraft documents on the cabin walls were torn free and whisked through the aft door. Headsets ripped free and just zapped out of sight. I hit both smoke generators as fast as I could move my hand and as soon as that white smoke streamed back, and a crewman inside the cabin on each side held up a big red sign proclaiming JUMP! everybody dove from the bird.

So we learned *that* lesson. Do not step into that critical juncture of wingroot and leading edge. *Never.* The airplane seems to go mad and the tail shakes wildly. In fact, Jim Garemore, flying in a chase SNJ, looked at us in disbelief. In the cockpit we managed to retain our headsets and heard Jim murmuring: "I think the tail's gonna come off if you don't quit that."

Back to Square One. Let's do it from the left wing only. More sense there than we'd figured, and suddenly we were thrust back into the thicket of learning some basic aerodynamics. How many of us really *live with* changing center of pressure and changing center of lift, massively altered camber, violently disrupted airflow, and crazy imbalances and mangled center of gravity, to say nothing of a mob crawling and stomping around the wings of your airplane?

We did. We made more tests with people along the fuselage. It didn't work out well because *Annie* is slab-sided and doesn't like that. The flow disturbance back to the tail is disastrous, the tail shakes, winds itself into a whirl mode and the yoke goes bananas. We tried it with different power settings, with varying degrees of flaps. We made dozens of flights and we relearned the rule that one must render unto the gods their tribute by obeying the invisible rules that abound on and about airfoils.

For example, if we had put out nine people on each wing, with several of them back behind the wing props, we would have done so in disregard of some basic rules. Most of the lift from a twin-engine plane — and we're a twin with an extra power package up front — takes place inboard of the propeller tips. If you kill the lift between the outside arc of your prop tips and the fuselage on just one side of the plane you can wipe out 30 to 40 percent of your lift. If you keep a gang out there on each side you can lose 60 to 80 percent of all your lift, and that means coming out of the sky like a great finned bomb.

We flew a test with 12 people on the wings, and, figuring we'd need every ounce of lift available, we used 15 degrees of flaps. As I said, a big mistake, but it took us a while, plus the help of Professor John Hoover of the University of Florida's Aerodynamics Office to find out why. We lowered the flaps and signaled the jumpers to take up their wing positions, this time spreading outward from the fuselage in a line, and crouching down low. All of a sudden the Ju-52 snorted, put its nose down sharply, and pounced for earth with a devastating pitchdown. We waved off the jumpers and pulled out.

We met that same day with Dr. Hoover, told him what happened, and listened to him chuckle. When we rolled in 15 degrees of flaps the ailerons also came down and so we had cambered the entire wing for maximum lift. But the bodies strung along the wing gave the left wing a super camber, a center of pressure that moved aft, a center of lift that went forward, an airflow disturbance that un-loaded the tail and let it go *up*, and the normal drag and buffeting we'd expected. The net result was an airplane configured for an immediate steep dive. Hey, no more flaps, man.

We did a flight test with the wingwalkers in position and full power from the engines. I had six guys hanging onto the ropes and 2250 RPM and I went through the gate on the throttles to get 34 inches at 11,000 feet. This test was to see what happened when I held full power *and* tried to hold the nose *up*, to maintain level flight and hold altitude.

We found out what happened, and fast. *We heard the angels sing, that's what.* Everybody was outside and I kept shoving those throt-tles forward and *Annie* was shaking and buffeting like mad and wanting to drop her nose and I was hauling back on the yoke to keep the nose up. The shock waves were hysterical. It was like being slammed in the neck with a two-by-four. *Annie* was descend-ing in a flat attitude and she got behind the power curve, where the power is useless, and I felt her trying to kick down the wing, and then, *boom!* it went. The left wing snapped down and the nose went up and we were whirling through some kind of crazy snap roll. As she came over on her back everybody on the wing jumped and I gave her hard opposite rudder and killed the power and hauled back on the yoke. That must have been some kind of bastardized split-S. It took my legs five minutes to stop dancing on the pedals.

The way we figured it, then, was to anticipate that we would *have* to fall. The trick was to let her come down along a ballistic line, the lift spilled off the left wing, and race with time-gravity-lift-distance-speed, trying to make them all match.

We made final plans to have two men go out first to take positions along the wingroot and we'd just have to endure the buffeting. They'd act as windbreaks to let the wedge of eight more people build up behind the left engine. Then nine more would come out and this last bunch would have it easy, because with air howling *over* them they could dance and prance if they wanted.

Some of the numbers show what you can do. We removed all the seats and put in heavy floor eyebolts for jumper security on takeoff, hung M-18 grenades under the wingtips for red smoke, built a great camera boom on the left-wing leading edge to which Ken Lindsley stuck a couple of cameras, hung cameras all over the airplane, and stuffed Mike Fuller with camera, powerpack, parachute, and himself into the cargo tunnel for a 300-pound load. Don Yahrling rode right seat, and we had our crew chief and 19 walkers. We played it careful with a bunch of camera and chase planes to ride shotgun for air traffic and communicate with Jacksonville Center. To my right was the SNJ with Jim Garemore, behind us an AT-11 flown by John Silberman, a Cessna 206 to our left with another camera, and well above us a Skylane with Brent Holman at the controls and Phil Paxton in charge of everything.

We had 24 people aboard and 400 gallons of fuel, which took us to an even 23,000 pounds at takeoff. I used Runway 35 at Palatka with 25 degrees of flaps and minus 1.5 degrees on the stabilator trim. Before winding up to normal max power for takeoff (36 inches and 2250 RPM) I told everyone aboard that if we were not airborne within 3000 feet of starting the takeoff roll I'd chop power and abort the takeoff (with plenty of stopping room in front of us). That airplane never fails to amaze us. We wound it up and cut the brakes and just about 1200 feet from starting the takeoff roll, with only a gentle breeze, the Ju-52 lofted easily from the runway without even tugging back on the yoke.

It was a perfect day, with ice-crystal clouds all about us to add a touch of fantasy to our surroundings. At 8500 feet I started on the final run with the power set at high cruise and an airspeed of

120 mph indicated. I cut them loose. "Let 'em go," was my quiet release, and as an afterthought I brought in the props to 2100 RPM for any faster power response if I needed it. The first six went out fast. Dave Kanamine took point position behind the left engine and Mike Maguire pulled himself forward along the fuselage. They blocked the worst of the wind for everyone else.

They were going outside steadily, I got the expected buffeting, and immediately saw a rate of descent of 1000 feet per minute and the speed start building. I could *feel* the effect of those bodies out there, but I was ready for all this with the months of practice behind us.

My first real big surprise came with a sudden severe yaw of the nose to the left. She really started clawing in that direction and I kicked right rudder as hard as I could to bring her around. Our speed went to 140 mph indicated, which was faster than I believed, and she put her nose down as that gang kept pouring out on the wing and the plunge became damned serious as the rate of descent came right around to 4000 feet per minute. And *then* the shaking went wild.

For a while I didn't think I could hang on to her. Don Yahrling was helping me all the way through, but I had no time to look at what he was doing; I *felt* his hands and feet working with me. He was beautiful. The airplane was shaking like mad. The buffeting was wild, really bad. We got into a pogo effect, a weird and frightening up and down. What I didn't know (and the films showed later and the wingwalkers explained) was that the left wing was twisting wildly, they could *see* it flexing like mad, and the right wing was drumming like a washboard, and then we got this terrific KA-BOOM! KABOOM! sound. She was oil-canning (metal expanding rapidly in and out) like one fast explosion after another. Our speed built up to a true 190 mph, and the yaw was just tremendous, and I was holding full left rudder to keep the ball centered, and of course she was trying to roll over on her back, and now I had in full right aileron, so there we were, coming out of the sky at nearly 200 mph and something like 5000 feet a minute, fully crossed controls, and I began to have doubts the airplane, or any airplane, could stay together under this beating.

We were slamming up and down in the seats and my head hit the top of the cockpit and the gauges were barely visible through the blur. Several times I told myself to hit the emergency smoke switches to stop this madness, because it began to dawn on me

We did it! The World's Greatest Wingwalk on November 14, 1981 — *and* the All-Time World Wingwalk Record, to boot. Nineteen skydivers crowd the left wing of the Ju-52. Starting out at 8500 feet, we came down like a lopsided bomb. Pucker Factor was 103 percent. *Photo by Ken Lindsley*

that with all their gear, *I had 4000 pounds of people standing on one wing.* It looked like *Air India* out there. Things were getting so violent I had to cut power fully and now I was aiming the airplane in a dive with crossed controls. A hell of a way to fly. In addition to all that weight out there I had to overcome the tremendous drag and buffeting that was reducing control in the tail area.

I finally glanced out at the left wing and I didn't believe what I saw. *The wing was twisting and rippling before my eyes.* I yelled to the crew to *"Get them the hell off!"* and I started reaching with my right hand for the emergency smoke switches. Someone yelled "They're going!" but it couldn't be too soon for me at that point.

The vibration was really bad, we were being banged around in the cockpit, the noise was unbelievable, and I was convinced by now I had to have been completely mad to do this. Garemore in the SNJ told me later that the right wing had become a blur like a vibrating diving board and he couldn't even make out details with all the twist-flex-bend-ripple motion, but even as all this was happening I felt it all easing swiftly as bodies left the airplane. I couldn't see any of them, of course, but the airplane responded with every single form that flew away behind us, and the forward slip eased, and the thundering buffeting began quickly to calm down, and then, with astonishing abruptness, it was pure glass up there.

I mean, absolutely smooth. Silken flight. The maniacs had been dancing and running and jumping and doing sidesteps and backflips off the wing, and they were forming stars and squares on the way down in their chutes, and I snarled something about counting the damned chutes and they gave me a report of twenty canopies in the air. Yahrling and I stared at one another. Twenty? It turned out that Art Barchie, the jumpmaster, had become so excited with everything that he threw himself out of the airplane even before all the wingwalkers had sailed away.

Once we knew that everyone was safe on the ground we put the nose down and turned on the smoke generators and did a fast beat-up of the field, came around and landed, parking on the grass, and out came the cigars and the beer and shouting and yelling and by God, we had the world's wingwalking record, and who said there's no fun in flying anymore?

☆

Comments from the Wingwalkers and the Crew Chief —

———————— ☆ ————————

Six people outside and *Annie* begins to shiver. Ten, then eleven, and the shivers become shakes. She begins to act rough and it's hard to walk inside the aircraft. The horizon is tilting, and, bouncing from side to side, I grope for the door. I've never been so glad to get out of an airplane in my life. When I jump I feel weightless as I float gently over the wing, but this ends abruptly as I smash into a wall of wind like nothing I've ever felt.

CHARLIE BURNETT

———————— ☆ ————————

We got on the final run, and when I started outside I didn't know if I could fight my way out to start the wedge. The winds were wild! The plane started buffeting and we began to pound real hard, like crazy. We were dropping like a stone and I was hanging on as hard as I could . . .

DAVE KANAMINE

─────────────── ☆ ───────────────

It was murder out there. I was fourth man and that meant pushing into a thundering wind that made it hard to work forward. It was very intense and wildly exciting.

TROY WHITE

─────────────── ☆ ───────────────

I was surprised with how smoothly the actual wingwalk went, even though there were problems. The buffeting was worse for other people than it was for me. When the plane is sinking like it was there's no wind in my position, number six. I was in a burble. When I left the wing I was still in that burble and I stepped back and it was gentle, but once I got behind the trailing edge of the wing, my God, it was like being hit with a sledgehammer.

STEVE WEISS

─────────────── ☆ ───────────────

Riding on that wing was like riding a bucking bronco.

CARL COLE

─────────────── ☆ ───────────────

When we were out on the wing, whenever I tried to frame a picture with the helmet camera, and Jim Barker moved his head, the wind would blast my head off. Both Maguire's and my pack flaps were blown open. We had an intense, tremendous speed.

GORDON HARDAGE

─────────────── ☆ ───────────────

I was hoping Marty in the cockpit wouldn't feel the tremendous vibration we had on the wing because if he did I believed he would hit the emergency smoke signal for us to get off. It was marvelous.

263

End of a perfect ride as the skydivers team up in stacks "for the hell of it" after completing the world-record wingwalk. *Photo by Gene Chevalier*

We held on outside and they stayed with it inside. We all made a great team.

NORM ROSS

———————— ☆ ————————

When we were on the wing and it started to buffet I was afraid they would call it off, that I would see the white smoke. It got pretty bad out there for a while. It was like trying to walk in an earthquake. The exit off the wing was easy, until I went back from the wing, and then, *THWAP!* It was like being smacked a terrific blow by a giant hand.

ALICE RAGLE

——————— ☆ ———————

I was number seventeen so there was plenty of time for the wing to load up with people, and by then, with all that drag and weight, the plane was a bucking bronco, really slamming up and down.

CLYDE BEATTIE

——————— ☆ ———————

It was unreal because it became so violent. Once the group was really piling up on the wing and the drag and turbulence became severe, the front of the airplane was a madhouse. We were shaking like crazy and we got this tremendous up-and-down motion along with everything else, a deep booming sound like the world's biggest drum . . . and then I saw the left wing flexing and twisting like mad even while it was bending up and down and I wondered if the plane was coming apart. You can't get much closer than that to a feeling that you're going to die . . .

BILL THARP
(800 jumps; crew chief)

——————— ☆ ———————

14

The Best Seat
in the House

I like women in flying. I've always got
room for 120 pounds of recreational
equipment.

PETE SHERMAN

The lady is an incurable romantic who indulges in a love affair
with the skies. She follows the sun and lofts gently through high
clouds, is friendly with curling mists and loves to watch (at a re-
spectful distance) brooding pillars of dark looming high above
earth. She keeps a careful distance from lightning (when she can)
despite shockingly close encounters, and she's had most unpleasant relationships with tornados. She gambols on grass strips and
has drifted earthward beneath shroud lines and silken canopies.
She floats cross-country in wicker baskets beneath great swollen
bags heated with propane fire, and she's known aerobatics in
everything from ragwings to howling jets. Her own logbook records a satisfying variety of homebuilts to bombers, Spam Cans to
jet choppers.

But what she likes best of all, it seems, is what she calls the best
seat in the house. Sometimes that's the left seat, on other occasions
the right seat, and quite often the back seat. "That way," she ex-
plains, "I've flown with some of the best pilots in the world, done

things I could never do on my own, and had *the* grandstand seat in airshows and aerobatic performances only a few are ever privileged to enjoy. Besides, it's a hell of a lot of fun to have some of the greatest pilots who ever flew turn to me when it's over and worry about how *I* liked the flight!"

The lady is, among other things, very independent when it comes to her flying. She'll tell you at the drop of a flight cap that she's earned that right and she'll brook no nonsense on the matter of getting grease on your clothes and dirt beneath your nails when there are airplanes to be maintained and long weekends to be spent helping other pilots in a warbird rebuilding effort. We met Dee Dee earlier in these pages, especially through Jack Kehoe in his chapter, "Coming Up Sixes." But I have a different role for my wife to play.

Having flown that "best seat in the house" so often, she has the best perspective to share with the reader: that rare vantage of what the airshows and aerobatic sessions and madcap flying are really about. Hers, in this case, is the position of the observer. How often have we said, "I'd love to be there *just watching* . . ." Well, she said it, and she did it, and from her diaries and logbook I've prevailed upon Dee Dee to share with you the events she shared with the people who drive the ragwings and the heavy iron.

Join her now in one of the mightier Mustangs . . .

———————— ☆ ————————

Whenever I see a beautiful blue sky speckled with soft, puffy clouds my mind is always drawn back to March twenty-seventh in 1977. That was my greatest Mustang flight of all that I've made, and it was in a very special Mustang with a very special friend, a 2300-horsepower fighter flown by Pete Sherman.

We — the airshow pilots, ground crews, aircrews, wives, children, friends — were part of a great airshow at Ft. Lauderdale Executive Airport, just north of Miami in Florida. We flew the show for two purposes. It wouldn't be the truth if I didn't say the first purpose was the flying itself, but the second was about as important to everybody involved. We were raising money for an orphanage. Together, those two reasons brought a terrific turnout by the warbird people.

We had about seven P-51 Mustangs, our own Ju-52, a *purple* Messerschmitt Me-109 flown by Don Whittington, the usual mob of T-6, T-34, and T-28 trainers, a mixture of different fighters and

267

bombers and transports. At the pilot briefing the leaders decided to open the main part of the airshow with the Ju-52 and the Me-109 strafing the flight line. The fighter pilots would then scramble to their aircraft, start them up, taxi out, and take off in a "wild melee" and form up once they were airborne. The whole idea was tremendously exciting.

I was still fairly new to airplanes in terms of being a pilot or flying in a warbird, but I did have *some* experience. I had already crashed in the Messerschmitt and had flown right seat in *Iron Annie* when the left engine was burning. I had some fifty hours of flying time on my own, but best of all, Pete Sherman and I were close friends, and I flew with Pete two months earlier at another airshow. I felt completely comfortable with him.

The fighters were all neatly lined up on the flight line, and about twenty minutes before show time all the passengers for the fighters were strapped tightly within the confines of rear seats. The "passenger seat" for the Mustang originally held radio gear, so that should give you some idea of how much space there was back there. The position of your body is similar to that when you're milking a cow — hunched over with very little room for your head and constantly kissing your knees. Now all we had to do was wait. The pilots were talking in small groups out on the flight line while the passengers baked in the airplanes. Thank goodness this was March instead of August.

Then came the signal to scramble! *Annie* came thundering toward the field and steepened into a dive directly at the flight line, with Don doing rolls and some pretty wild maneuvers as the two planes beat up the field. Sirens went off and people began running about in different directions.

Of all the airshows to which I have ever gone, this one really sticks in my mind, especially this moment. With the pilots scattering to their planes you really *felt* the sense of urgency. There was a professional (call it military) crispness, a feeling, because you just *knew* these pilots were going to save the day!

Pete pulled his chocks, leaped onto the wing, and climbed in. I already had my headset on so that when Pete talked to the other pilots I heard every word. We would take the lead, so Pete started his engine at once. Good Lord, what a roar! I'd forgotten he had the super-powerful engine in this thing. Pete taxied right out, with the others close behind. We went through some sort of checklist as we were taxiing, but stopped just short of the runway to complete the runup. Some of the other fighters were going to do formation takeoffs but we did it solo; maybe because of the larger engine or because we were leader. But I did know that with all that power up front you don't go to full throttle at once! Pete rolled onto the runway, straightened out on the centerline, and *eased* in the power.

Once the tail comes up (in seconds) the visibility from the back seat really makes this the best seat in the house. It's unmatched by any other plane I've ever flown, including the jets. Pete had a special racing canopy on his bird, so that from front to back there isn't even the first seam, nothing but clear Plexiglas. The view was clear in front of me, to the sides, and behind me. When we built to take-off speed the Mustang refused to stay on the ground, but Pete didn't horse her off. He lifted her gently from the ground and waited a bit to cycle the gear. Pete loved his bird and it showed in everything he did.

Once airborne we headed into a fantasy world of towering clouds. There might have been an airshow waiting for us on the ground, but Pete always heard siren calls in the sky and he could never resist taking a special look all around him. We circled one cloud and we seemed to levitate, to float along without any effort as Pete sliced his wingtip into frothy wisps of white. I heard the other fighter pilots calling out their locations, trying to team up with us, but to me it was the child's game of blindman's buff: see if you can find us. We were making swooping curves and shallow turns around the cloud banks and I kept looking for other fighters. There! But the instant I caught sight of one of the other planes, Pete also had him in sight and we raced about a cloud. Hide-and-go-seek; it was marvelous.

I think I finally hit on an expression to convey the feelings that swept through me then: you are a child again and all around you are the wonders of which dreams are made, floating in the sky and laughing, and hiding and playing among the valleys and mountains in the sky. When you're a pilot you're aware that at any time something can go wrong, but on a day like this, for a few moments you "forget" the dangers, and you enjoy dancing among the angels.

When the other birds finally started to catch up with us (because Pete finally came way back on the power of that huge engine), I spotted Johnny Williams's *Color Me Gone* edging up on our right, and Scott Smith in *GiGi* sliding onto our left wing. The other fighters were forming up slowly, and soon we were a great wedge riding through the cloud canyons.

269

"Mustang Lead from Airshow One." I heard the call to Pete on the headset. "Marty and Don are coming around for a final run, and you are cleared for a formation low pass down the runway." Pete checked with the other pilots and we began the descending wide turn for the "attack" in front of the crowd. From our altitude I saw three airports, but couldn't make out, really, just where we were. All *my* attention had been spent up here! I saw two airfields that *could* have been ours, and then my attention was back on the flying.

Pete put the Mustang into a beautiful slow dive and the sky fell away from us in a marvelous swooping motion, all the guys with us following in perfect order. This was *exciting* — to look behind me and see so many P-51s bouncing and bobbing in the air through turbulence and yet keeping perfect formation. And everybody *diving!*

As we dropped lower, the ground details became more than tiny distant specks and the outline of the airport before us became much sharper. Somehow the details didn't seem right to me, but then, I wasn't familiar with this area. And neither was Pete, as it turned out.

The first real clue I had that we weren't where we were supposed to be when we came diving down through a thousand feet, the whole swarm of Mustangs, really getting it on, and I saw an Eastern jetliner on the runway, *and I knew that Executive Airport didn't have any airliner traffic.*

We weren't more than two or three hundred feet up, ripping past the jetliner, when an agitated voice came through the headsets. "This is Airshow One to Mustang Leader. Where the hell are you guys?"

Pete answered calmly. "We're making the bounce, ah, *now.* Right on the deck —"

And we were, screaming down the runway, right on the deck, in perfect formation, *at the wrong airport!* We had just completed an unscheduled, uncleared, unannounced, and beautiful buzz job of Fort Lauderdale *International* Airport! We got a close-up view of airliners and the tower crew staring at us in disbelief, and they got the greatest view of their lives of a swarm of Mustangs tearing by right before them.

Pete broke out to the left and we continued in a steady wide turn at better than three hundred miles an hour, everybody still in perfect formation, and headed for the right field. The show was delayed somewhat until we hit Executive Airport, and from a different heading than we had planned, and we got loud razzberries from the Ju-52 and the Me-109 as we flashed beneath them.

Pete Sherman never heard the end of the hazing he got from the rest of the pilots for his Wrong Bounce formation attack. But to me it only made the day all the greater, because through it all I had everybody in sight and had a double airshow pass. There have been some fantastic moments in the skies since then, but this is the flight I always remember when I soar into a beautiful blue sky filled with the marble-white clouds that soar upward, on and on and on . . .

☆

Sometimes the best seat in the house can be the most frightening thing in flying. Especially if you're a pilot yourself. I am, even if my category is neophyte in the logbook department. But I've had enough experience and have flown with some of the finest pilots in the business *to know when to be scared.* So climbing into the copilot seat or even the back seat can be very trying, indeed. After all, you know what *you* can and can't do. But if you don't know the pilot who's flying the plane into which you strap your body, it can get very hairy. There are also times when you find out *quickly* what people can do when the boom lowers without warning. I found that there's equal value in the bliss of ignorance, when I took a flight in a Messerschmitt bf-108B in Harlingen, Texas, back in 1976.

Behind me at that time were six months of fairly steady and hard flying on my own. I'd already found the heart-squeezing joy of aerobatics and spins, and I'd been bitten deeply by the flying bug and I was eager (sometimes *too* eager) to fly with anyone in anything. I just love to fly. Just before the 108 junket, I'd spent an hour in a Breezy, that homemade contraption of flyweight aluminum girders for a fuselage, all of it naked and without a shred of covering. The wing had it, so I shrugged. I put on a Red Baron helmet and goggles to keep the bugs out of my eyes and remembered not to smile too broadly in the air. You can mash a grasshopper pretty far into your teeth that way. And it was a new experience to have a pusher engine and propeller well behind us.

The old man who helped strap me into the front seat was a dear; and he was seventy-eight years old! I felt as if I were sitting on the far end of a horizontal flagpole. There was no canopy over me, nothing to the sides, no doors, a whole open world in front of me. All I had was the seat to which I was strapped and a floorboard on which to rest my heels, with my feet on the rudder pedals. And a throttle and control stick. That's it! Breezy has small tires, and it felt as if I were seated on a stool with a skateboard beneath me.

I was *so* unknowing at this time about what to be afraid of that I never questioned climbing onto that stuck-together contraption. Breezy took off at sixty, cruised at sixty, and landed at sixty, or so it seemed to me. I didn't pay much attention to the numbers, because starting down the runway was like rushing toward the portals of a whole new world.

Everything was . . . so finely tuned, is about the way I would put it. The roar of the engine was so much louder because we were completely in the open, and to hear the wind and *feel* it against my face and body was almost like a miracle. And the *flying!*

I felt as free as a bird, breathless, excited. I wanted to clap my hands and shout with delight, to laugh with the wind. There was *nothing* around me — only the whole world! The wind tugged ever stronger, my hair blew wildly, and I could see everywhere! And the turns! I should have been frightened when we banked and there was nothing visible between me and the earth. When we came back to land it was the first time I'd ever felt the airplane was holding position in midair and the earth just rose to meet me, expanding its details until the runway suddenly appeared all around us, and I could feel and smell the heat off the ground and we were rolling and bumping.

If that wasn't enough, as I was leaving Breezy and grinning like an idiot child, Walt Wooten waved me over to the Messerschmitt and offered me a flight. Now, let me explain that going from Breezy to a Messerschmitt is almost like going from a Piper Cub to a Mustang fighter. Terry Ritter, our crew chief for the Ju-52, came rumbling over and climbed into the back seat. Walt Wooten took left seat and I strapped in by his side. The door hinges from a forward post so that it latches at the rear and swings forward, and I kept it open a few inches to keep cooler air flowing into the cockpit. Talk about your taildraggers; the 108 engine blocked everything from sight straight ahead. Walt S-turned to the runup area, I closed and latched the canopy, he went through the runup, and we eased onto the runway. I was still blind to a forward view but then Walt brought up the tail and the world snapped into view, and that little sucker wound up and grabbed at the air about us.

We went across the flat countryside at about five hundred feet, rolling into steep banks and soaring about and having a marvelous time. Walt Wooten was a magnificent pilot; by now I had come to recognize the touch of the superior fliers, from all the men with whom I'd flown. After a while Walt turned to me. He couldn't conceal his own grin. "You want to try it?"

Does a bird fly? I took the controls and, of course, *over*controlled. Was this thing ever sensitive! After a few minutes and trying coordinated maneuvers, everything fell into its proper place and I had time to marvel at the crisp and smooth response of this little airplane. I crossed an irrigation ditch and turned so I could do S-turns down the ditch to see how well I was doing.

The crash was deafening . . . but we were still in the air! What had happened? I had just experienced my first complete and instant engine failure. One moment we were flying smoothly and in the next instant we were in a heavy glider. Wooten's hand snapped to the stick, and his other hand flew about the engine and fuel controls as he tried to restart the engine, *very* quickly, considering our altitude. No way; that engine was deader than an anvil.

Walt scanned the countryside to which we were descending without hope of stopping that descent, called in a mayday, switched off the fuel, made certain the gear was up, and prepared to crash-land the airplane in a plowed field. In all honesty I must say I wasn't frightened, and for two reasons. There wasn't time enough for the luxury of being scared — and I was fascinated! The ground rushed at us but that wasn't anything new, and Walt eased up the nose until we felt the ground scraping beneath us. *That* wasn't smooth! We started bouncing around and a wall of trees seemed to be racing toward us, and I remember that Walt still had enough speed for the rudder to be effective and his foot slammed down hard; even with the gear up we skidded into a sideways ground loop that stopped us as if we'd thrown out an anchor.

I have a *very* clear memory of cotton plants swirling over the canopy, and dirt flying about, and the hammering-skidding of the fuselage along the rutted earth. When we came to a sudden stop I heard a voice that wasn't my own, but it *was* coming from me, and it said, "Let's get the hell out of here!" and I shoved open that side canopy. In a flash we were on the ground running from the airplane, Walt on one side of me and Terry on the other, and only then did I realize they each had grabbed an arm and my legs were running but my feet weren't touching the ground. When we were far enough from the plane that we wouldn't be hurt if she suddenly blew or burned, we turned to look back at the 108. In a calm voice, almost resigned, Walt said, "That's the *seventh* time she's just quit like that."

The farmer was so mad at us for messing up his field he wouldn't let us use his phone! It was a long walk back.

☆

Formation flying is an art. I learned that quickly from the back seat of trainers and fighters, from the right seat of bombers, and more than a hundred hours of airshow flying in the right seat of the Ju-52, and some more time than that either in the cabin or strapped into the turret shooting movies of the madcap adventures about us.

As an art it takes a *lot* of practice and patience. You start out learning any one of a number of ways. Some pilots go upstairs, a couple planes at a time, and take turns "forming up" on one another, and I'll tell you now, after having flown with the old pros, that is *not* the way to do it. Other pilots have someone "talk them through"; that is, keep on their butt all the time with a steady flow of verbal instructions. That isn't the greatest way, either. My own preference is to be taught by the best, and that would be one of the all-time truly great instructors, and have him in front of me in a T-34 trainer. The name would be (and is) Bob Casey. He's a retired air force colonel, and he's spent his entire life driving airplanes; every kind of airplane. He's one of the greatest formation pilots I've ever flown with and been instructed by, and had the privilege of watching from the ground, and hearing other pilots exclaiming in wonder and respect at his skills. To quote my husband: "I've flown with that dude in a lot of iron, and I'll tell you right now, when Bob Casey latches onto your tail, you can't shake him off because no matter what you do he's gonna stay with you like a leech."

I wanted to know *how*, and flying with Casey is an event of five particular formation flights I'd like to share with you.

We returned from a huge whoop-de-do airshow in the Carolinas, with the warbird crowd breaking up into different groups and going their own ways. I'd flown up in the Ju-52 but I was coming home with Casey in the T-34. I loved the airplane; low-wing, good power, very maneuverable and responsive. In the two and a half hours after takeoff, Casey drilled me through the initial introduction to formation flying. How to spot where you want your plane

274

to end up, how to come in from below, or pitch out sooner than you believe you'll need to because you have an invisible enemy in your formation work. It's called *momentum,* and it may carry you belly-first into the plane on which you're formating. So it's jockey up from below and get into position, using the elevators, ailerons, rudder, *and power.* Power is above all the single most important element you need to maintain your tight formation.

We needed another plane to practice what I was being taught, and there's nothing better than *Iron Annie.* She's perfect because she is so big and is relatively slow in cruise. We used *Annie* for our classroom. Once we got into position to really tighten it up, I learned to slowly, *slowly* ease the airplane into that space between the trailing edge of the huge Junkers wing, the leading edge of the horizontal stabilizer, and the fuselage. We did this again and again, and I was amazed every time at how Casey would bring it in real tight in a space already tight to begin with. Again and again Casey "parallel parked" with the Ju-52 and made me go through the drill with him, until I did it on my own.

Was I ever proud of me!

Until Casey said, "I've got it, Dee Dee," and I released the controls. We backed off from the huge shape of the Ju-52 and Casey thumbed his mike switch: "Ju, this is Casey. Think you can hold that thing straight and level for a while? And don't even twitch until I call you again?"

I won't repeat what my husband said, but he did agree. Casey called me on the intercom. "Put both hands on top of your head." I did as he told me and my eyes widened as Casey then did the same with his own hands, *and then slowly, using his feet on the rudder pedals and bracing the stick between his knees, he edged the T-34 back into that same tight space and held perfect formation with our wing overlapping the Ju-52!*

Look at the picture!

☆

On two of my next formation flights I had entered a new world of flying. I knew enough now to understand what was going on about me, and you can spell that as knowing enough to be scared.

I had the rare opportunity to fly in a Russian Yak-11C fighter-trainer, a wicked little machine about the size of a T-6, but with 750 horsepower. To give you an idea of this machine's incredible performance, it has only 150 hp more than the T-6, but is about 80 miles an hour faster! Anthony Hutton of England flew some air-shows with us, and some months later shipped the Yak-11C to our hangar in Florida, where we all reassembled the tough little air-plane. My husband went roaring off with Tony in the Yak, and both came back grinning like kids. They'd tossed the Yak around and run through a bunch of wild airshow passes, and now it was my turn. I wasn't *that* used to having a parachute strapped to me, and the helmet and goggles for *inside* the airplane also made me a bit uncomfortable.

The Yak is a *hard* airplane. Everything it does, happens with a *BANG!* There's nothing smooth about it. The exhaust is a constant exploding roar. The brakes are air-pressure systems, and they smash and bang every time they're used. There's nothing smooth about the airplane except when it gets into the air; even then those huge cylinders thrashing within that engine impart a real body-bruising vibration. And let me tell you, when an airplane is really tossed around the sky, the back seat is *not* the place to be. All the forces are increased on your body, and, well, rapidly I found myself more and more uncomfortable.

One of the ways I feel about flying in a plane is that if anything went wrong with the pilot, can *I* land the thing? It doesn't even matter if I can actually do it; just if I *think* I can. I really didn't believe I could land the Yak if Tony Hutton keeled over or some-thing. Everything is written in Russian, the systems work with air pressure, the gauges were incomprehensible to me.

Even when we formed up on the Ju-52 I did not feel comfortable. I found I was bracing myself with both hands through every ma-neuver. It wasn't Tony; he's a brilliant pilot. It was just the whole miserable situation.

When we pitched out it was like banging two steel bars together, and I wondered if this airplane could ever land without a crash. I felt perspiration down my face and running over my lips and mouth, and I also felt silly at my reactions.

When we parked, I found out that I was bleeding profusely from my nose, a result of the pitchout and pulling of those hard g-forces.

☆

The last airplane I ever expected to be frightened in, on a clear day, in smooth air, and with two engines (both running), was an Aero-star. We were returning from Leesburg to Gainesville after an air-show, and the Aerostar owner had talked Martin into letting him

"I see it but I don't believe it . . ." Bob Casey up front and Dee Dee Caidin in the back seat of the T-34 as they hold formation, *wings overlapping*, with the Ju-52. "Look, ma — no hands!" *Photo by Becky Ritter*

fly right seat in the Ju-52. In return, he offered me a flight in his airplane to be flown by his pilot. Air conditioning and a comfortable seat and a cool drink in an airplane I'd never flown in before? You bet.

What a mistake! I should have remembered that it was 106° F in the shade that day and we'd be flying low, and the Aerostar has thin wings and the airplane does *not* like to fly slow. Martin would be flying both low and slow; he had six hundred gallons of fuel and sixteen people aboard. I learned we were going to fly wing-to-wing formation with the bigger airplane.

I saw *Annie* in the distance as we closed swiftly. Martin was flying only about 110 miles per hour. The airplane loomed faster and faster before us and the Aerostar pilot kept pulling back on the throttles to slow down so he could stay with *Annie,* and it dawned on me that *he couldn't*. Not unless he asked the Ju to open up on the power and pick up another twenty or thirty mph. But he didn't, and to stay alongside *Annie* he had to lower his gear and then his flaps and he kept increasing his angle of attack until we were rumbling, and I mean *rumbling*, through the air in a very nose-high attitude. The stall warning was blaring and the Aerostar was mushing. We were at only fifteen hundred feet and I knew this was very stupid, because we were on the edge of a stall for nearly fifteen minutes.

What was even more stupid was that I kept quiet. Lesson Number One: if you're uncomfortable or frightened of what's going on, *sound off*. Tell the pilot. In this case I could have called the Ju-52 by radio and simply asked Martin to increase his speed. Instead, I just sat there frightened half to death until our airport came into sight.

☆

The opposite side of the coin was a flight in a Messerschmitt Me-208 with Ray Martin. Talk about a *wonderful* experience! When I flew with Ray, it was as if I'd strapped the airplane to my back, and become one and the same with the machine. Everything *flowed* together. We did all sorts of maneuvers, formation work, and even airshow performances, and it was one of the loveliest and smoothest flights I ever had. The key was that Ray never *pushed* the 208 around. He caressed and talked to that airplane and she responded like the lady she was. Ray Martin is one of the greatest pilots with whom I've ever flown.

The occasion was an airshow with the Valiant Air Command at Ti-Co Airport, and it was a true gathering of the clan. Ray was discussing with my husband the details of formation work and some wild action before the crowd, and I happened to be in the right place at the right time. I asked Ray casually if I could fly the show with him. "Can I, huh, huh, *huh?*" He laughed and told me to hop in. Unlike the 108, the 208 has wide tricycle gear and it's a dream to handle on the ground. The visibility is superb and everything is like — well, honey-smooth. We took off first and climbed rapidly, circling the runway as the Ju-52 took off with the doors off and people in the doorways and a gunner in the turret. Watching a rare sight like that below me, I even forgot I was *flying*. I seemed to be on a magic carpet just floating through the air, and then we began to work our way in with the Ju-52.

278

The tough little Yak-11P, Tony Hutton and Dee Dee Caidin in the cockpit, warms up in front of the Ju-52 for the lady's first flight in the Russian fighter-trainer. *Photo by Ken Lindsley*

Ray had done this many times before and he called the Ju the finest airplane he'd ever worked with for maneuvering and formation work. I was amazed with how comfortable I felt, even when Ray called *Annie* and asked for a steady run, and then he eased upward until our propeller was scarcely a foot beneath that mass of corrugated metal, and the whole world above us was filled with the sight of that airplane. I was thrilled; absolutely wowed by the whole event. We were as light as a feather and as free as a bird and it is truly one of my most memorable flights.

How marvelous it is to fly with the best.

☆

Another super "hands on the controls" flight was one of many I've made in a T-6 with Jack Kehoe. He is my dear, dear friend and an old flying buddy of my husband. Two brothers were never closer. Jack and I flew out of Merritt Island Airport, just south of Cape Canaveral, and flew out over the Atlantic Ocean. We came back, pitched out over our home, and circled for a while, and without

warning I heard the invitation I always love to hear: "Take it —
she's yours."

I'd heard so many horror stories about the T-6 I couldn't believe
how solid and responsive the airplane was. Jack told me to stay in
the turn, and in that awesome moment when you become part of
the airplane, my right hand rested easily about the stick, my left
on the throttle, and my feet were at home on those big rudder pedals. I made shallow turns left and right, and we maneuvered
through climbing turns and chandelles and wingovers and I was a
piggy little girl rooting in seventh heaven!

I thought I'd found my ultimate thrill until a gang of T-6s came
up to join us. There were Jim Garemore and George Morris and
some other pilots and we all formed up into a great vee and Jack
told me to stay on the controls, he'd be riding with me if I did
anything wrong. Terrific! We all made a formation pass on the deck
down the runway of Patrick Air Force Base and the whole thing
was unbelievable — *me* flying the airplane with that mob.

Thank goodness Jack didn't ask me to land the airplane!

☆

A thrill of another kind. That's the best way to describe my first
flight in a T-33 jet with George Baker during a big airshow at Langley Air Force Base in Virginia. The T-33 is a jet fighter-trainer and
to me one of the sleekiest and sexiest machines ever to fly. Not
knowing *what* I'd be flying in, but told to put on jeans, flight boots,
and a jacket, I was driven to the flight line by the other pilots and
offered the T-33 as a surprise. It was! George Baker helped me on
with my parachute and then began the litany of emergency canopy
release and helmet and oxygen mask and then the ejection lever.

Ejection lever? Me? "George," I said in my best nonquavering
voice, "I've jumped before, remember? I don't want to do it again!"
George nodded, smiled, and helped me into the back seat and
again went over my mask and oxygen hose and all those foo-faddle
connections. He took the front seat and we checked the intercom.
I could hear myself breathing. I was hoping he couldn't hear me. I
was nearly panting, and at this rate we'd be out of oxygen in 15
minutes flat. And then, we were on the runway and George brought
in the throttle and —

We rolled. Faster and faster. And we continued to roll. Faster and
faster *and faster*. Was this thing *ever* going to take off? Finally (at
last!) the nose came up, the rumble of contact with the ground

faded, I heard all the garbage come clanking and banging into wells and doors closing and . . .

It couldn't be real. It was smooth beyond all comprehension. No thundering engine, no whirling propeller, no thrashing pistons about us. Just this incredible sense of power and the nose pointing up and up and up and we were going straight up into a blue infinity and just — like — *that* — we leveled at fifteen thousand feet.

George brought me on to those supersensitive controls very carefully, and I felt my way around the sky, a sort of prodding at 500 miles an hour, which must sound as silly to you as it does to me, but that's the way it *was*.

"Hey, Dee Dee, want to do some rolls?" George had his happy-youngster tone in his voice. "You bet!" I sang out.

Faster than I could blink or even realize what was truly happening, we whirled — that's *whirl*, not roll — around and around to the left, stopped on a razor's edge in level flight, and then the world was spinning the other way as George flashed through a series of rolls to the right. I couldn't believe it. It was just . . . just incredible.

"Want to take it for a while?" Those marvelous words of invitation again! Did I ever! "Okay, be sure to stay below seventeen thousand. That's the top of our clearance."

"Okay, George. Below seventeen it is."

He held both hands above his head *and I had a jet fighter under my hands* and I twitched, sort of, a bare reflex of my fingers, and ZINGO! we shot two thousand feet into the sky and busted hell out of that lid of seventeen thousand. So I had more learning to do. Everything in this bird is power boosted and you don't move the controls; you *think* at the controls and that's enough. It took a few minutes and finally I wasn't rocking the wings like a rowboat in choppy water, and my God in heaven, I felt like an astronaut. When I had torn enough holes in clouds, and George was laughing until he began to shake the airplane, he took the controls, dropped the nose, and we fell gently from the sky.

Gently. Like a meteor. I couldn't believe the landing. I didn't know when we stopped flying and started rolling.

Thank you, George Baker!

☆

There are few things in life more rewarding than being in the midst of pilots who live the lives cherished by other people. That's the

281

truth of it. I had become part of a clan that made Walter Mitty's dreaming a pale shadow. Who ever dreamed *I* would have the opportunity to fly in some of the greatest warbirds in history?

During the Homestead Air Races in 1979 I watched one of the old Queens, a marvelous B-17 Flying Fortress, going through her paces as the crew practiced touch-and-go landings on the main runway. I knew what was going on. That same crew had flown with us in the Ju-52 and were still shaking their heads with a ground roll after a landing of only six hundred feet. They were out to cut their normal landing roll down by a very hefty margin, and they were doing it, coming in each time slower and lower until they had everything where they wanted it, and went to full-stop landings in only a third the distance they normally used. It was beautiful and the crowd cheered them lustily.

The B-17 taxied by directly in front of the Ju-52 where I was sitting with my husband on the greenhouse over the cockpit. "Who owns that airplane?" I asked, and when I heard the name Scott Smith, my eyes widened. It is always the greatest advantage when you want to bum a ride, to know the *owner,* and Scott is an *old* friend from way back when. I climbed down from *Annie* and went charging up to the Fortress. "Want some ballast in the nose for your next flight?"

The crew grinned at me. They'd been *my* guest in the Ju-52 and were more than eager to return the favor. "Come on over as soon as you see us preflighting. We'll put you up front."

I ran back to the Ju, snatched up my movie camera, pausing only long enough to kiss my husband goodbye before I returned on a run to the B-17. Does this sudden personal moment intrude on this story of flight? Don't consider it that way. I learned very early in this business that, one, you never pass up an opportunity to fly a rare warbird, and, two, you always kiss your love goodbye. The reality is that you may never have that chance again. We have lost too many dear friends not to *always* follow that rule with each other.

I climbed aboard the Fortress through the rear cabin door and started moving toward the nose. My head turned constantly. This was a whole new world. I couldn't believe all the exposed wires, tubes, lines, cables, rods — the airplane looked only half-completed. And the cabin was *dark*. Of course I was comparing all this to the Ju-52, where I had helped finish the interior to *cover* all this same stuff in our airplane. And we had lots of *big* windows.

End of a perfect day. Having flown this one day in six different warbirds, Dee Dee Caidin offers a farewell smile before taking the Ju-52 copilot seat for the return flight home. *Photo by Becky Ritter*

To reach the nose I had to first reach the cockpit, then crawl *beneath* the cockpit floorboards, and as I went forward a hand grasped my shoulder and I heard a warning voice. "Do *not* step onto that center floor panel. It's a breakaway paper covering in case we have to bail out of this thing in a hurry."

I almost turned around to crawl *out* of the airplane. A paper breakaway panel in the *floor?* And they had parachutes and I didn't? Terrific! I'd had enough nightmares, after my sky diving nonsense, about falling from the sky *sans* parachute to be so close to the real possibility! I stepped around the panel as if it were a land mine and could bite, and then took a careful look about me.

Behind the panel leading to the cockpit (which the pilots faced), I saw a nightmare of lines, hoses, wires, *chains*, cables, pulleys, and various other linkages bare and exposed, looped willy-nilly, held together by wire or string, and hanging in a great rat's nest in the air. What a mess! But it obviously satisfied the needs of this

283

crew, and reliability, not prettiness, was what they wanted.

Then the props began to turn, one at a time, until all four engines roared and the fuselage shook and trembled. Every time the vibration eased I shot movie film. The thunder increased and we started to roll, taxiing up to our takeoff point, and all I can remember seeing was the runway, the horizon and the tree line, and the blue sky. The nose of the B-17 is like a huge spider's web — nothing blocks your view except support beams. The glass is below you so you can see the ground. The glass bows out like a great punch bowl before you, and it was made to order for magic carpet flight.

The view was fantastic as we started to roll; the runway seemed inches away, the props were screaming right outside the side windows, and with an exaggerated nose-up attitude we took off. What a flying machine! This airplane spoke authority through every inch and with every move. She was stately, solid, majestic. She really picked up her skirts and ran, and in the air the B-17 was unbelievably smooth and light.

We circled the airport at a thousand feet and then the inevitable attack run began. The pilot lined up for a bombing run and came downstairs in a good dive, the howl of the wind growing ever louder and the sensation of speed picking up swiftly. The paper panel glared at me in my thoughts — what a strange time to be scared of that panel! We went lower, and lower still, and it dawned on me that with our gear up and any lower altitude we could be cutting grass with those propellers! The runway was an impossible, fabulous streaking gray blur, the world whipped by on each side with marvelous speed, and then we were at runway's end and I felt my jaw sagging as we went into a steep climbing pull-up. After all that time in the Ju-52 I recognized the maneuver as the pilots got ready to land: the gear came down and the flaps lowered, and with the nose high, we bled off the airspeed, and with the diminished wind sound the roar of props and engines became thunderous.

We came around slowly, lining up for the numbers, and through my body I could feel the smooth, the velvety touch of a great pilot. We eased across the numbers and she touched with the gentleness of a brushing feather. The runway went from a blur to a defined surface and then it stood still. The eagle had landed!

As we taxied back to the parking area I waved like a kid to the crowds waving at us. They parked that big beast as if it were a Cub and the props ground down and phumphered to a halt. Someone opened the infamous paper panel from the outside and I crawled over and dropped to the ground.

I was so ecstatic I think I bubbled for an hour.

How wonderful it has all been. How privileged I am to share all this . . .

———————— ☆ ————————

Postscript by the author:

We have an old saying in this business where you grasp at history and take your chances in the air with machines that were once and for many years abandoned wrecks that we had to bring back to life. And where you should never lose your perspective.
Teamwork is everything.
That's why a good pilot and copilot always go hand in hand.
But never through the terminal together.

——————— ☆ ———————

Index

287

289

293